INTERKULTURELLE BEGEGNUNGEN 6

Studien zum Literatur- und Kulturtransfer

Hrsg. von Rita Unfer Lukoschik
und Michael Dallapiazza

Federica Anichini

Voices of the body

Liminal Grammar in Guido Cavalcanti's *Rime*

Voci del corpo
Grammatica liminale nelle *Rime*
di Guido Cavalcanti

Martin Meidenbauer »

Die Deutsche Bibliothek verzeichnet diese Publikation in der Deutschen Nationalbibliografie; detaillierte bibliografische Daten sind im Internet über http://dnb.ddb.de abrufbar.

© 2009 Martin Meidenbauer Verlagsbuchhandlung, München

Alle Rechte vorbehalten. Dieses Werk einschließlich aller seiner Teile ist urheberrechtlich geschützt. Jede Verwertung außerhalb der Grenzen des Urhebergesetzes ohne schriftliche Zustimmung des Verlages ist unzulässig und strafbar. Das gilt insbesondere für Nachdruck, auch auszugsweise, Reproduktion, Vervielfältigung, Übersetzung, Mikroverfilmung sowie Digitalisierung oder Einspeicherung und Verarbeitung auf Tonträgern und in elektronischen Systemen aller Art.

Gedruckt auf chlorfrei gebleichtem, säurefreiem und alterungsbeständigem Papier (ISO 9706)

ISBN 978-3-89975-131-4

Verlagsverzeichnis schickt gern:
Martin Meidenbauer Verlagsbuchhandlung
Erhardtstr. 8
D-80469 München

www.m-verlag.net

Contents

Preface	7
I. Guido Cavalcanti, or of Lightness and Subtlety	11
II. Human Love in Darkness	
1. The Theory about Love and a Rhetorical Quest	31
2. Philosophers and Physicians in Thirteenth-Century Culture	39
3. *Auctoritates* of a Heretic: Avicenna's *Liber Canonis*	48
4. Imageless Love	52
III. The Body Speaks	
1. *Voces Gemituum, Dolorum et Suspiriorum*: the Words of a Pre-Verbal Language	61
2. Mapping the *Liber Canonis* in the *Rime*	75
3. 'Ché la 'ntenzione per ragione vale'	77
4. A World in Bewilderment	80
IV. Spirits in Storm	
1. The Debate about the Theory	87
2. Spirits Leaving the Body, Sighs, and the Poet's Craft	97
3. Pneumatic Circulation and Syntax in Sonnet XXVIII	108
V. Blinding Tears	
1. Experimental Colors: the *Ornatus* Is Made of Tears	115
2. Weeping Lovers in the Sicilian School	117
3. Guido and Dante	130
Appendix	147
Abstract	185
Bibliography	189

Preface

The degree of familiarity reached with a literary author after years of work on his or her oeuvre borders on the impudent, and is one of the many privileges of a persistent reader. Beyond such a private adventure, my book deals with a poet who belongs to a nonpareil category of thinkers. The slender collection of Guido Cavalcanti's verses that go under the title of *Rime* is the encryption of an intellectual undertaking of vast proportions. Traditionally considered within the context of his dispute with Dante Alighieri, Guido, in fact, presents his ideas braving a much wider front of opponents, one that consists of the theological stronghold ruling Western Europe in his day. By explaining love, the medieval template for knowledge, in terms of an operation of the senses, Cavalcanti describes a path that fell short of the divine vision granted to the *Divine Comedy*'s pilgrim at the end of his journey. The ultimately terrestrial perfection that Cavalcanti offered to humans was an affront to his 'primo amico,' Dante, as well as to an entire, firmly established cultural milieu. Despite the fact he was in the cultural minority, despite the obscuring of the texts he used as sources taking place at a major university in Europe, Cavalcanti did not yield. He entrusted his poems with a message that remapped the soul and made it mortal (a proposition of serious consequences in thirteenth-century culture): he crystallized a knowledge that was on the verge of being banned from the European history of ideas.

In this book, I look at the exiguous yet complex system of poetry that Cavalcanti created mainly from the perspective of his linguistic experiments and achievements. The investigation into Guido's rhetorical laboratory is introduced in the first two chapters. In chapter I, *Guido Cavalcanti, or of Lightness and Subtlety*, I outline the twofold tradition of Cavalcanti, which emerges from his lines, as well as from the character that was created by chroniclers and novelists, Guido's immediate successors. In the chapter I present the documents that gave origin to an author who from the very beginning was legendary and, at the same time, elusive. The most influential contributors to that tradition, Dante Alighieri and Giovanni Boccaccio, were among the most determinant agents in building Guido's profile as a textual lacuna. Yet, by looking at the body of Guido's work I demonstrate how this was Guido's own strategy, revealed by one of his sonnets, in which he depicted himself as a sequence of impalpable sighs. In chapter II, *Human Love in Darkness*, I introduce the object of my investigation, the 'minor' rhymes, that is, the body of Cavalcanti's work that complements his major Canzone *Donna me prega*. In this text Cavalcanti formulates the principle, which is also the theoretical foundation of his poetry, that an individual is such strictly on the grounds of his senses. This is the conclusive interpretation of the canzone reached in the course of an extensive exegetical tradition stretching from the commentary of Dino Del Garbo—a fourteenth-century Florentine physician whose reading still constitutes the base for understanding *Donna me prega*—to current studies. The theory about love formulated by Cavalcanti declares his philosophical affiliation with radical Aristotelianism, a current of thought whose assumptions, shortly after it appeared, were banned as heretical errors. Cavalcanti's conclusion that love is an experience restricted to the body is an indication that his sources belong to the sphere of natural philosophy. Among them, I selected Avicenna's *Liber Canonis*, a physician's handbook circulating massively in the thirteenth and fourteenth centuries. In the same chapter, I also outline the evolution of medicine in the thirteenth- and fourteenth-century academic world, with specific reference to the links connecting medicine to other, theoretical subjects.

In chapter III, *The Body Speaks*, I present the 'voices of the body,' which I highlighted and made the main object of my inquiry. The demonstration of the theory formulated in the philosophical Canzone *Donna me prega* lies in the 'minor' rhymes. These poems portray the *Rime*'s protagonist, the lover, as figuratively beheaded, that is, unable to retain the ideas he has produced through his perceptions. This confinement into sensorial capacities, and into the realm of matter where the senses work, carried linguistic consequences: the grammarians coeval to Guido had concluded that words are the product of abstract concepts. To solve this predicament, in a section of his *Rime* Cavalcanti employs a special language produced by the body of the lover while his venture unfolds, while his body is acted upon by the sight of the lady and exposed to a chain of violent, physiological responses. The 'voices of the body' are made of these involuntary responses employed as semantic units. In particular I consider two 'voices,' sighs and tears, that I explain by referring to Avicenna's *Liber Canonis*. By weaving into his text the material of a physician, Cavalcanti treated sighs and tears from the medical perspective and subverted the lyric tradition immediately preceding him. In addition to the medical source, I also employ the linguistic theories that were spreading in those centuries, especially those of Modism, a fringe movement engaged at the end of the thirteenth century in the first systematization of grammar that included, albeit at its extremities, *voces* uttered in the absence of concepts.

The last two chapters consist of the close reading of Cavalcanti's minor rhymes. In chapter IV, *Spirits in Storm*, I focus on Sonnet XXVIII, traditionally dismissed as self-parodic, but reconsidered in my reading as a model for an experiment conjugating language and physiology. The interpretation of the sonnet is framed by the historical debate regarding the notion of 'spirit' in Cavalcanti's time. In chapter V, *Blinding Tears*, I examine the theme of weeping in the context of the lyric tradition to which Cavalcanti belongs and, more specifically, in the light of the intellectual exchanges between Guido and Dante. For the latter, I mainly consider the *Vita Nova*. On the ground of the investiture coming from Dante himself, those are the pages in which the dialogue between the two 'primi amici' is launched and most conspicuous.

The *Appendix* of this book contains a list of excerpts transcribed from the *Liber Canonis*, selected on the basis of the vocabulary of the *Rime*. Some of these excerpts constitute the main material I employed for the close reading of Cavalcanti's poems.

Notwithstanding the weightless character that Giovanni Boccaccio, one of his first readers, built around him, Guido Cavalcanti has stood as an alternative center of gravity, active at the periphery of medieval culture. A champion of threatening forces that arise at the margins of any mainstream culture, Guido depicted a battlefield, which the love dramaturgy he staged left in its wake, representative of that which results from the imposition of one orthodoxy at the expense of contrasting doctrines. From that battlefield Cavalcanti withdrew and left behind, like a lantern defying the dark, the burning heart that in Sonnet XLIV[b] illuminates his corpse, doomed like a sinking ship: 'ché di me fa lume/lo core ardendo in la disfatta nave.' That illumination still marks the intellectual construction of his *Rime*, and makes it a living legacy.

I owe the deepest debt of gratitude to Maria Luisa Ardizzone, for the excellence of her work and, beyond that, because she walked me into the magnetic fields of her thoughts, and into the world of research that shapes lives. The privilege of having been a student of John Freccero is likewise precious. A few crucial observations I included in the last chapter are thanks to an illuminating conversation I had with Mary Carruthers. Nicola Gardini offered me his advice, which was essential at the onset of this work. I cannot imagine a more accomplished, perceptive and witty editor than Christine Streit Guerrini, who was a master in guiding me through the maze of a foreign language. Sara Bonechi was the impeccable editor of my transcription from the *Liber Canonis*. I thank Ennio Ranaboldo, the most expert and voracious reader I know, who made my first, mindful audience. Special thanks go to Lucia Benini, Gengi Bernardi, Daniela Costa, Emanuele Crocetti, Chiara Ferrari, Yvonne Freccero, Mark Froeba, Claretta Guatteri, Chiara Marchelli, Pier Nicola Pacini, and Nicola Ventricini: while I was engaged in this project they proved themselves indefatigable friends and gave me roots and wings, more than they can imagine. My family is the strong and patient shore that allowed my journey and constantly buoyed me along.

The material support for the production of this book was the desk of Julio Anguita Parrado. I inherited it after Julio died, in April 2003, while serving as an embedded journalist in Iraq. In my work, I have tried my best to be up to Julio's intelligence, determination, and vision: that is the legacy we have been left with to help us endure the void of his absence. My very close friend Stefano Albertini is the main component of the elective family I have found away from home. I dedicate this book to Julio's memory, and to Stefano.

CHAPTER I
Guido Cavalcanti, or, of Lightness and Subtlety

Undoubtedly Guido Cavalcanti was, with Dante Alighieri, among the first vernacular writers to be deemed *auctoritates* by readers accustomed to restricting that category to classic authors. The cultural rank achieved by Cavalcanti is attested by the proliferation of commentaries that from the thirteenth century on were produced about his philosophical Canzone *Donna me prega*. Cavalcanti's poetic production is slender; its groundbreaking content, however, nourished the legend surrounding this long-lived character, whom the incisive portrayals of his contemporaries considered a powerful icon[1] and who, centuries later, was even chosen to represent one of the values that Italo Calvino, in his *Six Memos*, wished to pass on to the next millennium.[2] The tradition acknowledging Guido Cavalcanti as an *auctoritas*, therefore, has developed along two lines: his poetry and his character. The beginnings of this tradition are complex and, as is the case for any message retrieved from medieval culture, full of gaps. In addition to the collection of exegetic works produced around *Donna me prega*, the most important sources are on one hand the literature that created his legend as a distinguished character, and on the other the Dantesque oeuvre. Although Guido Cavalcanti's caliber as an author and a prominent Florentine is widely documented, a great many of the traces he left in history result from his friendship with Dante. Dante recognizes this privileged fellowship with Guido early in his work, in the *Vita Nova*, where he coins the long-standing epithet of 'primo amico.' Inquiry into this 'prima amicizia' has been the focus of centuries of scholarship because chronologically and thematically this phrase appears at the onset of a new literary tradition written in vernacular. The *Divine Comedy* instead betokens a breakup. Given the

---

[1] 'Non c'è forse esempio, nella storia delle nostre lettere, tanto più ai loro inizi, di fortuna pari a quella di cui ha goduto Guido Cavalcanti già da vivo; fino a quando almeno non si cominciò, con Dante e con Petrarca, a provvedere, come all'altrui, così alla propria fama. Se è da tener conto dell'eminenza del personaggio, di famiglia cospicua nella sua città, e imparentato col grande Farinata degli Uberti, è anche vero che è sul valore e sul significato della sua opera poetica, per giunta esigua (l'eventuale falcidia del tempo non costituendo elemento discriminante come non sua esclusiva) e non di largo consumo, per non dire elitaria, è su quella che sin da allora apparve una sublime esclusività e insomma sul "nome che più dura e più onora" che è fondata la sua presenza e la memoria di lui nei secoli ed è cresciuta la stessa sua leggenda.' *Introduzione*. In: Cavalcanti, Guido: *Rime*. Ed. Domenico De Robertis. Turin: Einaudi, 1986, pp. xi-xii (all quotations from Cavalcanti's poems are taken from this edition).
[2] Calvino, *Leggerezza*. In: *Lezioni Americane*, pp. 5-30.

acknowledgment rendered in the *prosimetrum*, Guido's absence from the Dantesque journey and his indirect damnation for heresy in the first Cantica are striking facts. The final verdict is announced in *Inferno* X, 58-72, in the course of a well-known dialogue in which the pilgrim identifies Guido, *in absentia*, as the disdainful son of the Epicurean Cavalcante.[3] In fact, despite the rift that this dialogue came to signify, Dante never abandons Guido as one of his favorite, albeit problematic, interlocutors. Notwithstanding his marked ideological contrast with Dante and his disappearance as a character in the progression from Hell to the successive realms, Guido remains actively in dialogue with Dante throughout the text of the *Comedy*. As I will demonstrate in Chapter 5, Guido's presence spills out of the few lines of canto X and emerges from behind other damned souls who disclose unmistakable Cavalcantian features. References to Guido as an author are scattered not only in the *Purgatorio* and the *Paradiso* but also in Dante's entire poetic production.[4] In no other author's text, in fact, does Cavalcanti's work filtrate to such an extent. In terms of its intertextuality with Guido's verses the Dantesque work remains unparalleled. Dante is occupied with Guido's cultural import throughout his work, and his writing is among the major agents in the making of the Guido Cavalcanti tradition. Supposing that the strategy laid out in the *Inferno* aims at univocally erasing Guido, it proves counterproductive in that it actually acknowledges Guido's undisputed role in the intellectual debate of his time. However, in his intense colloquium with his former 'primo amico,' Dante also exhausted Guido's ideological import. In fact, given the scant direct references to Cavalcanti's text except for those found in Dante's writing, it is as if the banishment suggested by the controversial line 'forse cui Guido vostro ebbe a disdegno' in *Inferno* X simultaneously marked the overshadowing of Guido's work in the Italian tradition and the ending of a poetic mode, the 'adventure in hell' of which Cavalcanti's poetry and Dante's *Inferno* represent the last example.[5]

---

[3] Widely documented research of Dante's multilayered condemnation of Guido in *Inferno* X is found in: Freccero, pp. 41-54.

[4] Contini's conclusions are germinal, and firm in establishing that Guido 'aveva salato il sangue a Dante' (Contini, *Cavalcanti in Dante*, p. 445.) De Robertis (*Un altro Cavalcanti?*) summarizes the references to the Cavalcantian memory in the *Divine Comedy*.

[5] Mario Luzi, in his essay *L'inferno e il limbo*, claims that after Dante's *Inferno* the Italian poetic tradition abolished any contact with 'le episodiche circostanze della vita e, volendo ancora estendere il termine, con l'inferno.' Luzi outlines the Italian lyrical tradition as stemming from Petrarch, rather than from Dante, and specifically from the enclosed realm of the spirit established by Petrarch's poetry: 'Accettando Petrarca la nostra letteratura si trovò fin dai suoi inizi, a compiere delle capitali e definitive rinunzie. Esse riflettono in apparenza il mondo della

The recurrent allusions to Cavalcanti's works throughout the Dantesque corpus suggest that, after the *Vita Nova*, Dante evokes Guido's text following a precise strategy: to darken his former but persistent first friend while working on the foundation of an authoritative vernacular canon pivoted on his own name. As has been convincingly remarked, the famous indirect damnation in *Inferno* X is aimed at one specific aspect of Guido's poetry, i.e. the very 'obscure' way in which he organizes his text.[6] And this is the same obscurity that Dante never ceases to cast on him by identifying him as the heterodox *auctor* among the fourteenth-century vernacular poets. The effacing strategy we see at work in Dante's text affects both the making and the perception of Cavalcanti's character; as we shall see, however, this coincides with Cavalcanti's own strategy. Replicating the destiny of the protagonist of his poems Guido has already portrayed himself as a vanishing author: after an amorous encounter he hovers over the darkened stage as the imperceptible blowing of sighs which remains among the verses, the last sign of life after a battle. With such a self-portrait, Guido ultimately undermines the attempts on his cultural import and gains, via lightness and subtlety, a secure status in the poetic tradition.

Though the theoretical legacy of Guido Cavalcanti has had to strive to conserve its importance, Cavalcanti's character itself has enjoyed a longstanding and rich life, filling the spaces left by the limited documents on his life. He is included, mentioned and evoked in some of the most crucial literature of the Trecento and Quattrocento, both fictional and nonfictional.[7] Although he was the product of a culture that, on the basis of *scientia inflat*,[8] associated authorship with anonymity, Guido's legend began when he was still alive and continued to be expanded and shaped over time. The documents that contribute to the making of Guido's legend belong to different genres: mainly short stories, *Divine Comedy* commentaries and

---

materia e della quantità e a prima vista aumentano il dominio della purezza e dello spirito, il quale non riconosce più altro oggetto che la propria solitudine e il proprio sistema circolare e chiuso.' Luzi, *L'inferno e il limbo*, pp. 62-63.

[6] Maria Luisa Ardizzone in her study compares Dante's lines in Inferno X to the novella VI 9 of the Decameron as both texts share reference to the concept of 'obscurity' as it is elaborated by Cavalcanti in *Donna me prega* (*A Note on Dante's 'Inferno" X*. In: *Guido Cavalcanti. The Other Middle Ages*, pp. 65-70.)

[7] The documents are reported in any work dedicated to the Tuscan poet. Maria Corti resumes the main points of this tradition in *Una diagnosi dell'amore*, in: *La felicità mentale* (1983). Now in: *Scritti su Cavalcanti e Dante*, pp. 9-41.

[8] Saint Paul's statement, in his first letter to the Corinthians, is quoted as one of the defining sources for medieval authorship in Schmidt, pp. 1-8.

Florentine chronicles. These provide a body of quasi biographical information which is at times difficult to grasp as a coherent whole, although all the sources concur in mentioning a few traits: his solitariness and scornful attitude, his philosophical background and subtlety of thinking.

'Sottiglianza' is a poetic element commonly discussed in the course of the animated literary debates of the time, and one of the grounds of the well known polemic launched by Bonagiunta da Lucca in *Voi ch'avete mutata la mainera* against the forerunner of the 'new style,' Guido Guinizzelli. Guido Cavalcanti himself includes 'sottiglianza' in the semantic field of the teaching of Love, therefore of philosophy.[9] A philosophical penchant is the most persistent feature attached to Guido's character, as should be expected in the case of an author mainly identified through one text, *Donna me prega*, which from the very beginning was acknowledged as a philosophical treatise and accordingly read and interpreted. Among the decisive factors in attributing a scientific status to the canzone was the fourteenth-century commentary written by a physician, Dino Del Garbo, whose strictly technical interpretation of *Donna me prega*'s lines definitely became the cornerstone for the subsequent literature regarding Guido and his canzone.[10]

The philosophical importance of the canzone was soon acknowledged, yet the definition of its content remained a complex issue. Guido's compromising with heretical sources was widely disputed. Other than the precedent in *Inferno* X, in which Dante alludes to the application of Guido's subtle mind to nonorthodox learning, the Trecento literature that mentions Cavalcanti does not acknowledge his heresy. The only exception is the text that for authoritativeness and incisiveness stands out in the making of Guido's legend. Recalling the conversation staged between the pilgrim and the heretics' souls in *Inferno* X and assuming that the definition of Epicurean cast on Cavalcante Cavalcanti also implicitly regards his son, Giovanni

---

[9] See Cavalcanti's Sonnet L^a to Guido Orlandi (emphasis mine): 'Perché sacciate balestra legare/e coglier con isquadra archile in tratto/e certe fiate aggiate Ovidio letto/e trar quadrelli e false rime usare,/non pò venir pur la vostra mente/là dove insegna Amor *sottile* e piano/di sua manera dire e di su' stato.' It is precisely the poem's new philosophical content that opens up a new and selective basis for poetic writing. The topic of *subtilitas* as one of the characteristics of the Stilnovo ('Proprio nella sottigliezza, e cioè nel carattere intellettualistico e filosofico della nuova poesia, consisteva una delle discriminanti che identificavano l'avanguardia stilonvistica rispetto ai seguaci della maniera provenzaleggiante dei siculo-toscani.') is presented and discussed by Francesco Bruni, *Semantica della sottigliezza* (p. 4).

[10] A sylloge of the exegetical tradition regarding *Donna me prega* is compiled in Fenzi.

Boccaccio makes Guido Cavalcanti a protagonist of one of the *Decameron*'s short stories. In the novella VI, 9 Guido strolls about Florence until he finds himself among the tombs in front of San Giovanni, where a group of his fellow citizens surrounds him. The 'brigata' has approached him with the intention of testing his mind on his alleged atheism: 'Guido, tu rifiuti d'esser di nostra brigata; ma ecco, quando tu avrai trovato che Idio non sia, che avrai fatto?' Faithful to his reputation of being 'uno de' migliori loci che avesse il mondo,' as Boccaccio himself has introduced him to his readers, Guido retorts by forging a sophism: 'Signori, voi mi potete dire a casa vostra ciò che vi piace' and then leaps over the tombs, leaving behind, through Boccaccio's pen, one of the most incisive images of himself: 'e posta la mano sopra una di quelle arche, che grandi erano, sì come colui che leggerissimo era, prese un salto e fusi gittato dall'altra parte, e sviluppatosi da loro se ne andò.' In his novella Boccaccio not only connects Cavalcanti's fame as an Epicurean to his belief that the individual soul does not survive the death of the body but, also, as has been observed, by attributing to Guido Cavalcanti an ambiguous reply, the author of the *Decameron* insists on the Cavalcantian feature of obscurity, in the wake of *Inferno* X.[11]

Boccaccio's early portrayal of Cavalcanti deeply influenced those which followed. Since it is the only document other than Dante's *Inferno* that reports on Guido's heresy, it induced some readers to question the trustworthiness of Boccaccio's account and to suggest that the *Decameron* novella is a textual construction aimed at obscuring the real Guido. Their conjecture is reinforced by the literary caliber of these first two authors shaping Guido's character, Dante and Boccaccio, whose writing, it has recently been argued, certainly suggests a self-promotional subtext.[12]

---

[11] See n. 6.

[12] This issue has been recently raised by Zygmunt G. Baránski. On the grounds of a preliminary distinction between the historical Cavalcanti and his textual constructions, Baránksi refers specifically to two of the main testimonies of Guido's legend, the *Decameron* and the *Divine Comedy*, and he writes: 'Indeed, the highly particularized nature of Dante's and Boccaccio's recourse to Cavalcanti appears to be confirmed by the fact that, in each instance, Guido is utilized as a vehicle through which both authors attempt to establish their own literary identity.' Baránski, G. Zygmunt: *Guido Cavalcanti and his First Readers*, p. 150. Maria Corti's conclusions explain the inconsistencies within Guido's legend by means of his disconcerting originality: 'Allorché si parla degli effetti del tempo, abbondano nei discorsi degli uomini le ripetizioni; d'altronde non è possibile tentare schizzi di storia letteraria di epoca medievale senza riflettere su quanto il tempo ha soppresso dandoci l'impressione che siano oziose rispetto a quelle poche che esso ha conservato. Sicché quando il Boccaccio o il Sacchetti da un lato, Filippo Villani, Giovanni Villani, Dino Compagni, Benvenuto da Imola dall'altro abbozzano un ritratto di Guido Cavalcanti come di uomo dal nobile portamento, intellettuale solitario, coltissimo, loico

The hypothesis about the fictional nature of the profile of Guido in the *Decameron* was first suggested by Antonio Cicciaporci, curator and prefacer of the 1813 edition of Cavalcanti's *Rime*. The edition, included in the Leopardi library in Recanati, deserves greater attention since it indicates a comparative reading that still needs to be fully explored.[13] In his preface, Antonio Cicciaporci starts by presenting the poetry collection as a substitute for a biography of Guido Cavalcanti that the fugitiveness of Guido's character prevented him from producing.[14] Cicciaporci proceeds with an impressionistic interpretation that leads him first to acknowledge Guido's unique 'profondità' widely recognized even by Guido's contemporaries,[15] only to conclude a few pages later that Guido's poetry contains a sort of 'rozzezza' and 'oscurità' as should however be expected at the beginning of any literary tradition.[16] Beyond such cursory remarks, which nonetheless include an interesting reference to a *Grammatica* allegedly written by Guido,[17]

---

sottile, "filosofo naturale" dagli atteggiamenti sempre aristocratici, ora ironici ora sdegnosi o lievemente macchiettati di snobismo, elegante a cavallo, buon giocatore di scacchi, subito affiora il sospetto che dietro quella frequenza di giudizi affini non ci sia tanto una fonte unica di informazione e per noi Boccaccio (questa è diffusa *lectio facilior*), quanto un personaggio che la sua originale arditezza scombussolava e confondeva le menti dei contemporanei. Ma più in là non si può andare; e men che meno si va con Dante, nonostante i quintali di bibliografia dantesca accumulati nei secoli.' Corti, *Una diagnosi dell'amore*, p. 10.

[13] A few important indications related to the comparison between Guido Cavalcanti and Giacomo Leopardi are provided by Domenico De Robertis in his study: *Leopardi. La poesia*. Edizioni Cosmopoli. Bologna, Roma, 1996, p. 322. As for the presence of Cavalcantian echoes in Leopardi's poetry, see also the article by Alessandro Carrera, in which the critic indicates the battle of the glances (meant as the breaking of the solipsistic conception of love) as the topic of the 'missed' dialogue between Guido and Giacomo (Carrera, *"Per gli occhi venne la battaglia in pria"*. *Fenomenica dello sguardo tra Cavalcanti e Leopardi*).

[14] 'Pensai di tessere per esteso la Vita di Guido, ma ciò mi fu tolto dalla scarsità delle notizie, che da lui sonoci pervenute, perocché quel che fu di lui da diversi autori scritto è poco, e detto sol di passaggio; talché intorno ad esso non potei raccogliere che scarse memorie tratte da ciò che sparsamente ne dissero varj Scrittori. Credei cooperare maggiormente alla sua gloria col pubblicare le di lui *Rime* sì edite che inedite, mi è avvenuto di rintracciare.' Cicciaporci, p. vi.

[15] 'Tutti gli scrittori contemporanei di Guido [...] si accordano tutti in celebrarlo per uomo profondo [...]. La profondità, che nelle sue opere si ritrova, non è certo comune agli altri poeti dell'età sua.' Ibid., p. xxv.

[16] 'De' poeti antichi a me sembra che far si possa come de' Pittori, cioé le loro maniere e stili differenziare. Che ciò si verifichi anche riguardo a Guido parmi indubitato, poiché alcune delle sue Rime fanno ancora sentire quella rozzezza, ed oscurità, che nei primi Rimatori si osserva, ed altre poi son tali, che all'amico di Dante convengono.' Ibid., pp. xxxii-xxxiii.

[17] 'L'ornatissimo e dottissimo Sig. Jacopo Morelli Bibliotecario della Marciana in Venezia mi avvisa trovarsi in questa Biblioteca un rarissimo Libro che ha per titolo *Introduzione alla lingua volgare* di Domenico Tullio Fausto. Quest'opera è citata dal Crescimbeni nell'*Istoria della Poesia*

Cicciaporci's preface is important since it raises the doubt that Guido's Epicureanism might be fictional given the lack of evidence supporting it. His conclusions are that the attribute of Epicurean attached to Guido is merely a result of the *Decameron's* narrative strategies: 'come al Boccaccio è piaciuto farlo credere.'[18] In listing some of the sources composing the intellectual and biographical profile of Guido, Cicciaporci concludes that Boccaccio's labeling of Guido as an Epicurean is unsubstantiated and must be considered an effect of the famous indirect damnation in *Inferno* X:

> Per lo contrario poi nulla esiste che Epicuro comparir lo faccia come al Boccaccio è piaciuto farlo credere. Il Conte Mazzucchelli nelle sue erudite note alla Vita del Cavalcanti, scritta da Filippo Villani, da tale solenne ingiuria il difende; [...] nelle Opere di Guido nulla ritrovasi, che tale lo dimostri, quando non vogliasi dedur ciò dall'aver lui spesso favellato di amore [...] e quanto a questa accusa può agevolmente credersi, che fosse ciò mera opinione della gente volgare, facile per la sua ignoranza, specialmente in que' tempi, a interpretare in male, quel che in realtà è bene. [....]. Si può anche sospettare che una tal credenza nata fosse dall'aver Dante posto tra gli Epicurei Messer Cavalcante padre di Guido, e perciò si supponesse che anche il figlio fosse attaccato dallo stesso errore; [...]. Pare che il Boccaccio stesso riconoscesse poi per falsa quest'imputazione, poiché replicando nel suo Comento sopra Dante quelle cose, che avea dette di Guido nella citata Novella Nona, tace quella, che egli fosse Epicureo, e lo chiama in quella vece costumatissimo, ottimo loico, e buon filosofo. Cristoforo Landino, nel commentare quel luogo del s.c. Canto X dell'Inferno, dove Dante ragiona di Cavalcante, venendo a parlare di Guido non dice che egli neppur pizzicasse di Epicureo. [...]. Pure Domenico d'Arezzo nella fede di Dante soltanto lo asserisce Epicureo, tuttoché questi del padre, e non del figlio, abbia favellato. Alessandro Zilioli nella sua Istoria de' Poeti Italiani anch'esso come seguace di tal setta lo accusa, senza dire però su qual fondamento appoggi la sua asserzione. [...]. Anche Lorenzo de' Medici in una sua lettera diretta a D. Federigo d'Aragona, figliuolo di Ferdinando Re di Napoli, di Guido così favella senza alcuna menzione di vizio epicureo: [...].[19]

(On the contrary, there is no ground to make him into an Epicurean, as Boccaccio indulged in describing him. Count Mazzucchelli, in his erudite notes to the Life of Cavalcanti by Filippo Villani, shields him from such an insult. [...]. In Guido's works one can find nothing proving his Epicureanism, unless this is induced from that fact that Guido wrote

---

Volgare t. 2 a pag. 301. In questo libro dunque il Fausto in un capitolo intitolato *Dell'ordinare la Prosa* dice: "Delle parole bisillabe e trisillabe alcune sono aspirate come *honore* alcune hanno geminato le liquide come *novella, fiamma, anno, carro, lasso*, consonate dopo muta doppia, *fabbro*, ovvero muta in mezzo liquide, *sepolcro*, e cotali Dante chiamò nella sua Volgar Eloquenza, e Guido Cavalcanti nella Seconda Parte della sua Grammatica, *irsute*; e chi facesse combinazione di queste senza dubbio seria dura e roggia orazione." Convien dunque dire che realmente Guido abbia composto quest'opera [...] riguardare esso si deve come uno dei primi cooperatori all'avanzamento del bello ed ameno nostro volgare linguaggio, dando ad esso forma.' Ibid., p. xxxi.

[18] Ibid., p. xiv.
[19] Ibid., pp. xvi- xviii. Translation is mine.

often about love [...], therefore we can easily conclude that this accusation is simply the product of some ordinary people, naturally predisposed, out of ignorance, to interpret as bad what is, in fact, good. [...]. We can also imagine that this belief was originated by the fact that Dante had put Messer Cavalcante, Guido's father, among the Epicureans, therefore the son was guilty on the same charge; [...]. Further, it looks as if Boccaccio himself had acknowledged this imputation as false, because in his Commentary to the *Comedy*, while he recalls what he had said in the above quoted novella ix, he makes no mention of Guido's Epicureanism, and instead defines him as extremely virtuous, as an excellent logician, and a good philosopher. Cristoforo Landino, in his comment to those lines of *Inferno* x where Dante writes about Cavalcante, doesn't even remotely call Guido Epicurean. [...]. And Domenico d'Arezzo calls him Epicurean only because he believes what Dante wrote, although Dante was talking about the father, not the son. Alessandro Zilioli, in his *Istoria dei poeti italiani*, also calls Guido Epicurean, but fails to substantiate his conclusion. [...]. And Lorenzo de' Medici, in a letter he addressed to D. Federigo d'Aragona, son of Ferdinand king of Naples, talks about Guido without any mention of his Epicurean vice: [...].)

In more recent times, similar suspicions were shared with readers of Cavalcanti by Giovanni Parodi. In his 1915 article, Parodi argues that the disbeliever Guido of the *Decameron* is a fictional character and notes that Boccaccio treats Guido Cavalcanti from two distinct perspectives: one for the *Decameron* VI, 9, and the other for the *Inferno* X's commentary. He invented the material for the former and used historical documents for the latter (where, in fact, no mention is made of Guido's heresy). Parodi supports his claim by indicating the probable source behind the fictional Guido Cavalcanti of *Decameron* VI 9: Boccaccio based the characteristics he attributed to Guido on the ones that Frate Salimbene's *Chronicle* imputed to Frederick II, whose intellectual quest, like Guido's in the Decameron, is openly and dangerously focused on proving the death of the individual soul.[20]

The questioning of Cavalcanti's heresy was also rooted in the fact that although he was called an Epicurean by Dante and was attributed a heretical dogma by Boccaccio, no mention of Guido's heresy is made in the

---

[20] 'Tanto Federico quanto Guido cercano di provare *per scientiam*, come direbbe Benvenuto, che la verità rivelata non sia. Il non ornato latino di Salimbene si può tradurre alla lettera quasi con le medesime parole del Boccaccio: "Federico era epicureo e pertanto era tutto in cercare nella Sacra Scrittura, da sé o con l'aiuto dei suoi sapienti, ciò per cui trovar si potesse che altra vita non fosse dopo la morte." *Per se et per sapientes suos....*Par di vederli questi sapienti, loci, senza dubbio, 'de' migliori loici che avesse il mondo', e 'ottimi filosofi naturali', tutti intenti, con metodi medievalmente sofistici e cocciuti, e non senza un tremito nel cuore, a cercar nelle Sacre Scritture le prove contro le Sacre Scritture! Il Boccaccio con la sua viva fantasia e il suo lieto spirito di libero uomo di mondo ha intraveduto in uno di essi il suo Guido.' Parodi, p. 43.

Trecento literature that regards Guido; and notwithstanding the dramatic dialogue between the pilgrim and Cavalcante in *Inferno* X, neither is any mention made of the rift between Guido and Dante. The Trecento authors who make reference to Cavalcanti insist on the philosophical nature of his writing as being detrimental to his poetic achievement, and not as conducing to heresy. Guido Cavalcanti is, for instance, a 'valentissimo uomo e filosofo,' albeit 'furioso,' in the short story LXVIII of Franco Sacchetti's *Trecentonovelle*, where Guido's character serves to illustrate the cliché of the illiterate bystander (a boy, here) that with 'sottil malizia' plays a trick on the already renowned intellectual capacities of the poet-philosopher.[21] Further, these sources recognize Guido's inclination toward philosophy as the most manifest mark of his difference from, not his contrast with, Dante. The distinction between the two poets' fields of interest does not trouble their fellowship, which remains undisputed.

The major non-fictional works of the Trecento that contribute to the depiction of Guido Cavalcanti's character are chronicles and *Divine Comedy* commentaries. All the major fourteenth-century historians writing on Florence include Guido among the leading figures of those years in the city. In Dino Compagni's *Cronica* Giudo is identified as possessing what seem to have become his traditional characteristics: 'Un giovane gentile, figliuolo di messer Cavalcante Cavalcanti, nobile cavaliere, chiamato Guido, cortese e ardito ma sdegnoso e solitario e intento allo studio,'[22] in Giovanni Villani's *Cronica*: 'tornonne malato [from his political confinement in Sarzana, in 1300] Guido Cavalcanti, onde morìo; e di lui fu grande dammaggio, perocché era, come filosofo, virtudioso uomo in più cose, se non ch'era troppo tenero e stizzoso,'[23] and in Filippo Villani's biographies: 'Costui scrisse, intorno all'amore che si applica ai sensi più che alla ragione, disputando con grande sottigliezza intorno alla natura di questo, ai suoi moti e alla sua disposizione, una canzone straordinaria, nella quale da un punto di vista filosofico affrontò temi inauditi, con grande ingegno e molto estesamente.'[24]

---

[21] Sacchetti, p. 199.
[22] Compagni, p. 1.
[23] Villani, Giovanni, VIII, p. 42.
[24] 'Hic de amore qui in sensualitate potius quam in ratione versatur eiusque natura, motibus et affectu subtilissime disputando elegantissimam et mirabilem edidit cantilenam in qua philosophice inaudita actenus ingeniosissime et copiose tractavit.' Villani, Filippo, XLIV, 1, p. 146.

Interesting contributions to the making of Guido Cavalcanti's character are also found in the *Divine Comedy* commentaries. A rapid inquiry into them makes it manifest that the main focus of the pages concerned with Cavalcante's appearance in *Inferno* X is Guido and Dante's fellowship. As a result, the 'cui' of line 63 is unanimously interpreted as Virgil, i.e. poetry, which Guido Cavalcanti disdained in favor of philosophy. All the authors (except those that make little or no mention of Guido, such as Jacopo Alighieri and Jacopo della Lana)[25] cite the distinction between Guido's and Dante's profiles—a philosopher, the first, a poet, the second—as the reason for the different development of their work, never as grounds for questioning their friendship. The first commentaries to the *Divine Comedy* tended to normalize the text's asperities, to smooth away its cruces;[26] therefore it is not unexpected that the contrast between the two Florentine poets is resolved in terms of an undisturbing difference in their fields of interest. Graziolo Bombaglioli introduces Cavalcanti as 'amicus specialis et sotius Dantis';[27] the Ottimo lists the many common interests and experiences of the two as the unshattered ground of their fellowship: 'onde è da notare, che l'Autore e Guido Cavalcanti, figliuolo di Messer Cavalcante, furono contemporanei, cioè ad uno tempo, e amicissimi; la quale amistade si creò in loro per similitudine di abito scientifico, e per similitudine di costumi, e di passioni d'animo, e di vita, e di parzialitade, e di cittadinanza: le quali similitudini tennero in amistade congiunti li animi dell'Autore e di Guido, quanto Guido visse; amendue studiarono a Firenze, amendue amarono per amore, amendue parlarono in rime, canzoni, e altre specie di

---

[25] Jacopo Alighieri ignores Cavalcante's son (Alighieri, Jacopo: *Chiose all'Inferno*. Ed. Saverio Bellomo. Antenore. Padova, 1990), while Jacopo della Lana considers simply the issue of the aorist: 'Dice che perché Dante disse: *forse cui Gyuido vostro ebbe a disdegno*, il padre del detto Guido notò quella parola *ebbe*, che significa tempo passato, e ad esso, dubitando, domandò: come di tu *ebbe*? non viv'elli ancora al mondo? quasi: tu dovresti dire cui Guido vostro *hae* a disdegno.' *Comedia di Dante degli Allagherii col commento di Jacopo della Lana bolognese*, p. 214.

[26] 'Il desiderio dei commentatori di ricollocare la *Commedia* in un terreno mediano, ideologicamente e artisticamente sicuro e non controverso, si nota pure in altre loro scelte esegetiche. Per esempio, è rarissimo che un commentatore si fermi su contraddizioni presenti nel testo. [...]. Di conseguenza, consideravano parte della loro responsabilità di esegeti non solo quella di elucidare la lettera e l'allegoria del testo, ma anche quella di rettificare, neutralizzandoli, gli aspetti più perturbanti, pericolosi e problematici della *Commedia*.' Baránski, "*Chiosar con altro testo*". *Leggere Dante nel Trecento*, pp. 22-23.

[27] 'Hec umbra fuit pater Guidonis Cavalcantis, nobillissimi et prudentissimi viri, amici specialis et sotiis Dantis, qui, cum vidisset Dantem carissimum amicum et sotium Guidonis filii sui, amirabatur quam plurimum quod filium non videbat cum Dante, et propterea interrogavit eum de filio, ut sequitur.' Bombaglioli, p. 83.

dire con misura di piedi, e di tempi sillabati, amendue seguitarono un volere in governare la Repubblica di Firenze, per la quale con gli altri furon chiamati Bianchi, e per quello volere cacciati furono di Firenze con gli altri [...].'[28] Such a well established fellowship is certainly not jeopardized because Dante, unlike Guido, chose to incorporate in his text the tradition of classical poetry.[29] The most well-established commentator of Dante's sons, Pietro Alighieri, is also firmly intent on underlining the philosophical quality of Cavalcanti's writing, which serves him as the grounds for emphasizing the role of his father as poet.[30] Pietro acknowledges Guido's great mastery in the use of written vernacular language but at the same time notes his lack of concern for more specifically poetic issues.[31] Guglielmo Maramauro and Francesco da Buti present Guido as the 'perfecto filosofo'[32]

---

[28] *L'Ottimo commento della Divina Commedia*, p. 178.

[29] '61. *Ed io a lui ecc...* Qui l'Autore mostra che non per sua sufficienza cerca questi luoghi, ma per grazia di Dio, che li mandò innanzi Virgilio, lo quale fu di lui motore col libro dell'Eneida, dove elli introduce Enea all'Inferno sotto il conducimento di Sibilla; e qua come la ragione il guida e scorge questo argomento. Ch'elli fosse motore, per questo libro si conferma: per simile infra capitolo vigesimo primo *Purgatorii*, quivi-*Al mio ardor fur seme le faville ec.-Dell'Eneide dico ec.* dove dice che l'detto libro fu motore di Stazio. E dice l'Autore, che forse Guido ebbe a disdegno questo libro di Virgilio, e li altri suoi; e nota che dice: elli ebbe, non elli ha, per lo quale dire *elli ebbe*, il detto Messer Cavalcante intese che Guido fosse morto, e indi concepette dolore e tristizia.' Ibid., p. 179.

[30] 'Pietro, then, possessed ideal qualifications for Dante commentary: an intimate, first-hand knowledge of the full range of Dante's poetry and thought, daily contact with erudite and enthusiastic Latinists, and the native wit and independence to hold such divergent forces together. Once Pietro had committed himself to commentary he persisted with it for some twenty years, producing some three recensions of his *Commentarium*. [...]. Pietro's revisions reflect his desire to explain the bases of Dante's thought with ever greater clarity, concentrating (in humanist fashion) upon the letter of the text rather than upon extra-literary sources of inspiration. The *Comedy* is seen as the work of a "glorious theologian, philosopher, and poet," rather than (as in Guido's account [*Guido da Pisa*]) of a prophetic visionary. Pietro sees Dante, in essence, as a learned poet of classical stature; and the key term here is *poet*.' Minnis, *Medieval Literary Theory and Criticism c.1100-c.1375 The Commentary Tradition*, p. 451.

[31] 'Capitulum decimum Inferni. I. "[...] patris Guidonis, probissimi inventoris in materna rima, contemporanei ipsius Dantis. Qui Guido adhesit libris philosoficis magis quam poeticis, et hoc est quod tangit hic auctor, dum dicit quod ipse Guido vilipendo Virgillium, idest eius poema et alios, per consequentes, vates, solummodo secutus est philosophos; [...]" II. "Guidonis, viri acutissimi ingenij et comitis contemporanei huius auctoris, qui, quamvis fuerit magnus rimator in materno stillo, nullatenus tamen dellectabatur in poesia, sed pocius in philosophia, ut colligitur hic in textu, in eo quod dicit sibi auctor quod dedignatus fuerat studere super Virgilio; [...].' *Il Commentarium di Pietro Alighieri nelle redazioni Ashburnhamiana e Ottoboniana*, pp. 187-188.

[32] 'Il qual miser Cavalcanti ebbe un figlio chiamato Guido, gioveno assai virtuoso e literato, dotato di nobilissimi costumi, pregiato da tuti' Fiorentini, perfecto filosofo; e fu nel tempo de

who expanded his interests in matters that could not possibly be rendered poetically. In Francesco da Buti's commentary, Virgil, waiting aloofly for Dante's conversation with the two heretics to come to an end, stands for the very poetry Guido showed disdain for: '*Colui, ch'attende là*; cioè che m'aspetta colà, *per qui mi mena*; cioè me Dante: questi era Virgilio, *Forse cui Guido vostro ebbe a disdegno*; questo dice l'autore perché Guido dispregiava li poeti, e Virgilio come li altri; e dice *forse* per parlare più onesto. [....] quando dice che Virgilio l'aspettava, vuole intendere che a parlamentare con questi suoi Fiorentini non usava la ragione pratica della poesia, perché finge che parlassono di cose che non si stendevano a poesia; e così si dee intendere, quando dice che Guido ebbe a disdegno Virgilio.'[33] In addition to the commentary of Ottimo, who, as has been noted, draws a connection between the Epicureans and Averroistic theories,[34] the only commentator who hints at the possibility that Guido was guilty of heterodoxy is Benvenuto da Imola, whose exegetical effort unquestionably sets him apart from the group of commentators we are considering.[35] Benvenuto praises Guido and Dante, the *duo lumina Florentiae*,[36] and explains that Guido's absence from the *Commedia* was due to his philosophical bent, his *error*, which, moreover, not only precluded his producing a literary project as

---

D., e delectossi multo de dir in rima volgare e disse assai bene. Vero è che esso non se delectò sapere poesia, per la qual cosa non li fo opo studiare V.' Maramauro, p. 213.

[33] *Commento di Francesco da Buti sopra la Divina Commedia di Dante Alighieri*, p. 285.

[34] Ardizzone, *Guido Cavalcanti. The Other Middle Ages*, p. 198 n. Maria Luisa Ardizzone indicates a possible intersection of Epicureanism and radical Aristotelianism which would give historical substance to Boccaccio's account: '*Donna me prega* therefore contains a philosophical theory of happiness based on physics and matter, which was crucial to the Epicurean theory of happiness. In *Donna me prega* the central focus is on the sensitive soul, where love has its seat. This part of the soul is perishable according to "elli è creato" because it is part of the material world ruled by generation and corruption. A theory of happiness emerges that is related to the perishable nature of the individual soul. The fact that logic organizes the reasoning for earthly happiness as the direct consequence of the theory of matter and the denial of the survival of the individual soul can be considered among the reasons for Cavalcanti's fame as an Epicurean. It is this reputation that Dante introduces and Boccaccio expands upon.' Ibid., p. 126.

[35] It is a topos in Dante criticism to consider Benvenuto's commentary as original in the tradition of the Trecento: 'Benvenuto dice di essersi fatto macro su questo commento, come Dante sul poema; e, conscio del suo cospicuo sforzo di esegesi letterale e storica, non manca di segnare la propria disistima per predecessori quali Iacopo della Lana o il figlio stesso di Dante, Pietro; riserva il suo rispetto al solo Boccaccio.' Contini, *Letteratura italiana delle origini*, p. 874.

[36] '[...] fuerunt duo lumina Florentiae, unus philosophus, alter poeta, eodem tempore, de eadem parte, amici et socii [...].' Benvenuti de Rambaldis de Imola, p. 340.

grand as the *Commedia*[37] but also made him guiltier than his father, since in declaring the death of the individual soul he made a stand *per scientiam* that Cavalcante merely made *ex ignorantia*.[38]

As documented by the quoted excerpts, the Trecento readers focused heavily on Cavalcanti's philosophical interests, without considering them necessarily conducive to heresy, and undervalued his poetical achievement. Only during the Quattrocento did Guido Cavalcanti's philosophical profile cease to overshadow his literary one and was the *Donna me prega*'s author officially included in the vernacular Canon. The intellectual environment of the Laurentian age assimilated his oeuvre to such an extent that the *Donna me prega*'s exegetic tradition entered a Neoplatonic phase,[39] which was later considered unsound. The mediator essential to the recognition of Cavalcanti's literary importance was Antonio di Tuccio Manetti who, following Marsilio Ficino's suggestion, assembled and edited the first historical codex of Cavalcanti's poetry.[40] Although the Manetti codex still encloses Cavalcanti within the boundaries of his philosophical canzone (the sylloge also includes the major *Donna me prega* commentaries produced until then), it also has the merit of starting the circulation of the first Cavalcantian *canzoniere*. Shortly afterwards, Agnolo Poliziano and Lorenzo il Magnifico included Guido Cavalcanti as one of the most important

---

[37] '*per altezza d'ingegno*, quasi dicat: filius meus Guido fuit non minus perspicacis ingenii quam tu, et ex istis verbis potes perpendere, quomodo Dantes iverit ad Infernum; quia scilicet per altitudinem ingenii et altam speculationem animi. Et subdit autor responsionem suam ad quesitum, et respondet breviter quod Guido non potest facere istam descriptionem Inferni, quia non est poeta sicut ipse;' Ibid., p. 341.

[38] 'Modo ad propositum Guido, sicut et aliqui alii saepe faciunt, non dignabatur legere poetas, quorum princeps est Virgilius; sed certe Dantes alium honorem et fructum consecutus est ex poetari, quam Guido de solo philosophari, quia errorem quem pater habebat ex ignorantia, ipse conabatur defendere per scientiam.' Ibid., p. 343.

[39] The exegetic contributions of the Florentine intellectuals of the time are dismissed as an 'imbroglio' by Cavalcanti's later readers whose studies have firmly linked the *canzone* to Averroistic learning, such as Bruno Nardi: 'Invece i commentatori posteriori cominciarono a imbrogliare questo concetto, facendovi entrare elementi dell'amore inteso alla maniera platonica, che a poco per volta dovevano prendere il sopravvento. Così Marsilio Ficino poté vedere sintetizzate in questa canzone tutte le tesi sostenute dai partecipanti al *Simposio* di Platone, e attribuire al Cavalcanti la distinzione d'un duplice amore: l'uno acceso nell'appetito sensibile dalla forma corporea entrata in noi per la vista; l'altro suscitato nella volontà dalla forma intelligibile che riluce nella mente; il primo riposto nella voluttà sensibile, il secondo nella contemplazione intellettuale d'una pura idea.' Nardi, *Dante e la cultura medievale*, p. 83.

[40] For the philological issues regarding the *Rime*'s tradition see: De Robertis, *Antonio Manetti copista*; Tanturli, *Filologia cavalcantiana fra Antonio Manetti e Raccolta Aragonese*; Tanturli, *Proposta e Risposta. La prolusione petrarchesca del Landino e il codice cavalcantiano di Antonio Manetti*.

representatives of vernacular literature in their anthology: the *Raccolta Aragonese*, to which the Manetti codex probably served as a philological precedent.[41] In the dedicatory *Epistola* addressed to Federico d'Aragona—the letter was composed by Poliziano and signed by Lorenzo—Guido is still a 'sottilissimo dialettico e filosofo del suo secolo prestantissimo,' but he is also presented as extraordinarily competent in rhetoric and therefore celebrated for his poetic achievement: '[…] nelle invenzioni acutissimo, magnifico, ammirabile, gravissimo nelle sentenze, copioso e rilevato nell'ordine, composto, saggio e avveduto, le quali tutte sue beate vertù d'un vago, dolce e peregrino stile, come di preziosa veste, sono adorne.' When Poliziano cannot avoid recording flaws that emerge especially from a comparison with Dante, he justifies them by emphasizing Guido's intense work on his philosophical Canzone *Donna me prega*, which understandably exhausted all of his creative energy: 'Il quale, se in più spazioso campo si fusse essercitato, averebbe senza dubbio i primi onori occupati; ma sopra tutte l'altre sue opere è mirabilissima una canzona, nella quale sottilmente questo grazioso poeta d'amore ogni qualità, virtù e accidente descrisse […].'[42] A similar explanation for Cavalcanti's rhetorical weaknesses is also in

---

[41] Tanturli interprets the quick sequence of Cristoforo Landino's course on Petrarch and the Manetti *codex* as the evolution of a taste, from the Landino, who in his attempt to refound the vernacular tradition according to Humanism saves only Petrarch, to the more inclusive repertory that the *Raccolta Aragonese* will conclusively made into a canon: 'Qui c'è la scoperta di un poeta intero, non solo il poeta filosofo della canzone, e di uno stile, magari non ben definibile nei termini consueti e familiari alla cultura umanistica, cioè alla retorica classica ("non so che più che gli altri bello"), ma di indubbia qualità. Perché questa avvenisse, e nel giro assai breve di una decina d'anni, forse piuttosto meno che più, ci voleva la duttilità e l'umiltà di leggere i testi secondo i loro principi, anche prima di averli scoperti e definiti, senza schemi e propositi preconcetti, la disponibilità e la curiosità a ritrovare e riassaporare i frutti di una civiltà letteraria, di cui sotto altre urgenze si era perso il gusto. Di questi requisiti era fornito di certo Angelo Poliziano: l'umanista non ciceroniano, il filologo che predilige la latinità argentea, il poeta volgare che pratica solo i metri e i generi più marginali e popolari.' Tanturli, p. 225.
[42] Contini, *Letteratura italiana del Quattrocento*, p. 132. The *Raccolta Aragonese* is among the first Italian literary collections. Despite Lorenzo il Magnifico's signature, Agnolo Poliziano is the author of the dedicatory letter as well as of the whole project: 'Anche l'attività del Poliziano scrittore volgare ha un inizio filologico: è il lavoro o perlomeno la collaborazione alla cosiddetta Raccolta Aragonese. Questa silloge di poesie toscane antiche e coeve (che fra l'altro contribuì potentemente a livellare le rime siciliane e affini e a introdurre altri ammodernamenti) fu inviata dal Magnifico a Federico d'Aragona (il futuro Federico I re di Napoli), con un'epistola introduttiva, l'anno dopo un loro incontro in Pisa del quale Michele Barbi e altri hanno congetturato dover essere quello del 1476, non del 1465 come s'era pensato un tempo. Il Barbi stesso e altri studiosi hanno poi dimostrato che l'*Epistola*, come ha un antico manoscritto, si deve al Poliziano (in quell'epoca cancelliere di Lorenzo), che certo non si sarà limitato alla

the Quattrocento commentary to the *Divine Comedy* by Landino, whose claim is that excessive philosophical meditation prevented Guido from cultivating a proper style: 'Ma per tornare onde ci partimmo, di Cavalcante nacque Guido non solo nella vita civile excellente ma anchora in ogni spetie di speculazione exercitato; ma *precipue* acutissimo dialetico, et philosopho egregio, et non poco exercitato ne' versi toscani, e quali anchora hoggi vivono pieni di gravità et di doctrina; ma poiché datosi del tutto alla philosophia non curò molto leggere e poeti latini: né investigare loro arte et ornamenti manchò di quello stile et leggiadria la quale è propria del poeta.'[43]

Beside being celebrated as a philosopher, Cavalcanti finally gained undisputable recognition during the fifteenth century for poetry-making as well. Nevertheless his readers never ceased to turn to the lines of *Donna me prega*, whose ideological affiliation remained a predominant issue.

It is the tradition of the exegesis of the canzone that provided solid ground for confirming Cavalcanti's 'damnation' and that surpassed all the hypotheses concerning its fictional nature, such as the ones ventured by Cicciaporci and Parodi. After the crucial testimony of Dino del Garbo, the Florentine physician who composed the first important commentary of the canzone in the early fourteenth century (I will return to this text in the following chapters), a few crucial exegetes of *Donna me prega* in particular ratified Cavalcanti's heretical positions and conclusively rooted Cavalcanti's thought in the problematic ground of forbidden learning. After the lively debate in which Bruno Nardi and Guido Favati engaged between 1940 and 1955,[44] the canzone was definitely identified as a document of Averroism, or radical Aristotelianism. Nardi was proven right thanks to a crucial document. In 1952, in the library of Stuttgart, Paul Oskar Kristeller discovered a manuscript containing a moral treatise by Magister Jacobus de

---

prefazione scritta in nome del suo patrono: la pima riflessione critica sulla nostra poesia, se si prescinde dal *De Vulgari*, appartiene dunque al Poliziano, che vi usa una prosa affine a quella del Boccaccio dantista.' Ibid., p. 128.

[43] Landino, p. 587.

[44] The Nardi-Favati *querelle* starts with two essays by Bruno Nardi: *L'averroismo del primo amico di Dante* (1940) and *Di un nuovo commento alla canzone del Cavalcanti sull'amore* (1947), now included in *Dante e la cultura medievale*. While Nardi attributes full reliability to the fourteenth-century commentary to *Donna me prega* by Dino del Garbo and therefore claims the *canzone* is rooted in Averroism, Favati locates the theoretical background of the Cavalcantian manifesto within the more general area of a 'dilagante neoaristotelismo scolastico' (Favati, *La glossa latina di Dino del Garbo a 'Donna me prega'*, p. 77). In his: *Noterella polemica sull'averroismo di Guido Cavalcanti*. In: *Rassegna di filosofia* (1954) No. III, pp. 47-71, Nardi replies to Favati and establishes *Donna me prega's* ideological frame of reference, which remains decisive.

Pistoia, the *Questio disputata de felicitate*, among other uncatalogued writings. It had been written in Bologna and bore the dedication: *amico carissimo Guidoni Cavalcantis*. Kristeller concluded that the *Questio* was a product of Averroism, as well as evidence of an intersection between Averroism and the poets of the Stilnovo.[45] Kristeller's decisive discovery substantiated Nardi's reading of *Donna me prega* first, and secondly that of Maria Corti, consequently settling the question of the philosophical affiliation of the canzone.

The material composing the Cavalcanti tradition, as well as the ways in which this material was assembled and used, confirm the profile of a controversial author and an elusive yet crucial character. Further, these features reflect the dominance of Dante's writing in the classification of the vernacular repertory since they are a response to the source available when the profile was being made, the few lines included in *Inferno* X. The aloofness attributed to Guido Cavalcanti throughout the literary vernacular tradition was almost directly influenced by the void he inhabits during the dialogue in *Inferno* X and by the even more general strategy laid out by Dante: to obscure Guido's intellectual space in order to purge the established *auctoritates* of the heterodox ones that the *Donna me prega*'s author incorporates into his text, as well as to found a new set of vernacular *auctores*, led by Dante himself. However, as I previously suggested, this is also Guido's strategy. As if anticipating and counterbalancing Dante's move, Guido enacts his own disappearance and leaves his page void of its author, his lines adespota. Guido represents his own effacing in line 10 of Sonnet XVIII (emphasis mine):

> Noi siàn le triste penne isbigotite,
> le cesoiuzze e 'l coltellin dolente,
> ch'avemo scritte dolorosamente
> quelle parole che vo' avete udite.
>
> Or vi diciàn perché noi siàn partite
> e siàn venute a voi qui di presente:
> la man che ci movea dice che sente

---

[45] The treatise is the *Questio disputata de felicitate*, which had first been discovered in another manuscript by M. Grabmann. The dedication 'Viro bene nato et mihi dilecto et pre aliis amico carissimo Gwidoni domini Cavalcantis de Cavalcantibus de Florencia' is what convinced Kristeller that philosophical studies were cultivated in Bologna and that a direct relationship between the Averroist philosopher magister Jacobus and Guido Cavalcanti could be established. His finding also gave documented evidence to Nardi's interpretation of *Donna me prega* (Kristeller, *A philosophical Treatise from Bologna dedicated to Guido Cavalcanti: Magister Jacobus de Pistorio and his Quaestio de felicitate.*)

cose dubbiose nel core apparite;

le quali hanno destrutto sì costui
ed hannol posto sì presso a la morte,
ch'altro non n'è rimaso che sospiri.

Ora vi preghiàn quanto possiàn più forte
che non sdegniate di tenerci noi,
tanto che un poco di pietà vi miri.

(We are the poor bewildered quills, the little scissors and the grieving penknife, who have sorrowfully written those words that you have heard. Now we tell you why we have left and presently come here to you: the hand that used to move us says it feels dreadful things that have appeared in the heart, which have so underdone him and brought him so close to death *that nothing else is left of him but sighs.* We now beg you as earnestly as we can that you do not scorn to keep us for so long as a little compassion suits you.)[46]

Guido Cavalcanti emerges from thirteenth-century memory with this self-portrayal fashioned by the tools on his desk and delivered to his readers, the Faithful of Love. This is the picture that quills, scissors, and penknife, the only witnesses to have survived the destruction wrought by 'cose dubbiose,' have created: Guido, a ghost-like presence lingering in the background of a desolate scenario and reduced to only his own sighs, can barely be heard. Cavalcanti commits his character and his lines to this almost undetectable profile; accordingly, his character moves across the centuries resisting the historical grounding of its main features, and his lines occupy a satellite position in the literary canon.

Sonnet XVIII has been singled out in specific essays, such as the ones by Italo Calvino and Maria Corti, although not in terms of a self-portrait. According to Calvino, with this sonnet Cavalcanti makes himself the initiator of modern poetry. The emphasis he places here on the material processes inherent in literary activity is an anticipation of what is taken up again many centuries afterwards by Mallarmé, who engages in a similar clash between the page's whiteness and the author's writing. Maria Corti concludes that in this sonnet Cavalcanti highlights the materiality which serves to deliver his poetry and in doing so he also includes the element of formality among the identifying marks of the Stilnovo fellowship.[47]

---

[46] All translation of Cavalcanti's poems are from: *The Poetry of Guido Cavalcanti*. Ed. and trans. Lowry Nelson. Jr. Garland. New York and London, 1986.

[47] Italo Calvino begins an essay about Saul Steinberg by recalling sonnet XVIII as a testament to Cavalcanti's modernity: 'Il primo a considerare gli strumenti e i gesti della propria attività come il vero soggetto dell'opera è stato un poeta, nel XIII secolo. Guido Cavalcanti scrive un

I believe Sonnet XVIII contains further information. In it, Cavalcanti Cavalcanti forges a new relation between *auctor* and *agens* as yet another ground for the troubled dialogue with Dante. The *Divina Commedia* originates in an important distinction between the *auctor* and the *agens*, who are different by nature as well as distant in time: 'Ah quanto a dire qual *era è* cosa dura/esta selva selvaggia e aspra e forte/che nel pensier mi rinnova la paura!'(emphasis mine). The distinction is crucial since it is the tool Dante employs as the narrative mechanism through which the pilgrim's conversion at the core of the poema unfolds: the progression of Dante's journey corresponds precisely to the overcoming of that distinction. In Cavalcanti's poetry, on the other hand, the writing offers no redemption since the distance between *auctor* and *agens* is shortened, if not reduced to zero. The act of recording the experience does not take place from a safe later perspective as is the case for the *Divine Comedy*; it happens simultaneously to the experience.

Rather than resulting from an act of writing, the *Rime*'s composition could be compared to the tracing of lines of an electrocardiogram. As the protagonist gazes at his love object, the reactions taking place in his body are registered on the blank page; the tracing records the sequence of events encompassed between the first glance directed at the love object and the obscurity that inevitably, as we shall see, follows. Such synchronicity between the events and their recording is produced in the reader's eyes by the superimposition between *agens* and *auctor* of which Sonnet XVIII is an example. In it, the protagonist and author of the amorous encounter are

---

sonetto in cui chi parla in prima persona sono le penne e gli strumenti per tagliarle e appuntarle, che si presentano fin dal primo verso: *Noi siàn le triste penne isbigotite,/le cesoiuzze e 'l coltellin dolente.* [...]. Guido Cavalcanti apre con questi versi la poesia moderna. La apre e la chiude. Dopo di lui i poeti preferiscono dimenticarsi che mentre scrivono stanno scrivendo e non facendo qualcos'altro. [...]. Bisogna aspettare Mallarmé perché il poeta si renda conto che il luogo dove avviene la sua poesia si situa *sur le vide papier que sa blancheur défende*.' Calvino, *La penna in prima persona*, pp. 362-363. Maria Corti follows up Calvino's essay and observes that entrusting the poem's content to writing tools and then sending them as heralds to the Faithful of Love signifies the founding of the Stilnovistic fellowship in the formal delivery of poetry: 'Gli strumenti della scrittura vanno dai Fedeli d'Amore perché destinatari del discorso loro, anche se non sono nominati. Il fatto semanticamente di rilievo è che l'appello ai Fedeli d'Amore indica sostanzialmente un rifiuto del destinatario che non sia del gruppo, che non abbia la poetica stilnovistica, condizione indispensabile, secondo il Cavalcanti, per la comunicazione lirica. Il che equivale a dire che la partecipazione degli amici al dolore del poeta è, si badi bene, partecipazione alla *resa formale* del dolore amoroso, alla sua rappresentazione entro la scrittura, di cui sono appunto simbolo gli oggetti di cancelleria.' Corti, *La penna alla prima persona*. In: *Scritti su Cavalcanti e Dante*, pp. 44.

subject to the same destiny: the protagonist is driven into obscurity and stripped of his vital capacities by the encounter while the author remains detectable at the conclusion of that encounter only through the sighs that his writing tools convey to the readers. This sonnet bears the marks of a crucial text. Whether it should be considered the envoy of the whole *canzoniere* as has been suggested[48] or not, in my reading it serves as the model for a series of poems within the *Rime*, whose content is the representation of the phenomena resulting from the love encounter. These poems complement Cavalcanti's theory about love formulated in the major canzone because they represent the phenomenology of this theory: on the grounds that the notion of subjectivity must be intended in strictly sensorial terms, these poems show the sequence of effects upon the body of the *Rime*'s protagonist after his gaze has encountered the love object. By replicating the concatenation of events following the sight of the love object, the poems function as the laboratory in which Cavalcanti applies his theory on rhetorical grounds and proves it. In the following chapters, I shall investigate these poems by framing them in this perspective and casting light on the *auctoritates* Cavalcanti builds into his texts in order not only to demonstrate his conclusions about love, but also to preserve those *auctoritates* from the impending banishment threatening them in European academia at the onset of the thirteenth century.

---

[48] As noted by Domenico De Robertis in his introduction to this text: 'Da "scritte" a "diciàn" a "dice," è l'intera dimensione della parola cavalcantiana che si traduce (oggi si direbbe 'teatralmente') in assoluta dedizione. Per cui il sonetto, peraltro di limitatissima tradizione, potrebbe fare da epigrafe a epilogo all'intero libro delle sue rime.' De Robertis, *Rime*, p. 59.

CHAPTER II
Human Love in Darkness

II.1 The Theory about Love and a Rhetorical Quest

In this study I examine the lines of Cavalcanti's 'minor' rhymes. I use this definition conventionally in relation to his major Canzone *Donna me prega*, a philosophical manifesto about love. While the *Rime* gravitate towards the canzone as the center of their structure, the theory elaborated in *Donna me prega* circulates from the center to the margins, where, more specifically, this theory is tested on the grounds of its representability as well as of its conveyance. In the minor rhymes, in other words, Cavalcanti expands the theme of his major canzone by showing its phenomenology and by solving the technical issues it suggests: the quest for a language able to expound the human experience of love.

Signs of this quest, for a means of transmitting a content which is compelling but ineffable because it overwhelms the weak expressive power of language, can be found in the very origins of the vernacular lyric tradition. The leading author at the Sicilian court of Frederick II, the notary Giacomo da Lentini, had already remarked on the inadequacy of his poetic tools when he was called upon to describe the lover's experience; faced with his inability to speak about the conditions provoked by love, Giacomo da Lentini was troubled and disheartened.[1] In the Canzonetta *Meravigliosamente*, while searching for a saying ('detto') to describe how the lover is affected as he gazes at the woman, the Sicilian notary shifts to a semiotics of the suffering lover's demeanor—'Per zo s'io v'o laudato,/madonna, in molte parti/di belleze c'avite,/non so se v'è contato/ch'eo lo faccia per arti,/che voi ve ne dolite;/sacciatelo per singa/zo ch'eo vi dire' a linga/quando voi mi vedite' (I have praised you highly, my lady, in all your beauties. I do not know if you have been told that I do it with artifice, since you complain. Learn through signs what I would tell you in words when you see me, 37-45)—and ultimately resolves the impasse of his delivery by letting the lover's sighs speak for themselves: 'Si *'n corpo*, quando passo,/inver voi non mi

---

[1] 'Lo meo namoramento/non pò parire in ditto,/*ca sì* com'eo lo sento /cor no lo *penzaria* né diria lingua:/zo ch'eo dico è neente/inver ch'eo sono distritto/tanto coralemente:/' Giacomo da Lentini: *Madonna, dir vo voglio*, 17-22. The quotes from the Sicilian School are all from: Panvini, Bruno: *Le Rime della scuola siciliana*. Leo Olschki. Firenze, 1962. Translations are mine.

giro,/bella, per isguardare,/andando, ad ogni passo/sì getto uno sospiro/che mi faci ancosciare;/e certo bene ancoscio,/c'a pena mi conoscio,/tanto, bella, mi pare.' (If I do not glance at you when I walk by you, in person, at every step I give a sigh, which grieves me: and truly I am anguished, and I almost do not know myself, so beautiful you seem to me.)

Following in the notary's wake, Guido Cavalcanti replaces verbal language with visible bodily signs when he finds himself faced with the linguistic void threatening his writing. Cavalcanti, however, brings the topic of language deficiency to a radical conclusion. In a few poems of his *Rime*, he illustrates the crafting of a new poetic language by using the body's components and functions to convey meaning. In order to array the body's rhetorical capacities entirely, Cavalcanti disassembles it into its single members and furthermore makes the internal organs visible, as if the display were an anatomical section. In Sonnet XII, the reader is presented with the lover's wounded heart which bears the sign of a cross, described by an off-stage 'voce profonda' as the symptom of the sequence of events triggered by love: 'tanto che s'ode una profonda voce/la qual dice: -Chi gran pena sente/guardi costui, e vederà 'l su' core/che Morte 'l porta 'n man tagliato in croce.-' (Until a deep voice is heard to say: -'Whoever feels great suffering let him look at that man and he will see that Death bears in hand his heart cut into a cross.') This voice, which is demoted to noise in Ballad X (13-20), is autonomous of the author's expression: it testifies to the very detachment of the message from its author, who 'dies' from the experience. For Cavalcanti, this alienation is a direct result of the overwhelming chain of physiological processes set in motion by the vision of the beloved. The ostentatious presentation of the wounded heart serves a communicative purpose. The marks carved in the lover's heart convey the poem's meaning and exemplify the use of the lover's body as an active rhetorical tool. This special rhetoric results from the application of the theory of love, as formulated in the lines of *Donna me prega*, to poetic language.

The connection between love and ineffability is introduced in Guido Cavalcanti's poetry in the ballad we find at the beginning of the *Rime*:[2]

Angelica sembranza
in voi, donna, riposa:
Dio, quanto aventurosa
fue la mia disïanza!

---

[2] According to the sequence set in the Favati edition: Cavalcanti, Guido: *Rime*. Guido Favati ed. Ricciardi. Milano-Napoli, 1957. On this edition is based the commentary by De Robertis.

> Vostra cera gioiosa,
> poi che passa e avanza
> natura e costumanza,
> ben è mirabil cosa.
> Fra lor le donne dea
> vi chiaman, come sète;
> tanto adorna parete,
> ch'eo non saccio contare;
> e chi poria pensare - oltra Natura?

(An angelic semblance dwells, lady, in you: God, how lucky was my desiring! Your joyful countenance, in that passes and goes beyond nature and custom, is surely a wondrous thing. Among themselves the ladies call you goddess, and so you are; you appear so embellished that I know not how to describe it: and who could cast thought beyond nature?)

The inability to articulate, which comes with the inability to think: '/...non saccio contare;/e chi poria pensare - oltra Natura?' is explained through the unattainable object of the telling, the woman who lies beyond the boundaries of his perceptions, and therefore beyond his experience, she who '...passa e avanza,/natura e costumanza.' The setting introduced by this ballad, in which the lover is spatially separated from the object of his love, the former within nature and the latter beyond it, is repetitively presented in Cavalcanti's rhymes: it is love that makes the fracture visible.

This fracture of space is crucial. The separate spaces that the woman and the lover gazing at her occupy are also symptomatic of a crucial flaw in the lover's capacities, i.e., his impossibility to reach out beyond his sensorial ability. This constraint reflects the ideological stance at the roots of Cavalcanti's poetry as it is explained in his treatise about love: the Canzone *Donna me prega*. In the canzone, Cavalcanti elaborates his meditation upon the nature of love by answering a set of eight questions: 'là ove posa, e chi lo fa creare,/e qual sia sua vertute e sua potenza,/l'essenza – poi e ciascun suo movimento,/e 'l piacimento – che 'l fa dire amare,/e s'omo per veder lo pò mostrare.' (Where it [love] resides, who makes it exist, and what its virtue and potency may be, its essence next and each of its stirrings, and the pleasurableness that makes it called love, and whether one can show it to be visible.) The text, among the most complex in the Italian tradition, utilizes a dense and precise philosophical language that, because of an inadequate grasp of the cultural context to which the text belongs, has challenged many generations of scholars engaged in disentangling obscure cruces.

My study is grounded in the most recent and, I argue, convincing reading of *Donna me prega* in Maria Luisa Ardizzone's monograph: *Guido Cavalcanti. The Other Middle Ages*. Ardizzone presents and extensively supports her exegesis of the canzone in chapters II through IV of her book; in those chapters, she bridges the gap distancing modern readers from the canzone by connecting directly to its first interpretation, the lengthy commentary produced in the fourteenth century by the Florentine doctor Dino Del Garbo. Ardizzone's crucial contribution is her claim that Guido Cavalcanti's theory does not present love as dark (as Bruno Nardi and Maria Corti concluded)[3] but, rather, as diaphanous. By relating love to the diaphanous Cavalcanti imbues it with a state of potentiality: love contains both light and darkness, but is inevitably dark when experienced by humans. Ardizzone sets forth the diaphanous as the crucial metaphor active inside the text. The term is included in Aristotle's *De anima* and explained as 'transparent;' however, once incorporated into the theory of light and vision, the diaphanous is related to, and explained by, the field of accidentality.[4] The term 'accident' is employed to define love in *Donna me prega*'s first lines: 'Donna me prega,-per ch'eo voglio dire/d'un accidente – che sovente – è fero/ed è sì altero – ch'è chiamato amore:/' (A lady bids me, and so I would speak of an accident that is often unruly and so haughty that it is called love.) Accident and the diaphanous are the two Aristotelian terms that are essential to disclosing the meaning of *Donna me prega*. The former is included in Aristotle's works (although not among his *Categories*) and defined by juxtaposition with 'substance.' In his *Physics*, while making a distinction between the *substratum* and its possible mutations, Aristotle writes that those accidental mutations can be added to the substance but are not part of its essence, which, unlike them, is permanent.[5] Accident is also related in the

---

[3] Bruno Nardi, in particular, omitted to give importance to Del Garbo's commentary: 'Aware as he was of the long exegeses of the canzone, Nardi did not, however, take into account Dino Del Garbo's interpretation of these lines in his important fourteeenth-century commentary. Contrary to Nardi's interpretation, for Del Garbo the two terms 'diaphanous' and 'obscurity' are related rather than opposed. This point is crucial since it reveals Del Garbo's thorough knowledge of Aristotle's *De anima*, which he cites.' Ardizzone, *Guido Cavalcanti. The Other Middle Ages*, p. 54.
[4] Ibid., p. 48.
[5] 'Determinatis autem his, ex omnibus que fiunt hoc est accipere, si aliquis intenderit sicut dicimus, quoniam oportet aliquid subici quod fit, et hoc si numero est unum, sed specie non unum est; specie enim dico et ratione idem; non enim idem est homini et inmusico esse. Et hoc quidem permanet, illud vero non permanet; non oppositum quidem permanet (homo enim

De anima, and its commentaries, to the operations of the soul. Therefore, by defining love as an accident, Cavalcanti creates an ideological scenario in which he compounds physics and the science of the soul and subjects the processes of the soul to the same laws ruling the realm of matter. This connection between love and the theory of matter is recalled and endorsed by Dino Del Garbo in his commentary, specifically when he claims that 'love' is simply a name given *ad placitum* to the main topic of *Donna me prega*, which is 'passion.' The theory of passion is a key topic in the thirteenth-century intellectual debate and part of the theory of matter for medieval thinkers. Aristotle employs the category of passion in discussing perception in the *De anima*: 'to perceive' means to be acted upon, to be affected by the agent of the sensation. The category of passion, however, is elaborated mainly in the *De generatione et corruptione*: in it, passion is the category defining matter since matter is characterized by ongoing movements and transformations that require it to be passive to change.[6] Drawing from this composite philosophical ground and employing the same tools of logic at the foundation of Cavalcanti's method, Ardizzone discloses the meaning of the poem and demonstrates how, according to Cavalcanti's theory, love comprises by nature both light and darkness but is experienced by humans only as darkness. Although humans are drawn to follow the abstract image produced at the sight of the woman they are unable to, held back by an excessive physiological reaction which disturbs and ultimately interrupts the knowledge-acquiring process. Incapable of complete the phantasmatic process human beings fall back into the realm of the senses and of matter, that is, the realm where their individual sensorial capacities can be performed, while the phantasm joins the intellectual and universal dimension of the possible intellect.[7]

---

permanet) musicum autem et inmusicum non permanet, neque ex ambobus compositum, ut inmusicus homo.' Aristoteles latinus, *Physica*, I, 7 190a, 14-21.

[6] For a thorough explanation of the term passion and its implications in Cavalcanti's poetry, see Ardizzone, *Guido Cavalcanti. The Other Middle Ages*, pp. 75-77.

[7] On the grounds of her conclusions, Ardizzone reconstructs the connection between *Donna me prega* and the *Quaestio de Felicitate* by Giacomo da Pistoia. As I mentioned in chapter I, the *Quaestio* was employed by Bruno Nardi first, then by Maria Corti, as a decisive source for the deciphering of *Donna me prega*. In her chapter *Pleasure and Intellectual Happiness*, Maria Luisa Ardizzone contributes to the issue by proving that although Giacomo da Pistoia and Cavalcanti participate in the same debate, they reach opposite conclusions with regards to human happiness: in the *Quaestio de Felicitate*, Giacomo includes happiness among the attributes of the speculative intellect and defines it as the contemplation of the separate substances and especially God, while Cavalcanti theorizes the radical inability of human individuals to perform,

The possible intellect, introduced by Cavalcanti in the second stanza of his canzone, is a crucial tenet of his poem's interpretation and of his cultural affiliation, as we shall see. The theory elaborated in *Donna me prega* states that when engaged in a phantasmatic process, such as the one triggered by the sight of the love object, humans are unable to participate in the intellectual realm. Although they are part of the abstraction process when they produce the image (the phantasm), they are ultimately excluded from it. In lines 21-28, while answering the question 'chi lo fa creare' Cavalcanti describes the phase following the production of the phantasm: 'Vèn da veduta forma che s'intende,/che prende – nel possibile intelletto,/come in subietto, – loco e dimoranza./In quella parte mai non ha possanza/perché da qualitate non descende:/resplende – in sé perpetüal effetto;/non ha diletto – ma consideranza;/sì che non pote largir simiglianza.' ([Love] derives from a seen form that becomes intelligible, that takes up place and dwelling in the possible intellect as in substance. In that part [love] never has any power. Since [the possible intellect] does not derive from quality, it shines in itself as perpetual effect; it does not have pleasure but rather contemplation; and thus it can not create an image.) Once humans, affected by the love object, have produced the phantasm, it is attracted to the possible intellect, the realm where it belongs. This reference to the possible intellect has given grounds for supporting the claim of Guido Cavalcanti's alignment with a current of thought that in its short life-span became a dangerous threat to medieval culture. Radical Aristotelianism, or Averroism,[8] was a controversial fringe movement that surfaced between 1260 and 1277 at the Faculty of Arts in Paris mainly as a result of the massive introduction into medieval Western culture of a new body of works, including translations from Greek and Arabic of Aristotle's *Libri naturales* and their commentators (such as al-Kindi, Alfarabi, Avicenna, Averroes, al-Ghazali). By 1255, all of Aristotle's known works were officially included in the curricula of the Parisian Faculty of Arts. The entrance of the 'new' Aristotle, including the *De anima* and its

---

as individuals, an intellectual activity and, consequently, their exclusion from the happiness of the mind (ibid., p.130.)

[8] Van Steenberghen claims that the most accurate definition is 'radical,' or 'heterodox' Aristotelianism. The term 'Averroism,' on the other hand, was employed to indicate specifically believers in the unity of the possible intellect: 'Les données certaines sur lesquelles nous pouvons tabler se réduisent aux suivantes: un *courant philosophiques hétérodoxe* a existé à Paris entre 1260 et 1277; ce courant est fondamentalement aristotélicien et doit être caractérisé comme un *aristotélisme hétérodoxe* ou *radical*; au chapitre de l'âme intellective, certains de ces philosophes ont accepté l'interprétation averroïste d'Aristote en professant le *monopsychisme d'Averroès*.' Van Steenberghen, *La Philosophie au XIII siècle*, p. 335.

commentaries, led to the redesigning of the ideological scenario in Paris. Radical Aristotelianism was among the currents of thought (three, according to Van Stenbeerghen's conclusions)[9] that arose in response to the newly available Aristotelian texts. Among its most significant exponents were thinkers who rooted their ideas in the Aristotle commentary of Averroes, namely, Sigier of Brabant and Boethius of Dacia.[10] Their distinctive mark was the monopsychism they professed through the assimiliation of the concept of the possible intellect: the collective and immortal soul as had been elaborated by Averroes from the Aristotelian theory of separate substances.

The specific conclusions supported by Sigieri and Boethius, and the scientific theories that entered the University classrooms, soon constituted a threat to the theological fundaments which could not possibly absorb some of their assumptions. The inevitable clash between these new theories and the established scholastic ones reached its climax between 1270 and 1277, when the Parisian theological stronghold acted and banished some of the newly introduced theories from University milieus. In 1270 Thomas Aquinas wrote his *De unitate intellectus contra Averroistas* in which he directly disputed Sigieri's theories. In the same year Étienne Tempier, the Bishop of Paris, composed a list of thirteen 'errors' and prohibited the Parisian professors from incorporating them into their teaching under threat of excommunication. There were four main heretical errors: eternity of the world, negation of divine providence, unicity of the intellective soul, and determinism.[11] A few years later, in 1277, Bishop Tempier was pressured by

---

[9] 'En utilisant et en complétant les travaux de ses devanciers, Mandonnet montre que l'attitude prise vis-à-vis d'Aristote a déterminé l'orientation des principaux courants doctrinaux du siècle. Attitude d'opposition à Aristote chez les augustiniens: [...]. Vers 1240, Albert le Grand inaugure une nouvelle école et crée l'*aristotélisme latin*; son œuvre est continuée par son disciple Thomas d'Aquin; [...]. Enfin vers 1250 ou un peu plus tard apparaît un troisième courant, aristotélicien comme le précédent, mais tandis qu'Albert et Thomas s'efforçaient de créer un aristotélisme chrétien, Siger de Brabant professe un aristotélisme hétérodoxe, car il interprète Aristote à la manière d'Averroès et sans souci de respecter les enseignements de la révélation chrétienne et de l'Église: Siger est le fondateur de l'*averroïsme latin.*' Ibid., pp. 13-14.

[10] Averroes' commentary to Aristotle's works started circulating in the Latin West after 1230, first in the court of Frederick the II, then at the University of Bologna and finally at the University of Paris. The main agents in this process were Frederick II and Michele Scoto, the philosopher and magician who, invited to the Court of Frederick, led a team of translators converting the corpus of Averroes into Latin. The documents attesting the growing importance of Averroes in medieval culture are examined and chronologically organized by Roland De Vaux in his: *La première entrée d'Averroès chez les Latins.*

[11] Van Stenberghheen, *La Philosophie au XIII siècle*, p. 337.

the Pope to take action again and in the end emanated a second condemnation of 219 propositions. Following this banishment, several teaching careers, including Sigieri's, were terminated.

The decisive theme that Cavalcanti transfers from radical Aristotelianism to his poetry is the theory of monopsychism. Following the Averroistic tenet of the possible intellect, Cavalcanti establishes that humans are individuals within the boundaries of their senses but, as individuals, have no participation in the intellectual realm that is by definition universal. The fracture separating individual senses and the collective intellect is made clear through the experience of love. That experience starts as senses-bound, through the eyes, and develops into the production of a phantasm. This production, which corresponds to the process of abstraction, can be either completed—the phantasm is attracted to the collective soul all humans share only through a momentary *coniunctio*—or interrupted, as is the case when the disturbances occurring in the lover's body are excessive. Regardless of the outcome of the phantasmatic production, individuals are bound by their sensorial perceptions and subjected to the laws ruling the realm to which their perceptions apply, that is, matter.

Human confinement within the realm of matter has ethical repercussions. The consequences of Guido Cavalcanti's conclusions are that humans are subject to the same determinism at work in matter. In the *Rime* the poet records the lover's behavior as a sequence of reactions to the sight of the woman that are as involuntary as any other alteration occurring in the natural world. These alterations constitute the object of the minor rhymes and the reason why the minor stand as the phenomenology of *Donna me prega*'s theoretical conclusions. However, the theoretical and phenomenological elaboration does not exhaust Cavalcanti's quest, which regards rhetorical issues as well. The poet's task in the *Rime* therefore also includes an illustration of his expressive technique, the display of the laboratory in which he crafted the tools able to describe his poetry's content: *cesoiuzze* and *coltellin* (the quills and the penknife) that, in order to represent the painful love venture, are described in Sonnet XVIII as 'grieving.' In correspondence with the object of his poetry, Cavalcanti forged tools that have been affected by the same painful sequence of reactions as the protagonist of the love venture and that are, therefore, in pain. That is to say, Cavalcanti, in a specific portion of his rhymes, elaborates a language assembled in obedience to the features that characterize love: coaction, passivity and darkness.

Responding to the predestined destruction which awaits the *Rime*'s protagonist, Cavalcanti creates a language whose vocabulary and syntax obey the rules of passion. The relation between the minor rhymes and *Donna me prega* becomes more defined: the minor not only dramatize the changes that take place in the body as a result of the 'accidente fero,' they also make the rhetorical consequences of the major canzone's assumptions explicit for the reader. In the close reading of the following chapters I have selected a group of rhymes that offer radical rhetorical solutions since in them the violence of the lover's physiological reactions disrupts the formation of the phantasm and, as a consequence, all imaginative activity. Since love prevents the lover from retaining the image of the woman, it also compromises language production. To this, Cavalcanti responds by encompassing the language used to convey his poetry's object in the realm of nature and making it subject to the law of matter. In chapters IV and V, I will investigate his rhetorical solutions to the darkness produced by love, as well as the transformation imposed on the notion of authorship. In this chapter, I will show how the closely knit relation between language and object in the *Rime* becomes visible, and is indeed explained, by the investigation of the sources interwoven into the text.

II.2 Philosophers and Physicians in Thirteenth-Century Culture

I employ the word 'source' in the meaning of *auctoritas*, a concept at the very foundation of medieval literary production. As attested by the statement that John of Salisbury attributed to Bernard of Chartres, the medieval intellectuals perceived themselves as being vastly subordinate to a cultural past of undisputed importance.[12] In the shadow of the achievement nonpareil of the classical authors, the Middle Ages based the production of its written culture on the notion of authoritativeness preserved in the existing tradition. The authors who were recognized as *auctoritates* became the foundations of medieval culture as well as its principal, essential building material: following the scholastic procedure, which assembled excerpts connected by commentaries, the 'writing' of a text depended largely on the

---

[12] 'Dicebat Bernardus Carnotensis non esse quasi nanos gigantium humeris insidentes, ut possimus plura eis et remotiora videre, non utique proprii visus acumine aut eminentia corporis, sed quia in altum subvehimur et extollimur magnitudine gigantea.' John of Salisbury, *Metalogicon* III, 4.

inclusion of existing material.[13] The *auctoritates* constituted a collective patrimony that the medieval writer could readily avail himself of; drawing from it, he wove the old material into the new and, in this connection with the imported author, found his own intellectual identity. The imported authors, with their status of *auctoritates*, were worthy of credit, 'authentic.' And it was this very authenticity that guaranteed that the quotes from their works, in addition to filling the 'warp' of the new text (a *textus* is etymologically a fabric), also bestowed the status of authority on it, thus assuring the making of an intellectual tradition. The distinction of the two interfacing functions at work, on one hand the production of a text, on the other the passing on of authority, were clearly at the root of an orthographic variation regarding the word 'author,' which is rendered both as *actor*, from *aliquid agere*, to produce an artifact, and as *auctor*, from *augere*, to augment. It is also however linked semantically to *auctoritas*, to initiate an act in the juridical sense, and therefore to be trusted and obeyed.[14] This same twofold notion of 'author' is documented in the *Banquet* (IV, 6), where Dante indicates the two etymological derivations for 'autore' that explain his two

---

[13] Marie-Dominique Chenu wrote extensively about the notion of auctor in medieval culture. In his *Authentica et magistralia* he claims that the general clerical setting in which medieval culture develops is what explains why that culture is formed by adding on the margins of an already written book: 'Pendant le moyen âge, la mise en route de tout enseignement et tous les cadres de la culture s'organisent par des clercs: [...]. Il est donc normal que la théologie soit la science suprême, étant la première et suprême curiosité de ces esprits. Or la théologie est la science d'un livre, le livre des livres, la Bible. Elle l'est de droit, car, science de Dieu, elle trouve dans ce livre la parole de Dieu, la révélation de Dieu; elle le fut de fait, car l'enseignement s'en établit spontanément et continûment sur le texte de cette parole de Dieu, sur la collation des textes d'une tradition qui l'interprète en s'agglutinant autour de lui. L'autorité, les "autorités", sont la loi de son travail.' Chenu, *Authentica et magistralia*, pp. 352-353.

[14] 'C'est cependant au moyen âge, au moment où les confusions sembleraient devoir se multiplier et amener une facile équivoque, que les deux mots vont, dans leur emploi technique et malgré les négligences des copistes, se différencier nettement et se spécialiser, avec un curieux déplacement de sens. C'est *actor* qui va revêtir le sens de *auctor* = auteur d'un ouvrage, selon une précision qui renforce, sans le limiter du reste, le sens de *aliquid agere*; et *auctor* va prendre une valeur spéciale en direction et en dépendance de *auctoritas*, où se bloquent l'idée d'origine (*auctor*: qui prend l'initiative d'un acte) et l'idée d'autorité, de dignité; il prend ainsi la couleur juridique de tout le système de vocabulaire qui, dès l'antiquité, s'était développé autour du concept d'*auctoritas*. [...]. C'est d'ailleurs ce qui va introduire une seconde équivoque, avec le nouveau mot, ou mieux la nouvelle graphie *author*, que suscitait évidemment le rapprochement entre *auctor* et *authenticus*.' Chenu, *Auctor, Actor, Author*, pp. 82-83. Chenu explains the transmission of the function of authority through the semantic evolution of the term auctor, beginning with its first employment in Latin in the field of private law (Chenu, *Authentica et magistralia*, p. 354.)

tasks: to tie together, to harmonize as when composing music, and to pass on his authority, his 'being worthy of faith and obedience':

> È dunque da sapere che 'autoritade' non è altro che 'atto d'autore'. Questo vocabulo, cioè 'autore', sanza quella terza lettera C, può discendere da due principii: l'uno si è d'uno verbo molto lasciato da l'uso in gramatica, che significa tanto quanto 'legare parole', cioè 'auieo'. E chi ben guarda lui, ne la sua prima voce apertamente vedrà che elli stesso lo dimostra, che solo di legame di parole è fatto, cioè di sole cinque vocali, che sono anima e legame d'ogni parole, e composto d'esse per modo volubile, a figurare imagine di legame. [...]. E in quanto 'autore' viene e discende da questo verbo, si prende solo per li poeti, che con l'arte musaica le loro parole hanno legate: e di questa significazione al presente non s'intende. L'altro principio, onde 'autore' discende, sì come testimonia Uguiccione nel principio de le sue *Derivazioni*, è uno vocabulo greco che dice 'autentin', che tanto vale in latino quanto 'degno di fede e d'obedienza'. [Onde, con ciò sia cosa che Aristotile sia dignissimo di fede e d'obedienza,] manifesto è che le sue parole sono somma e altissima autoritade.
>
> ('Authority' means the activity proper to an author (*auctore*). This word, (*auctore*, without its third letter, C) can be derived from either of two sources. One is a verb, *auieo*, which has largely dropped out of use in Latin; it has the meaning of 'to tie words together'. An attentive person will clearly recognize from its form in the first person of the present tense that the word itself makes it own meaning plain, for it consists entirely of what ties words together, that is, entirely of the five vowels. [...]. 'Author' as having its origin and derivation in this verb is used only of poets, who have tied their words together through the art of music. With the word as used in this sense I am not concerned here. As Uguccione indicates at the beginning of his *Derivations*, the other source from which 'author' (*autore*) is derived is the Greek word *autentin*, which is equivalent to the Latin meaning 'worthy of being trusted and obeyed'. From this comes the word with which we are concerned, 'authority.' It is clear, then, that 'authority' means the same as 'an activity worthy of being trusted and obeyed.' I need only establish that Aristotle is entirely worthy of being trusted and obeyed for it to be clear that his words are of the greatest and most revered authority.)[15]

Given the theoretic and procedural settings at the basis of medieval literary production, the first investigation to be conducted on a thirteenth-century text regards its sources, the material the author employed as the authoritative filling of the text. In the case of Guido Cavalcanti, the field of inquiry is defined by the ideological affiliation established in *Donna me prega*. As recapitulated above, in his canzone Cavalcanti articulates a meditation about love by pivoting it around the tenet of passion, therefore grounding the text in the field of natural philosophy. Thirteenth-century natural philosophy, or physics, was based on the *Libri naturales* by Aristotle (*De anima, Physics, Meteorologica, De coelo, De generatione et corrutione, Parva Naturalia,*

---

[15] Dante Alighieri, *The Banquet*. Ed. and trans. Christopher Ryan. Saratoga: Anma Libri, 1989, pp 133-134.

De animalibus) and had a central and propaedeutical role in university teaching. Its vast field of study comprised the terrestrial as well as celestial bodies, which are all subject to change, that is, to movement.[16] Inside the boundaries set by natural philosophy, the sources dealing with the human body that cover the main topics in the field of psychology, such as the *De anima*, are the ones most connected with the thought of Guido Cavalcanti, a poet whose penchant for science distinguished him from his contemporaries. Giovanni Boccaccio introduces Guido's fictional character as a 'natural philosopher' (*Decameron* VI, 9) and, furthermore, as a 'loico' who conducted his quest scientifically, via 'natural dimostramento' (*Donna me prega*, 8), and reached the threatening conclusions in his philosophical canzone that humans are confined in matter; therefore, individual souls are mortal. The transmission of authority in the *Rime* relies upon sources from natural philosophy since they correspond to the poetry's object: love as passion. Although not the only ones, as demonstrated by a canonical critical edition of the Rime,[17] these sources are particularly significant since not only are they in direct relation with the theoretical assumption of *Donna me prega*, but they also shape the text's rhetoric, Cavalcanti having forged his poetic tools from the same realm of matter as, according to his theory, encloses the experience of love.

Modeling my reading method after Cavalcanti's method of composition, I interpret the poems by employing excerpts from his scientific sources as a footnote apparatus. These sources describe the same processes at work in the *Rime* to demonstrate that love, i.e., human knowledge, develops from the senses and ends with the production of an image that detaches itself from the human subject and joins the universal and single realm of possible intellect. The theory that abstraction is not within individual capabilities is articulated and presented as a manifesto in *Donna me prega*. I have already introduced the distinction in the *Rime* between the major canzone and minor rhymes, with the claim that the former serves a theoretical purpose, while the latter present the theory's phenomenological and rhetorical consequences. In my close reading I deal specifically with the minor rhymes

---

[16] 'In its broadest sense, then, natural philosophy in the Middle Ages was concerned with the study of bodies undergoing some kind of change. [...]. The domain of natural philosophy thus was nothing less than the entire physical world, because motion and movable things occur everywhere in both the celestial and terrestrial regions, the two major parts into which Aristotle divided the cosmos.' Grant, pp. 135-136.

[17] The edition by Domenico De Robertis, who in the introductions to some of the single poems (e.g. II, IV, XXVI) gives a predominant role to scriptural sources.

that describe the collapse of the cognitive process before the abstraction of the phantasm can take place, as is the case when the physiological reactions induced are excessive: shaken by an unbalanced circulation of the internal humors, the lover's body shuts down. My reading of those poems addresses the transformation of the writing process when the battle of the phantasm against the senses staged by Cavalcanti ultimately destroys imagination. Before dealing with the texts, my investigation regards the choice of the *auctoritates* that Cavalcanti incorporated into his lines: natural philosophy sources concerned with the body and the body's alterations, that is, sources from the medical literature.

The alliance between natural philosophy and medicine, before becoming an institutional reality in the major European universities of the time and the topic of debate often overshadowing the obvious purposes of medicine,[18] was instrumental in determining the preference for Aristotelian texts and their commentators, among others, on the part of translators active at the geographical and cultural boundaries between East and West in the late eleventh century.[19] Once translated from Arabic into Latin, and before reaching the Faculty of Arts in Paris, these texts were in fact employed as handbooks in the centers for medical learning that marked the discipline's revamping after the early-medieval stalemate in Europe. Between the seventh and the eleventh centuries medicine, in particular, was absorbed into the clerical world: practitioners of 'monkish' medicine helped keep the tradition of texts alive albeit in a reduced form and quiescent state, contracting the basic medical literature into a small *corpus* (mainly of Greek

---

[18] Nancy Siraisi quotes the work by Peter of Abano, *The Reconcilier of Differences and Especially of the Philosophers and Physicians* as a document of the debate active around 1300 between scientists and physicians, i.e. between the Galenic tradition and the Aristotelian one (Siraisi, *Taddeo Alderotti and his Pupils*, p. 149). The debate is, as well, a sign of the physicians' prevailing interest in adding to such debate rather than in being successful practitioners: 'Extended accounts of physiological topics by medical writers are mostly to be found in learned Latin commentaries on general introductory works (notably the first part of the first book of the *Canon* of Avicenna) and hence fall within the most scholastic and bookish genre of medical discourse. Most of these expositions therefore show few if any signs either of therapeutic concern or of readiness to modify theory on the basis of evidence drawn from clinical experience.' Siraisi, *Medieval and Early Renaissance Medicine*, p. 80.

[19] 'Les nouveaux textes aristotélicien provenaient donc, tant en Espagne qu'en Italie, des cercles s'intéressent surtout aux sciences exactes, aux sciences naturelles et à la médecine; il n'est donc pas étonnant qu'ils aient été utilisés d'abord précisément par les représentants de ces domaines du savoir.' Birkenmajer, *Le rôle joué par les médecins et les naturalistes dans la réception d'Aristote au XIIe et XIIIe siècles*, p. 75.

origin) that did not offer, one can imagine, much opportunity to educate physicians let alone assure any development in the field.

This static scenario began to change in the wake of the general renascence that had begun to spread all over Europe by the end of the millennium. The nucleus of what would become a homogeneous medical curriculum was coalescing, consisting of recently translated Arabic texts as well as the already available Greek ones, mainly Hippocratic and Galenic works. Thanks to this addition, medicine began to achieve a scientific status which would soon be institutionally recognized. The Arabic texts gave a fresh start to European medicine because they reflected a culture that, unlike the Western one, had continued to add on to and develop the medical tradition; furthermore, many of the Arab authors were also philosophers and by touching upon issues of philosophical relevance in their works they certainly facilitated the theoretical expansion of European medicine.[20] The most important points of entry of Arabic medical knowledge into the West were located in Spain and in Southern Italy. In twelfth-century Spain, Gerard of Cremona and his circle translated texts, such as Avicenna's *Liber Canonis*, that would dominate Western medical education until the seventeenth century. In Southern Italy, Constantine the African, a monk and teacher of medicine at the convent of Montecassino, provided the Latin-speaking world with Greek and, more importantly, Arabic medical texts, including Haly Abbas' *Pantegni* and Al Dschazzar's *Viaticus*. Constantine's translations became the handbooks at an institution of great moment for medical education: the School of Salerno. Initially a congregation of practitioners, the School began to flourish around the second half of the tenth century and developed into a center of theoretical learning with a renowned *Collegium doctorum*.[21] By introducing the use of

---

[20] 'It is worthy of note that some of the most important and influential Arabic treatises on medicine were written by Avicenna and Averroes, the leading philosophers and Aristotelian commentators, and that other medical writers in Arabic such as the Jew, Isaac Israeli, showed a great concern and familiarity with philosophical problems. This must mean that in the Arabic world, even more than among the Greeks, the same persons were professionally engaged in both medicine and philosophy, and this fact is important, not only in itself, but also in its impact on the Latin West where the Latin translations from the Arabic [...] played a very significant role.' Kristeller, *Philosophy and Medicine in Medieval and Renaissance Italy*, p. 31. A similar conclusion is reached by Siraisi, *Medieval and Early Renaissance Medicine*, p. 12.

[21] The documents are insufficient for a clear picture of the center in Salerno, especially until the twelfth century, although we have evidence of it merging with the University of Naples and structured as a *studium* (therefore including more *universitates*, or university associations) in the

medical literature as early as the eleventh century, the School of Salerno encouraged theory-based instruction. Wide evidence supports the fact that it was here that medicine was first studied through books and that a new methodological and theoretical approach to medicine was formulated and its connections to other disciplines defined, as stated in the prologue of the *Pantegni*.[22] The School of Salerno, where the definition of *physicus*, a doctor with a philosophical background, was introduced,[23] is also the place where the first medical handbook was compiled: the *Articella*, a selection of Greek and Arabic medical texts translated by Constantine which, by the end of the twelfth century, was also in use at the Universities of Montepellier and Paris. The utilization of the *Articella* triggered a production of commentaries on the *auctoritates* it contained, which was a further step towards the recognition of medicine's scholastic status.[24]

---

course of the thirteenth century. For an account of the existing documents, see Kristeller, *The School of Salerno*.

[22] 'Nel prologo della *Pantegni*, ritenuta opera di Costantino l'Africano, in realtà traduzione da Ali ibn Abbas, il problema è il rapporto della medicina con le altre scienze. Mentre infatti tutte le "seculares seu divine littere" sono soggette alla logica o all'etica o alla fisica, la "medicina litteralis" non può essere ricondotta ad una sola di tali discipline, ma esige il rapporto con tutte e tre "cum oporteat medicum esse rationabilem et rerum naturalium et moralium tractatorem."' Pesenti, p. 155.

[23] 'In classical Latin, the doctor is regularly called *medicus*, whereas the Greek term *physicus* is reserved to the students of natural science or natural philosophy. […]. It was not until the early twelfth century that the term *physicus* began to be used for the medical doctor, and it became gradually more frequent and remained in use up to the end of the Middle Ages. It still survives in the English term *physician*. This change of terminology has been made the subject of special studies for France, and the results thus obtained have been confirmed for Salerno, where the term *physicus* for doctors also occurs in the documents from the early twelfth century on and becomes more frequent thereafter. […]. I am hence inclined to believe that the new use of *physicus* had a programmatic significance and reflected a change in the very conception of medicine. It emphasizes the need for the medical doctor to have a thorough training in natural philosophy and science, and distinguishes him from the mere medical practitioner who lacks such theoretical training. The term thus forecasts, if it does not directly express, the close alliance between philosophy and medicine so characteristic of later medieval and Renaissance science. The term *physica* also shares the development of *physicus* and often came to mean medicine, especially theoretical medicine, but at the same time it preserved its earlier significance and continued to mean natural philosophy and science.' Kristeller, *The School of Salerno*, pp. 515-516.

[24] 'The collection as first compiled in the twelfth century (later other texts were added) consisted of two Hippocratic treatises, the *Aphorisms* and the *Prognostics*; a brief Galenic treatise known under various titles (*Ars medica, Ars parva, Tegni* or *Microtechnè*); an Arabic introduction to Galenic medicine known to the Latins as the *Isagoge* of Johannitius; and short tracts on the main diagnostic tools of the medieval physician, namely pulse and urine.' Siraisi, *Medieval and Early Renaissance Medicine*, p. 58. From Maurus' commentary found in a twelfth-century manuscript

By this time medicine had become a complex and fervently debated subject consisting of two separate fields requiring integration within the same discipline: theory and practice. Moreover, it became necessary for medicine to determine its proper place as well as define its functions inside the curriculum, since it touched on methods and issues relevant to other disciplines as well, namely natural philosophy and logic.[25] The distinction in medicine between *theoria* and *practica* dates back to the sixth-century medical schools of Alexandria and, as such, entered Western culture thanks to Constantine the African who used these two terms to translate the Arabic for *science* and *action* in the opening sentence of Johannitius's *Isagoge*: 'Medicina dividitur in duas partes, id est *theoricam* et *practicam*.'[26] The debate about the discipline's classification arose simultaneously to its entrance into the university curriculum, as is documented in the *accessus* with which the medieval authors prefaced medical *auctoritates*.[27]

Medicine's twofold structure led to the creation of a diversified body of professionals, ranging from surgeons to *literati* depending upon their ability to take advantage of the written sources, as well as to a development in this discipline both in its practical application and in the field of epistemology.[28] Given its complex capacity to expand, the disciplinary boundaries of medicine posed a much debated issue. The main concern with its practice was that medicine not be diluted into mere mechanics, in recognition of the rational background that had directed its practice; the topics of medical theory, on the other hand, were as we have seen mainly dictated by natural philosophy, with which medicine had established a relationship of *subalternatio*, of dependence (although, as some theoreticians specified, natural philosophy dealt with changing bodies but not actually with corporeal diseases and cures).[29] What emerges from the available documents

---

and dealing precisely with the texts composing the *Articella*, Kristeller infers that the *Articella* was first composed in Salerno (*The School of Salerno* pp. 513-514).

[25] Agrimi-Crisciani, *Edocere medicos*, p. 65.
[26] Jacquart, p. 103.
[27] Agrimi-Crisciani, *Edocere medicos*, p. 88.
[28] 'Solo un rigoroso *curriculum* legittima un esercizio professionale altrimenti qualificato come casuale sotto il profilo epistemologico, illegale sotto quello giuridico. *Illitterati*, non hanno letto i testi degli autori, non sanno scrivere, non hanno ricevuto un'adeguata istruzione da parte di maestri dotti oltre che esperti, e per questo "non bene exercent [...] neque sapienter neque sub certa radice".' Agrimi-Crisciani, *Edocere medicos*, p. 191.
[29] 'Thus Taddeo himself, in the introduction of his commentary on the *Isagoge*, emphasized the links between medicine and natural philosophy and the characteristics that entitled medicine to be defined as a science in the Aristotelian meaning of the term. [...]. Taddeo, however,

is that the discipline's two parts, *theoria* and *practica*, were in fact kept separate and did not affect each other: theoretical assumptions did not impose rigorous methodologies on medical practice and, conversely, practical operations did not serve to confirm or alter already established theoretical conclusions. In the twelfth and thirteenth centuries medicine does not appear to have been an 'applied science' in the modern meaning of this expression, and some of the definitions forged by the medical writers in Bologna, such as *scientia operativa* for the practice of medicine, denote the attempts on their part to find a middle ground on which the two aspects pertaining to medicine, *scientia* and *ars,* could be joined.[30] The theoretical background undoubtedly constituted medicine's most important asset: when it came to the transmission of learning, the *litterati* and not the empirics played the main role, especially when operating from within an institutional setting.[31] Teaching became of specific relevance in this respect since, through their teaching, the theoreticians could consolidate a *corpus* of authoritative texts which helped establish a likewise authoritative status for medicine and its disciplinary identity. Medicine could be delivered as a *traditio*, grounded in a textual substrate made concrete by the individual works brought to light by the *lectio magistrale.* Furthermore, the argumentations about didactics provided the link between *theoria* and *practica* by imbuing the discipline's twofold contents with the notion of *doctrina*, by claiming, in other words, that both *theoria* and *practica* are sciences precisely because they are both teachable.[32] This is also what allowed medicine to gain

---

introduced a different emphasis. He began by defining *scientia*, citing the *Ethics* and *Posterior Analytics*. *Scientia* is knowledge strictly demonstrable from premises. The subject of medical science is the human body; [...] medicine is also distinct from *scientia naturalis*, which does include the study of the human body as a mobile physical object, but not its health and sickness.' Siraisi,*Taddeo Alderotti and his Pupils*, p.121.

[30] '[...] according to the first book of the *Posterior Analytics*, this type of knowledge [*scientia*] could only be attained in disciplines that began from accepted first principles and proceeded by way of rational arguments to demonstrate universally valid conclusions.' *Ars*, on the other hand, is ' [...] a word used in different contexts for both crafts and liberal arts but always with implications of skills and ordered knowledge rather than of reasoning toward universal truths.' Siraisi, *Medieval and Early Renaissance Medicine*, p. 76.

[31] Agrimi-Crisciani, *Edocere medicos*, p. 192.

[32] Jole Agrimi and Chiara Crisciani present a survey of thirteenth-century commentaries to the *Tegni*'s prologue (by Gentile da Foligno, Pietro d'Abano and Pietro Torrigiano) to demonstrate how by focusing on the introductory term *doctrina*, they attribute a scientific status not only to medical theory but also to medical practice: 'Se questa specificità le [i.e. to medical practice] conferisce, certo, caratteristiche epistemologiche particolari, quali che esse siano, alla definizione in generale del suo valore di scientificità si lega dunque immediatamente la

a specific curricular place without compromising its necessary connections with natural philosophy and mechanics.

II.3 *Auctoritates* of a Heretic: Avicenna's *Liber Canonis*

Important traces of the discussion about the interfaces between medicine and the other curricular disciplines are to be found at the University of Bologna. Its faculty of arts and medicine,[33] established around the second half of the thirteenth century, is among the centers where medical learning found a strong theoretical connection with natural philosophy, as documented by Siraisi.[34] Although Siraisi is cautious about identifying a coherent school of thought, she assembles enough evidence to conclude that the men singled out in her study did constitute a group whose activities consistently aimed at establishing active links between medicine and philosophy, as sanctioned by the institution they worked in. The model of disciplinary integration was moreover embodied by the contiguous school

---

segnalazione della sua insegnabilità: "Practica est—giusta la definizione di Avicenna, con poche varianti, per tutti—scientia operativa, idest scientia que docet modum et qualitatem operationis." Scritta essa pure "in libro vel in anima magistri," insegna procedure e proprietà dell'operare senza identificarsi col singolo intervento e neppure con la *praxis*: piuttosto dirige quello tramite questa—"Practica docendo dirigter qualiter," puntualizza Tommaso Del Garbo nella *Summa*—; e può dirigere entrambi, perché ne espone—nell'accezione tecnico-didattica del termine—i modi e li trasmette: "dictio operationis—come la definisce Gentile da Foligno—idest pars que dat modum operandi." ' Agrimi-Crisciani, *Edocere medicos*, p.138.

[33] Although it is largely employed by many scholars in the field, Maierù questions the use of the expression *Facultas Artium* for the University of Bologna since 'at Bologna the situation does not allow us to speak of a faculty in the sense of a teaching body of one or more disciplines. The term is normally used as a synonym of "art" or more commonly as a synonym for "science." [...]. However, at Bologna (and perhaps other universities as well) the term *facultas* is linked to the conferral of academic degrees. [....]. In conclusion, in these texts and in the university statutes (the rubric of disputations) there is no support for the idea of a faculty of arts, understood as an organic entity, but the variety of courses and corresponding academic titles is affirmed. Thus, the idea of a *facultas artium* is not confirmed by the texts.' Maierù, *Bolognese Terminology in Medicine and Arts*, pp. 77-78, and p. 81.

[34] 'As the thirteenth century wore on, more and more of the medical men who congregated in Bologna ceased to apply to themselves the very general title *medicus*, a term that, as we have seen, could be used both for the pragmatic surgeon Ugo da Lucca and for the 'subtle and speculative' medical author Pancius. They began to assume the titles of *magister, doctor*, and sometimes *professor*, while some of them began to describe their art as *scientia physicalis*. This development suggests that the ancient tradition linking medicine with natural philosophy and with the other disciplines studied in the school of arts (see chapter five) was increasingly coming to shape the direction of medical study and teaching at Bologna.' Siraisi, *Taddeo Alderotti and his Pupils*, p. 18.

of law.³⁵ The bibliography at the core of the medical curriculum included an updated version of the *Articella*;³⁶ it was presumably introduced into Bologna precisely by Taddeo Alderotto, who also prescribed the study of the *Liber Canonis* by Avicenna who, with Hippocrates and Galen, constituted the *auctoritates* of the faculty's curriculum.³⁷ The masters at the faculty of arts and medicine were driven by an intellectual quest that pushed some of them beyond the approved boundaries and into the controversial field of radical Aristotelianism;³⁸ in this quest their attention veered to fields not directly related to their profession, such as Tuscan vernacular poetry, as Dino Del Garbo's commentary to *Donna me prega* demonstrates.³⁹ It is against this background that I have grounded the choice of the source employed in my close reading of Guido Cavalcanti, namely the *Liber Canonis* by Avicenna.

Avicenna's *Canon* stood out as a pivotal medical handbook immediately upon its first appearance in the 1200s, and remained in use for the following

---

[35] Agrimi-Crisciani, *Edocere medicos*, pp. 17-18.

[36] For the different hypotheses with regard to the original place from which the *Articella* was brought to Bologna see Siraisi, who claims it came from Siena thanks to Pietro Ispano (*Taddeo Alderotti and his Pupils*, pp. 98-99), and Pesenti, who instead supports the idea of a Parisian path (Pesenti, pp. 165-169).

[37] 'The works commented on by Taddeo and his students show that the chief source of their medical teaching were the aphoristic writings of Hippocrates, accompanied by Galenic commentary, the *Tegni*, several authentic and major works of Galen, and the *Canon* by Avicenna. Hippocrates, Galen, and Avicenna were regarded as preeminent authorities of equal weight; but in sheer bulk, Galen and Avicenna must have dominated the curriculum; and Avicenna, of course, incorporated much Galenic material into the *Canon*. It seems, therefore, that the claim that is now sometimes made that the Bolognese medical school of the early years of the fourteenth century knew relatively little of the authentic Galen holds good only for Galen's major treatises on anatomy.' Siraisi, *Taddeo Alderotti and his Pupils*, p. 106.

[38] Bruno Nardi, and Maria Corti after him, are firm in acknowledging Averroistic trends at the faculty of arts and medicine in Bologna (see, for all, Nardi's article: *L'averroismo bolognese nel secolo XIII e Taddeo Alderotto*). Other scholars, such as Nancy Siraisi, are more cautious: 'There is no doubt that Taddeo was familiar with the notorious Averroist thesis of the unicity of the Intellect, and his exposition of it has convinced some scholars that he shared the view he was describing. As we have seen, similar opinions have been ascribed, on less firm grounds, to Dino. Yet it remains to be seen whether these particular philosophical ideas attribuited to Taddeo and Dino played any considerable or consistent part in the medical teaching of Taddeo's school.' Ibid., p. 149.

[39] In terms of a direct acquaintance, Siraisi concludes that: 'There is no evidence for any personal connection between the physician and the poet, although it is possible that in his youth Dino was acquainted with Guido, his older contemporary. Dino almost certainly knew another Tuscan poet, the jurist Cino da Pistoia, who was his colleague in 1322 at Siena, where the number of professors was probably small.' Ibid., p. 82.

five centuries. In addition to reflecting the thirteenth-century scientific landscape, this work by Avicenna is also specifically connected to Guido Cavalcanti through the mediation of Dino Del Garbo, whose main achievement was to contribute to the array of the *Canon*'s commentaries. Further, the *Canon* was included in the library of Cavalcanti by Bruno Nardi, who in the essay *L'amore e i medici medievali* incidentally mentioned the *Canon* as one of the possible sources for the *Rime*, suggesting further study in this direction. In his essay, cutting short his long-lived 'polemica contra Favatium,'[40] Nardi reaffirmed Cavalcanti's Averroistic background, which had just assumed a validity which was difficult to dispute thanks to Kristeller and his article on the *Questio disputata de felicitate* manuscript dedicated to Guido. From the *Quaestio*, Nardi quotes the passage in which Jacobus introduces the 'affectiones et passiones appetitus sensitivi' as the common obstacle to happiness (which Jacobus defines as 'intelligere substantia separatas et precipue ipsum Deum') and includes, among these *passiones*, sexual desire. Nardi recalls that excessive attraction was described by Plato and Aristotle and then by the Arab medical tradition as a form of intemperate love to be treated as a disease and concludes that this is precisely the tradition followed by both Iacobus and Guido when they approached love according to such a 'comune o volgare'[41] meaning of 'disease.' From these premises, Nardi indicates medical literature as the critical material for Guido's interpretation and, in order to demonstrate how some topics related to 'love passion' were imported into thirteenth-century poetry from science, offers a preliminary probing into the *Canon*'s pages, specifically those in which Avicenna describes the symptoms of the *solicitudo melancholica*—'Et est spiritus eius plurimae interfectionis et reversionis, et sit multae elevationis, alteratur dispositio ipsius ad risum et laetitiam et ad tristitiam et fletum quum amoris cantilenas audit, et praecipue quum fit rememoratio repudii et elongationis...'—with a terminology and a thematic cadence that Nardi recognizes as being rhetorically transformed, but intact, in *Donna me prega* 45-47: 'Poi non s'adorna di riposo mai:/move cangiando color, riso e pianto/e la figura con paura storna.'[42]

---

[40] As Nardi defined the animated discussion which took place in the 1950s between Favati and himself about Guido Cavalcanti's more or less marked Averroism. The different phases of the discussion are reconstructed in chapter I, n. 44.
[41] As distinguished for instance from the metaphorical meaning attributed to love within the Platonic tradition (Nardi, *L'amore e i medici medievali*, p. 250).
[42] Ibid., p. 253.

With the incorporation of Avicennian material into his lines, which the close reading of the following chapters supports, Cavalcanti lays out his cultural project: to preserve, by enclosing it in verses, a content that contemporary culture was on the verge of banning. His choice of the medical *auctoritates*, and the philosophical affiliation this choice implied, had an effect on his poetry, which consists of an isolated branch that has produced little or no tradition at all. However, the experimental import of his language stands as a major contribution. The language fashioned by Cavalcanti in his poetry, pushed by this unorthodox content to its expressive limits, in turn produced its own unusual and rhetorically heterodox results, a liminal ground marked by the radical interpretation of natural philosophy. Modulating his verbal tools in obedience to the theory that love is a passion of the body, Cavalcanti stretched those tools to new expressive potential, anticipated in the synthesis that in a single line weaves together the 'cantar d'augelli' and the 'ragionare d'amore,' hinting at the possibility of a pre-verbal language as the perfect vehicle for love, a language that is furthermore included among the 'biltà' listed in his personal *plazer*, Sonnet III: 'Biltà di donna e di saccente core/e cavalieri armati che sien genti;/cantar d'augelli e ragionar d'amore;/adorni legni 'n mare forte correnti;/aria serena quando apar l'albore/e bianca neve scender senza venti;/rivera d'acqua e prato d'ogni fiore;/oro, argento, azzurro 'n ornamenti:/' (Woman's beauty and sage's heart and knights in armor that are noble; singing of birds and discoursing of love; embellished ships sailing swiftly on the sea; clear air when the dawn appears; and white snow falling with no winds; watered bank and meadow with every flower; gold, silver, azure in adornments.)

By tracing the Canon's material woven into the verses of the Rime, the close reading conducted in the following pages aims at locating common themes that are rhetorically forged without any loss in their scientific meanings. My investigation proceeds to acknowledge Cavalcanti's poetic language as an exact and literal tool which delivers a content unaltered for aesthetic purposes. A language, as Ezra Pound acknowledged, whose figures of speech are used strictly to convey meaning and never merely to add ornamental beauty:

> Leave all question of any art save poetry. In that art the gulf between Petrarch's capacity and Guido's is the great gulf, not of degree, but of kind. In Guido, the 'figure', the strong metamorphic or 'picturesque' expression is there with purpose to convey or to interpret a definite meaning. In Petrarch it is ornament, the prettiest ornament he could find, but not

an irreplaceable ornament, or one that he couldn't have used just about as well somewhere else. In fact he very often does use it, and them, somewhere, and nearly everywhere, else, all over the place.
[...]
When the late T. E. Hulme was trying to be a philosopher in that milieu [i.e. in what Pound himself defines as the 'British desert' of contemporary British philosophy], [...] I spoke to him one day of the difference between Guido's precise interpretative metaphor, and the Petrarchan fustian and ornament, pointing out that Guido thought in accurate terms; that the phrases correspond to definite sensations undergone; in fact very much what I had said in my early preface to the Sonnets and Ballate.[43]

II.4 Imageless Love

In his canzone Cavalcanti places human love—therefore human ontology, given the function attributed to love as a parameter for knowledge—in the semantic field generated by the concept of the diaphanous, the metaphor at the core of his theoretical manifesto. As recapitulated above, the diaphanous is connected to accident (introduced in *Donna me prega* as an inclusive definition of love) and therefore to the field of matter and of sensation. The concept of passion, which Dino Del Garbo discusses in his commentary and claims is *Donna me prega*'s ultimate topic, is linked to this group of contiguous terms. This vocabulary provides answers to the eight questions about love presented in the philosophical canzone, and also affects the portion of the *Rime* that deals with love phenomenology. The sphere of matter and sensation, which as postulated by *Donna me prega* encompasses the love experience, determines love's symptoms; therefore, it dictates the content of the minor rhymes. Furthermore, matter and sensation affect the expressive technique of love. Love manifests itself through a chain of sensorial, and accidental, reactions to the sight of the love object. The language conveying such content doesn't alter the nature of the necessity and immediacy of these reactions, and reproduces, as we shall see, their crucial outcome: the interruption of imagination. In order to narrate love, Cavalcanti fashions verses that capture the facts as they occur, erasing the chronological shift between the events and the writing process; further, the language these lines are made of is composed of semantic units that do not necessarily result from the rational processing of images, a phase that grammarians indicate as essential to language production.

By applying the laws of the sublunar world to his tools of expression, Cavalcanti employs a language that is imprinted with its content and

---

[43] Pound, *Cavalcanti*, pp. 154-155 and p. 162.

articulated within the same corporeal sphere as that of the love protagonist and his deeds. I define this language as being experimental because, as we shall see, Cavalcanti explores possibilities that the theories of his time considered borderline, virtually excluded from the sphere of linguistic signs. In the language of Cavalcanti's *Rime* the utterer is the body: the account of the body's alterations induced by love is entrusted to the 'voices' produced by the body itself. In order to shape this language of the body, Cavalcanti bends rhetorical laws and modifies the notion of the agent of writing, who corresponds in the *Rime* to the disassembled constellation of body parts and organs. Ultimately, it is the body's very modifications that function as the agents of communication and define the author's identity. This procedure is granted legitimacy by the medical sources that Cavalcanti established as the *auctoritates* of his poetry.

The prominent position of matter and sensorial perceptions is a decisive factor in Cavalcanti's elaboration of a crucial tenet in thirteenth-century lyrics: the phantasm.[44] In the previous pages I introduced the phantasmatic process in the context of Cavalcanti's Averroistic leanings, as revealed in the passage in *Donna me prega* that describes the production of the abstract image resulting from the sight of the love object, and the consequent *coniunctio* of that image with the possible intellect (lines 21-28):

> Vèn da veduta forma che s'intende,
> che prende – nel possibile intelletto,
> come in subietto, – loco e dimoranza.
> In quella parte mai non ha possanza
> perché da qualitate non descende:
> resplende – in sé perpetüal effetto;
> non ha diletto – ma consideranza;
> sì che non pote largir simiglianza.
>
> ([Love] derives from a seen form that becomes intelligible, that takes up place and dwelling in the possible intellect as in a substance. In that part [love] never has any power, since [the possible intellect] does not derive from quality, it shines in itself as perpetual effect; it does not have pleasure but rather contemplation; and thus it cannot create an image.)

These verses are aligned with a philosophical stand. As we summarized in the previous pages, in *Donna me Prega* the phantasmatic process is depicted based on the conclusions Cavalcanti has drawn from the Averroist tradition: the process is completed when the phantasm detaches itself from

---

[44] For a synthesis see Agamben.

the subject of the sensations, the individual who has produced it, and subsequently joins the sphere of intellection, the collective and universal dimension of the possible intellect. Dino Del Garbo is the first reader to provide an interpretation of *Donna me prega* in the framework of Averroistic thought. In his commentary he explains that the final recipient of the phantasm is the agent of the intellection of the phantasm, i.e., the *intellectus possibilis*: 'intellectus possibilis est ille qui recepit speciem rei, et recipiendo speciem rei cognoscit rem.'[45] The agent of the love experience does not participate in the process of abstraction—whose subject is the possible intellect: 'come in subietto'—except for producing, as the subject of sensation, the object of the process, that is, the phantasm: 'compriso – bianco in tale obietto cade.' On the grounds of these conclusions, the *coniunctio* that occurs between the two dimensions, matter and ideas, when the phantasm is formed corresponds, from a human perspective, to a division.[46] Human sensorial perceptions and intellectual abstractions belong to distinct spheres. The fracture separating them is embodied by the *Rime*'s love protagonist, who is repetitively depicted in his collapses into the sphere of matter, in which his sight and other senses are aroused; his sensorial capacities are his definition and his boundaries. Since they mark an insuperable limit, sensorial capacities are also the perfection of individual

---

[45] 'Hic autem est ordo in apprehensione humana, sicut declaratum est in scientia naturali: quod primo species rei pervenit ad sensus exteriores, ut ad visum vel auditum vel tactum vel gustum vel olphatum, deinde ab illis pervenit ad virtutes sensitiva interiores, sicut pervenit ad fantasiam primo, deinde pervenit ad cogitativam et ultimo ad memorialem. Ab istis autem virtutibus procedit postea ista species ad virtutem nobiliorem, que virtus in homine est altissima inter virtutes adprensiva, et ista est virtus possibilis, que dicitur possibilis ad differentiam intellectus agentis, qui etiam est in nobis. Sed quia intellectus agens non est de virtutibus apprensivis de quibus loquimur hic, sed intellectus possibilis est ille qui recepit speciem rei, et recipiendo speciem rei cognoscit rem, ideo dicit quod pervenit ista forma, primo apprehensa a visu, usque ad intellectum possibilem et non amplius procedit ad aliam virtutem, sed cognoscit quod non est alia virtus apprensiva que sit in nobis altior et nobilior quam si ista.' Fenzi, p. 100.

[46] 'The previous analysis shows that at the center of the process that speaks of the *coniunctio*, Cavalcanti deliberately focuses on the process of form as useful for designating the break between the sensitive qualities of the phantasm and the abstract being of the intellect through which the act of intellection is performed. This break has a precise meaning: the act of intellection does not belong to the sensible qualities of the phantasm. The break between the sensitive soul and the possible intellect in not just because they differ in genus (this was also present in Giacomo), and not just because the *coniunctio* is accidental, but rather because the properties of the sensible in this process are lost. This break shows that bodily perfection is completely different from the perfection of the intellect. In the *coniunctio* a human being does not perform an activity of intellection.' Ardizzone, *Guido Cavalcanti. The Other Middle Ages*, p. 118.

human agency, *prima perfectio hominis*, as Averroes declares in his commentary on the *De anima*.[47]

The recurrent warnings of the lover's death bespeak his collapses into matter. These collapses coincide with the appearance of the spirit of Love, and testify that love has occurred: 'L'anima mia vilment' è sbigotita/de la battaglia ch'e[l]l'ave dal core:/che s'ella sente pur un poco Amore/più presso a lui che non sòle, ella more.' (My soul is abjectly appalled by the battering it had from the heart: for if it feels Love just a little closer to it than it was before, it will die) explains Guido in Sonnet VII. In Sonnet XXII, the lover's fear (the 'pauroso spirito d'amore') is signaled to the woman he is gazing upon because it is depicted on his face, since the very encounter with the woman anticipates his impending death: 'Veder poteste, quando v'inscontrai,/quel pauroso spirito d'amore/lo qual sòl apparir quand'om si more,/e 'n altra guisa non si vede mai.' (You could see, when I encountered you, that fearful spirit of love that is wont to appear when one is dying, and otherwise is never seen.) The lover's soul is pale, 'nel morto colore,' as it is getting ready to die: 'allor si mise nel morto colore/l'anima trista per voler trar guai' (my soul then took on the color of death, wretched from the moans that it would heave.) Then, to add dramatic power to the encounter with the lady, the remaining lines describe a momentary suspension of the verdict: the soul 'sostenne' (it held back) because the woman's glance brings a brief 'dolcezza' to the lover's heart, filled with the pneuma impressed with the image of the woman, the 'sottile spirito che vede' that aids the weakened body. 'Dolcezza,' here, indicates that the production of the image is the supreme human achievement: 'ma po' sostenne, quando vide uscire,/ dagli occhi vostri un lume di merzede,/che porse dentr'al cor nova dolcezza;/e quel sottile spirito che vede/soccorse gli altri, che credean morire,/gravati d'angosciosa debolezza' (But then it held back, when it saw issuing from your eyes a gleam of favor that infused into my heart unusual sweetness; and that delicate spirit of sight rescued the others that thought they were dying, burdened by anguishing weakness.) That same impermanent 'dolcezza' becomes tout-court illusory in XIV, in

---

[47] 'Et est secunda quaestio magis difficile valde. Et est quod, si intellectus materialis est prima perfectio hominis, ut declaratur de diffinitione anime, et intellectus speculativus est postrema perfectio, homo autem est generabilis et corruptibilis et unus in numero per suam postremam perfectionem ab intellectu, necesse est ut ita sit per suam primam perfectione, scilicet quod per primam perfectionem de intellectis sim alius a te, et tu alius a me [...].' Averroes, *Commentarium magnum in Aristotelis De Anima libros*, III, 429 a24 158-165.

which the poet declares the apparent ('par') descent into his heart of a sweet love, while the true outcome of that pleasure is a deadly one:

> (...)
> e, qual si sente simil me, ciò crede.
> Ma chi tal vede - (certo non persona),
> ch'Amor mi dona - un spirito 'n su' stato,
> che, figurato, - more?
> Ché, quando lo piacer mi stringe tanto
> che lo sospir si mova,
> par che nel cor mi piova
> un dolce amor sì bono
> ch'eo dico: «Donna, tutto vostro sono».

(And he who thus feels like me believes this; but who sees (surely no one) that Love grants me a spirit of his own dignity which, once it is figured forth, dies? For when pleasure so wrings me that sighing begins, seems as if into my heart it rains so fine a sweet love that I say: 'Lady, I am all yours.')

Imagination is a crucial tenet in Cavalcanti's *Rime*, and closely linked to the *Rime*'s linguistic construction. Cavalcanti's treatment of imagination is drawn from a background including Aristotelianism with its Arabic commentaries, whose notions were active at the University of Bologna in the circle of Taddeo Alderotti. According to Aristotle's *De anima*, imagination is a voluntary faculty which consists of 'fingere formas,' molding and assembling mental pictures.[48] Mental pictures consist in a movement determined by another movement, such as a sensation.[49] The sense properly linked to imagination is sight, as implied in the etymology of the Greek word for imagination, φαντασίας.[50]

---

[48] 'Ymaginatio autem est aliud a sensu et aliud a distinctione. [...]. Quoniam autem non est cum intelligere et consiliari idem manifestum est. Ista enim passio nobis est quod voluerimus; possumus enim ponere in directo oculorum nostrorum, sicut res deposite in conservatione, et fingere formas.' Ibid., II, 427b 14-20.

[49] 'Ymaginatio igitur non est aliqua istarum, neque ex eis, sed sicut aliquid movetur per motum alterius, et ymaginatio existimatur esse motus, et impossibile est ut sit sine sensu, sed in eis que sentiuntur et in eis que habent sensum, et fit etiam motus ab actione sensus. Et oportet ut iste sit similis sensui (iste enim motus impossibile est ut sit extra sensum, aut ut sit in carente sensu), et ut sit illud quod habet ipsum agens et patiens multas res; et erit verus et falsus.' Ibid., II, 428b 9-18.

[50] 'Si igitur quod narravimus non est alio modo quam diximus, et illud quod narratum est est ymaginatio, ymaginatio igitur est motus a sensu qui est in actu. Et quia visus proprie est sensus, derivatum fuit ei nomen a luce; impossibile est enim videre sine luce.' Ibid., II, 428 b30-429 a4.

Imagination is located in the anterior hollow of the brain, and its functions are similar to those of common sense. As stated in the *De memoria et reminiscentia*, mental pictures, or images, are the material essential not only to imagination but also to the other post-sensationary faculties.[51] Post-sensationary faculties, or internal senses, are not treated by Aristotle as a separate category. In his *De anima* III and *De memoria et reminiscentia*, he mentions imagination, cogitation, and memory without however expressly addressing them as a group of distinct faculties as he does with the five external senses. The term 'internal sense' is employed by early authors of Latin philosophical texts to indicate one single faculty corresponding, at large, to Aristotle's common sense, which distinguishes and compares the data of the senses. The Arabic and Hebrew traditions, instead, specifically employed the general term 'internal senses,' by which they designated a detailed spectrum of post-sensationary faculties that ranged, depending on the single authors, from three to seven faculties. In the twelfth and thirteenth centuries, through the Latin translations from the Arabic, the different models of classification of the post-sensationary faculties also became known to, and assimilated by, the Scholastics.[52]

In its most complete form, the classification of the internal senses is made of seven faculties, such as the ones listed by Avicenna in his *De anima*;[53] among them is common sense, which, in addition to other functions, receives the impressions of sensible objects from the visual pneuma (as well as the impressions from all other senses) and imagination. On the grounds of its two functions, the latter is divided into retentive imagination (it retains the images of sensible objects received from the common sense even when the objects are not present) and compositive imagination (it composes and divide those images, thereby constructing

---

[51] Aristotle: *De Memoria et Reminiscentia*, 450a 13-14.
[52] A fully documented reconstruction of the tradition of the internal senses is in: Wolfson, *The internal senses in Latin, Arabic, and Hebrew Philosophical Texts*. With specific regard to imagination, Wolfson indicates as decisive the addition to the group of the internal senses of the estimative faculty, the animal equivalent of human reason. The estimative faculty is a term largely corresponding to the 'natural faculty' that Aristotle mentions exists in animals (by which animals react to indirect likes and fears, not just direct ones) as well as to the Scholastic term *aestimatio* (Wolfson, p. 90.) Its inclusion among the internal faculties determined, among other consequences, a semantic modification of one of the terms meaning imagination, which came to signify 'compositive animal imagination' (the combination of imagination and estimation) that was listed in addition to 'human compositive imagination' (the combination of imagination and reason).
[53] Ibid., p. 96.

unreal images out of real ones). Avicenna records two views: according to physicians (interested in the bodily location of the faculties) imagination and common sense are the two functions of one single faculty since they are located in the same anterior hollow of the brain; philosophers, who are interested in the different functions, consider them two separate faculties.

Against this background, by employing the term 'imagination' in this study, I indicate common sense and retentive imagination, that is, the two internal senses (or one, if considered from the medical perspective) through whose interaction the visual impressions of the sensible object are transformed into an abstract image. In his *Rime*, by alluding to the lover's death, Cavalcanti indicates the interruption of that process of abstraction.

Exposed to love as if it were a natural catastrophe, the lover is repetitively acted upon by the sight of his beloved and consequently subjected to darkness, to a lack of images he cannot escape. Locked in the realm of matter in which his perceptions define his identity, he is agitated by the passions that the sight of the love object elicits and simultaneously by the desire to attain the intellectual dimension he can contribute to only by producing the phantasm. As if on a battlefield, he is torn by the clash between his structural limitations and the impossible desire to participate in an act of intellection. The language describing the lover's death bears the signs of this confinement, on a chronological ground as well. As I stated earlier, the act of writing is not deferred: the love encounter occurs and, at the same time, the lover's body is exposed in order to reveal the marks that passion has impressed upon it, virtually engraving the story onto the body. The articulation of a language whose alphabet is impressed in matter, and whose utterers are body members and organs moving about without any central control finds its origins in the sense-based subjectivity shaping Cavalcanti's culture.

The language of the *Rime* is affected by sensation because Cavalcanti gives corporeality, which his culture considered an element of the psychological dimension, its ultimate expression. In Cavalcanti's lines, the emphasis upon the sensible features of the soul and on the material dimension these features apply to is radical. In his terms, the perceiving subject disappears into matter. Especially since the perceiving subject is the lover, who is thereby exposed to sudden and violent alterations of his senses, constrained by their overwhelming object: the woman. In the above-mentioned Sonnet XVIII, the agent of writing is tout-court replaced by his quills, scissors and penknife. The tools of the desk are entrusted with the task of speaking to the readers. They replace the poet—'Noi siàn le triste penne isbigotite,/le cesoiuzze e 'l coltellin dolente,/ch'avemo scritte dolorosamente/quelle parole che vo' avete udite./' (We are the poor bewildered quills, the little scissors and the grieving penknife, who have sorrowfully written those words that you have heard)—and announce the sensations experienced by the dismembered hand moving the writing tools: 'la man che ci movea dice che sente/cose dubbiose nel core apparite;/le quali hanno destrutto sì costui/ed hannol posto sì presso a la morte,/ch'altro non n'è rimasto che sospiri.' (the hand that used to move us says it feels dreadful things that have appeared in the heart, which have so undone him and brought him so close to death that nothing else is left of him but sighs.) As if pronouncing a solemn envoy to Cavalcanti's entire poetic production ('quelle parole che vo' avete udite,') the desk tools remain the last characters standing on the stage after the battles triggered by love have undone the poet. Proving his dispossession of both spoken and written language, he transfers the signification of his destruction to his own body, which, although dismembered into its single components, thus becomes the agent of communication.

In the next chapters, I will introduce the formation of the image in the context of language production, and I will present the close reading of a subsection of the *Rime*. These poems are grouped together because they reveal how the recounting of the love experience is inevitably affected by the outcome of the phantasmatic process, that is, by the lover's severance from the image he has produced and his subsequent 'death,' his being cut off from the process of intellection because bound to the sphere of passion.

CHAPTER III
The Body Speaks

III.1 *Voces Gemituum, Dolorum et Suspiriorum*: the Words of a Pre-Verbal Language

In Sonnet XVIII, Guido Cavalcanti makes the agent of writing disappear behind the tools of his desk. The pronoun 'noi' boldly opening the poem— 'Noi siàn le triste penne isbigotite,/'—marks both the new authorship and the completion of a rhetorical scheme that, laid out at the beginning of the *Rime*, aimed at solving the quest for a language capable of conveying the love venture. For humans, that venture is experienced exclusively through perceptions, therefore through senses. Matter, to which senses apply, is thereby the realm in which humans take part in love. Senses and matter, moreover, define the dimension from which the language describing that venture originates. Since matter is a realm that is not hierarchically organized, the facts described in the *Rime* are neither readable nor accountable from an outside perspective vertically removed from them. The author does not benefit from a panoptic vision. With a definition that became canonic among scholars of Cavalcanti's poetry, Gianfranco Contini called this equalizing process the 'parificazione cavalcantiana dei reali,' presenting it as Cavalcanti's original contribution to the development of coeval poetic themes.[1]

For the purposes of this research, I focus on the notion of the lover's body not only made equal to matter and things, but 'impressed,' the way matter is, by the love experience. The notion of 'being impressed' is strictly related in the field of medieval psychology to sensation, the main principle of the soul of an animal. A sensation consists in an alteration, in the being

---

[1] 'Che cosa poi sia in concreto «la gloria de la lingua», in quanto tocchi a Cavalcanti sopra Guinizzelli la riposta è nei fatti: basti raffrontare, nelle parti affini, i sonetti *Avete 'n vo'*, *Biltà di donna*, *Chi è questa*, *L'anima mia*, *Tu m'hai sì piena* e i guinizzelliani *Io vogl' del ver*, *Lo vostro bel saluto*, magari *Dolente, lasso*. [...]. Il geniale metodo analogico dell'iniziatore ("rassembro", "somiglio") mantiene i due poli attorno al "come", dove Cavalcanti fonde e unifica ("Avete 'n vo"); in colui permane una ruvida realtà esterna ("statüa d'otono"), che si smorza e diciamo pure introverte nella parificazione cavalcantiana dei reali ("di rame o di pietra o di legno"). Cavalcanti si rinserra e perfeziona nei limiti della sola analisi interna, movimentandola e drammatizzandola come le ombre cinesi delle ipostasi (lo lodano infatti di filosofo naturale, cioè di psicologo).' Contini, *Cavalcanti in Dante*, pp. 434-435.

moved and acted upon of the sense by its object.[2] The sensations are affections of the soul anatomically based, and explained through the picture of a form of the perceived object which, without its matter, is impressed on the sense in the same way that wax is impressed by a signet-ring.[3]

The material concreteness upon which the explanation of perceptions is grounded also permeates the pages of Aristotle's commentators. In his *Introduction sur la doctrine psychologique d'Avicenne* Gerard Verbeke emphasizes the strictly biological interpretation of sensations and the elaboration of sensorial data in Avicenna's commentary. Verbeke describes the assimilation of forms into the brain in metaphoric terms, as a metabolic process: the animal's cognitive activities must be considered a nutritive act, as essential to our brain as food is to our body.[4] As Verbeke explains, in the course of the process, passivity is of the utmost importance: the perceiving subject's sensorial capacities consist in the capacity to be impressed,[5] as in the aforementioned Aristotelian image when wax retains the form without the material that has impressed it. During this phase, the perceiving subject becomes similar to the form of the perceived object and, in doing so, achieves perfection.[6]

---

[2] 'Et cum iam determinavimus ista, dicamus iam in omni sensu universaliter. Dicamus igitur quod sentire accidit secundum motum et passionem, sicut diximus; existimatur enim quod est aliqua alteratio.' Averroes, *Commentarium magnum in Aristotelis De Anima libros*, II, 416b 32-35.

[3] 'In unoquoque igitur sensuum dictum est secundum descriptionem. Et dicendum est universaliter de omni sensu quod sensus est recipiens formas sensibilium sine materia, v.g. quod cera recepit forma anuli sine ferro aut auro, et recipit signum quod est ex cupro aut ex auro, sed non secundum quod est cuprum aut aurum.' Ibid., II, 424a 15-22.

[4] 'On pourrait dire que l'animal reçoit sa nourriture "cognitive" comme il reçoit sa nourriture matérielle et qu'il l'assimile, qu'elle devient sienne, qu'il s'enrichit par elle: car toutes ces formes sensibles qu'il reçoit ne sont pas simplement l'image éphémère d'un monde en devenir, elles pénètrent jusque dans le cerveau, où elles se rencontrent dans le sens commun; elles sont conservées dans l'imagination, elles sont combinées ou séparées dans l'imaginative et leur valeur est appréciée par l'estimative. Le monde sensible est l'aliment de l'activité cognitive de l'animal. De même qu'Aristote, Avicenne nous présente donc une interprétation «biologique» de la perception sensible.' Verbeke, *Introduction sur la doctrine psychologique d'Avicenne*, p. 63.

[5] 'N'oublions pas que, dans la perspective d'Avicenne, la sensation est une forme de passivité: la puissance cognitive est passive vis-à-vis de l'objet à connaître et en subit l'action à tel point qu'il devient semblable à la chose. Le premier terme de la perception, c'est la forme assimilée de l' objet, donc ce que le sujet connaissant perçoit, c'est en quelque sort lui-même, mais lui-même devenu semblable à l'objet.' Ibid., p. 57.

[6] 'Dans l'acte de la sensation, le vivant ne devient pas "autre": on ne se trouve pas devant une aliénation, mais devant un perfectionnement qui se situe dans la ligne de l'équipement naturel de l'animal. [...]. Selon Avicenne, toute sensation consiste à recevoir la forme abstraite de l'objet perçu; grâce à cette assimilation de la forme, le connaissant devient semblable à ce qu'il

Guido Cavalcanti dramatizes the material impression provoked by sensations in Sonnet VIII, in which, as a result of the body's exposure to love, the heart is left carved by a wound (lines 9-14). This wound is also a mark which signifies that the lover is dead, as an 'aperto segno' (that is, openly, but Cavalcanti also introduces here the abolition of the distinction between interior and exterior): 'I' vo come colui ch'è fuori di vita,/che pare, a chi lo sguarda, ch'omo sia/fatto di rame o di pietra o di legno,/che si conduca sol per maestria/e porti ne lo core una ferita/che sia, com' egli è morto, aperto segno.' (I go like one who is outside of life, such that, to the onlooker, he seems a man made of brass or stone or wood, that can walk only by artifice and that bears in [his] heart a wound that is a manifest sign of how he is dead.) The signifying wound borne by the heart is denoted as a cross in Sonnet XII, which epitomizes the encounter with love, as well as its conveyance:

> Perché non fuoro gli occhi a me dispenti
> o tolti, sì che de la lor veduta
> non fosse nella mente mia venuta
> a dir: «Ascolta, se nel cor mi senti»?
>
> Ch'una paura di novi tormenti
> m'aparve allor, sì crudel e aguta,
> che l'anima chiamò: «Donna, or ci aiuta,
> che gli occhi ed i' non rimagnàn dolenti!
>
> Tu gli ha' lasciati sì, che venne Amore
> a pianger sovra lor pietosamente,
> tanto che s'ode una profonda voce
>
> la quale dice: - Chi gran pena sente
> guardi costui, e vederà 'l su' core
> che Morte 'l porta in man tagliato in croce.-»

(Why were my eyes not extinguished or torn out, so that through their power of sight she would not have come into my mind to say: 'Listen if you hear me in your heart'? For a fear of fresh torments appeared to me then, so cruel and sharp that my soul called out: 'Lady, help us now, so that my eyes and I do not stay grieving! You have left them in such a state that Love came to weep piteously over them, until a deep voice is heard to say: -Whoever feels great suffering let him look at that man and he will see that Death bears in hand his heart cut into a cross.')

---

connaît, suivant l'adage ancien, préconisé par Empédocle, disant que le semblable est connu par le semblable.' Ibid., p. 49.

In the following pages, I will employ the image of the heart bearing a material impression of love as an introduction to the 'voices of the body' of which Cavalcanti's language is made. Before examining the special idiom Cavalcanti forged and adopted in his *Rime*, however, I set forth what I consider to be the theoretical background of this idiom. The engraved heart, I claim, represents Cavalcanti's poetic rendering resulting from the topics discussed in the ambit of linguistic theory coeval to him.

In his *De interpretatione*, Aristotle formulated a set of definitions in the field of linguistics which was pivotal in thirteenth-century culture, explaining words as the phonic or written symbols that describe the *passiones animae*, the affections of the soul that correspond to a general mode of how the sensitive powers of the soul are acted upon. These mental affections represent the objects that have impressed the senses.[7]

In the first chapter of the same work Aristotle established a threefold articulation: objects (*res*), *intellectus*, language (*vox*). Language is made of conventionally signifying symbols that connect mental affections to the concrete reality of things. Cavalcanti refers to the functional relation between language and the power of the mind that forms images in Sonnet VI, in which the apparition of the phantasm puts the lover's vital powers to flight and determines a simultaneous dearth of words that the poet begs his spirits to fill, and in Canzone IX (lines 15-18), where he points out that the author's lack of language is determined by his mind's inability to 'withstand' the phantasm of the woman, that is, to form that image: 'Di questa donna non si può contare:/ché di tante bellezze adorna véne,/che mente di qua giù no la sostene/sì che la veggia lo 'ntelletto nostro.' (One cannot describe this lady, for she comes adorned in so many beauties that no mind here below can withstand her to the point that our intellect might see her.) Cavalcanti makes clear that the capacity to 'think' about the woman, the capacity to produce images within the individual mind ('lo 'ntelletto nostro'), is prerequisite to the production of verbal expression ('contare'), which we may assume is rhetorically organized verbal expression in his case. The notion that words cannot be produced if conceptualizing images do not precede them becomes decisive when applied to the minor rhymes that are developed around one main event: the interruption in the formation of the

---

[7] 'Sunt ergo ea quae in voce earum quae sunt in anima passionum notae, et ea quae scribuntur eorum quae sunt in voce. Et quemadmodum nec litterae omnibus eadem, sic nec eadem voces; quorum autem hae primorum notae, eadem omnibus passiones animae sunt, et quorum hae similitudines, res etiam eadem.' Aristoteles latinus, *De Interpretatione* (*Translatio Boethii*), 16a 4-8.

phantasm due to the body's violent response. Since the lover's intellectual capacities are overwhelmed by the body's reactions to the sight of the woman, as indicated in Canzone IX, they not only become unable to form images but they also disrupt linguistic production. When the body is shaken by the effects of the encounter with the love object, mental activities are impeded because, as narrated in the dramatic description in Sonnet VII (and elsewhere)[8], the lover's mind is 'strutta':

> L'anima mia vilment' è sbigotita
> de la battaglia ch'e[l]l'ave dal core:
> che s'ella sente pur un poco Amore
> più presso a lui che non sòle, ella more.
>
> Sta come quella che non ha valore,
> ch'è per temenza da lo cor partita;
> e chi vedesse com' ell' è fuggita
> diria per certo: «Questi non ha vita».
>
> Per li occhi venne la battaglia in pria,
> che ruppe ogni valore immantenente,
> sì che del colpo fu strutta la mente.
>
> Qualunqu' è quei che più allegrezza sente,
> se vedesse li spirti fuggir via,
> di grande sua pietate piangeria.

(My soul is abjectly appalled by the battering it had from the heart: for if it feels Love just a little closer to it than it was before, it will die. It stands as one that has no strength, since out of fear it has forsaken my heart; and whoever saw how it fled would surely say: 'This man is lifeless.' Through the eyes came the first battering that at once routed all valor, so that the mind was killed by the blow. Whoever it is who feels most cheer, if he should but see the spirits take flight, he would weep out of his great pity.)

The poems that address the collapse of the mind and, therefore, the collapse of its power to produce images, raise a crucial issue: if language production takes place only provided that the human mind intervenes as a conceptualizing tool, what happens when rational activities are impeded? What linguistic solution does Cavalcanti adopt when faced with the lover having to tell of his mind's undoing? As I introduced earlier, Cavalcanti resolves the impasse by forging a language that results not from a process

---

[8] See also VIII, IX, XIII, XIX. The locution: 'strutta mente' is employed as well in Ballad XXXV.

complete with mental images but from the direct use of bodily affections as verbal signs.

The employment of an unconventional handling of the linguistic issue pertains, on the other hand, not just to the minor rhymes but to the whole body of Cavalcanti's poems. While the description of love semeiotics in the minor rhymes is grammatically challenging because affected by the interruption of the imaginative process, the theoretical undertaking of the major canzone, as has been acutely remarked, overpowers grammar tout-court, making the philosophical content, and the rules of logic, convey the meaning, to the extent that the rules of grammar are broken.[9] The grammar structure of the minor rhymes is, likewise, dictated and forced by their content. Unlike *Donna me prega*, whose content, the fracture between the two irreconcilable dimensions of matter and ideas, is expressed through a syntactical alteration that is grammatically inexplicable, the minor rhymes, which describe the undoing of the mind and the consequent impairment of imagination, require the employment of a language consisting of the affections of the soul. This language undermines the notion of authorship since, like mental affections, it is universal.[10] Further, while *Donna me prega* portrays the separation between matter and ideas, the minor rhymes originate in matter and are bound by it. They define the boundaries of matter and indicate the limits of the experience of human love. Their language is, accordingly, on the fringes. By replicating the liminal locus indicated by love phenomenology on the grounds of grammatical categories, Cavalcanti selected for the minor rhymes the terms that linguists had moved to the extremities of their taxonomy: *voces gemituum, dolorum et suspiriorum*. These are the 'voices of the body' I indicate as Cavalcanti's grammar, resulting from a mental process in which imagination does not actively participate.

---

[9] An example of the overpowering of grammatical conventions in *Donna me prega* is in stanza 2, where Cavalcanti explains the moment of *coniunctio* between the phantasm and the possible intellect, as highlighted by Ardizzone's study: 'In stanza 2 of *Donna me prega*, grammar is subordinated to the philosophical meaning. Of interest here is that Cavalcanti emphasizes the very thing that enables the reader to distinguish the being of intellect from the being of love. He organizes—through the "form"—an apparent continuity through different levels and exposes its content, breaking the continuity of grammar in order to expose the break that takes place in the process he is describing.' Ardizzone, *Guido Cavalcanti. The Other Middle Ages*, p. 115.

[10] As stated by the opening lines of Aristotle's *De interpretatione* quoted above (' […] eadem omnibus passiones animae sunt, […].' See this chapter, n. 7.

The use of the term 'grammar' in the thirteenth-century cultural context requires a reference to speculative grammar, a movement whose aim was to analyze language with scientific, methodical tools and which emerged in the major European intellectual centers as the result of the influence of *logica nova* (four works included in Aristotle's *Organon*: *Prior and Posterior Analytics, Topics* and *On Sophistical Refutations*) which entered the West and had strong bearing on both the intellectual debate of the time and university curricula, as well as, for our purposes, the evolution of grammar. Another factor that contributed to the evolution of the Western study of grammar during the last decades of the 1200s was the influence of the Arabic tradition consisting of the commentaries to Aristotle's *De Interpretatione*. The Arabic commentators, especially Alfarabi, sharply distinguished logic and grammar on the grounds of their respectively rational and linguistic nature. This distinction had, in fact, the effect of creating a reciprocal dependence between the two disciplines and ultimately contributed to the consideration of language as universal, therefore, as a topic for scientific study.[11]

Due to these multiple factors interacting with Western learning, the *ars gramatica* rooted in the works of Donatus and Priscianus and their commentators, that is, the study of how to speak and write correctly in addition to studying the literary tradition, underwent a radical change in status in the first decades of the 1200s. By the mid-thirteenth century the distinction between *artes sermocinales* and *artes rationales* had begun to blur, and pedagogical grammar, the tool for the study of classic literature and the Bible, gradually developed into a theoretical, philosophical discipline.[12]

---

[11] Deborah Black studied the tradition of Latin and Arabic commentaries on the *De interpretatione*, and makes a comparison between the different approach of the two traditions to some of the knots Aristotle deals with, mainly with regards to the rational and linguistic functions attributed to logic and grammar. In other words, how logic and grammar deal with linguistic phenomena (the first on the ground of truth, the second of congruity). In Black's conclusions, while the Latin authors 'assign to grammar, i.e., speculative grammar, what they believe to be properly philosophical consideration of the nature of language and linguistic construction,' Alfarabi, by sharply distinguishing the two disciplines, was forced to attribute linguistic and rational properties to both, and consequently promoted 'a model of logic as a science of reason which includes universal grammar as an essential part.' (Black, pp. 53-54).

[12] 'By 1215, classical authors were absent from the Arts course in the University of Paris and by 1255, only Donatus and Priscian remained of the ancient Latin authors; the plain fact is that the classical literary tradition which had been so superbly fostered by the cathedral schools of Chartres and Orleans died of sheer starvation, because the ideas which the study of Aristotle produced became too absorbing to allow the study of classical authors to remain important. Grammar, the weathervane of intellectual change, turned from the study of literature into a

Among the most important products of speculative grammar was Modism. The Modistae (whose presence is attested in Paris as well as at the University of Bologna, by the end of the thirteenth century) were strong agents in the course of this disciplinary reconfiguration, and their work was an impressive synthesis of tradition and new theoretical goals. Driven by the requirement for a grammar that could be classified as a 'science,' one that would deal with universal and immutable features of reality, the Modistae produced a general theory by assembling a set of rules systematizing the linguistic modes universally employed to describe reality. They focused their study on what correspondence could be found between the structures of reality and the concepts the mind produced as a result of contact with the reality of things. In the framework of such a general formulation, the Modistae did not focus on verbal expressions, which they considered subsidiary to their studies; furthermore, interest in the 'ways' of description often shifted the focus of their investigation from reference to sense, that is, from material to formal meaning, thereby detaching their theories from reality (and coincidentally raising the issue of the scientific nature of such theories).

The wide scope of their investigation merits their being referred to as the first 'linguists' in the current meaning of the term. Formulations considered preliminary to the Modistic conclusions can be found in the texts produced by the masters of grammar at Chartres between 1120 and 1154.[13] The author who however clearly marked a change in the objectives and tools of grammar and indicated the path to general theories is Roger Bacon. His *Summa gramatica* (1245) and later work *De signis* (1267) laid the groundwork for the speculative grammar that the Modistae systematized a few years later. Speculative, that is, 'in the sense that language mirrors the "reality" which, according to mediaeval metaphysics, underlies the phenomena of the physical world.'[14] Language expresses the two primary elements of the world of things: permanence (*nomen* and *pronomen*) and becoming (*verbum* and *participium*).

Although language and reality are described as specular dimensions, they do not correspond exactly to each other; what actually creates the specularity is the mind which, while it formulates words that reflect the

---

logical science, a speculative philosophical discipline, and its problems were no longer solved by reference to the best Latin literature, but by logic.' Bursill-Hall, p. 25.
[13] Ibid., p. 28.
[14] Ibid., p. 31.

properties of the objects, also works as a tool of mediation.[15] The Modistae explained the process involved in the production of language by means of a threefold scheme, which served the purpose of bounding reality and the single languages while preserving the capacity to reach universal conclusions. The three distinct, although strictly interconnected, elements of the scheme presiding over language production are the *modi essendi*, the *modi intelligendi*, and the *modi significandi*, the last two both described in a double form, as *activi* and *passivi*. The *modi essendi* define the qualities of the things perceived; the *modi intelligenti* consist of both the mental capacity to apprehend reality (*modi intelligenti activi*) and the closely related capacity of things to be apprehended (*modi intelligenti passivi*); as a result of these bilateral functions, the noises produced by humans, *voces*,[16] are imposed on by the mind's modes of actively giving meaning (*modi significandi activi*) and become signifying sounds, *dictiones*, which correspond to the modes of signifying of the properties of the things themselves (*modi significandi passivi*). It is after a further intellectual process that the *dictio* becomes a *pars orationis*, a grammatical unit on which the mind has bestowed the capacity to consignify and therefore to function syntactically. The triadic scheme of the *modi essendi*, *intelligendi* and *significandi*, corresponding to the *res, intellectus rei* and *vox significandi rem*, attempted to demonstrate how verbal elements can correspond to mental acts and, through these mental acts, to reality. Language is the final product of a system of bilateral and simultaneous relations, of an interplay between mental capacity and reality, the former perceiving and subsequently actively conceptualizing, the latter passively exposing itself to being conceptualized.

This is the background against which I support Cavalcanti's theoretical choices. The mapping of the sources for grammar employed by the thireenth-century Tuscan poets is still the object of a debate, which includes the inference that a direct contact between Guido Cavalcanti and the texts

---

[15] 'The word, in the Modistic scheme, is not just the imitation of a piece of reality but must pass through a 'filter of intellectual apprehension' which will impart to the word something of the subjective ideas of the creator of the word. On the other hand, the word, which will however not be entirely a figment of the mind but must have some correlate in the world of things outside the mind, will therefore be defined in terms of the properties of the thing meant; this amounts to a subjective evaluation of the being and its properties which the intelligence has perceived and is now seeking to signify.' Ibid., p. 40.

[16] As is made clear in all the studies about the Modistic theories, sounds are taken into account only insofar as signs, given that 'the Modistae excluded any physiological-auditory approach to linguistic analysis, phonetics being outside the province of the grammarian, a matter more for the natural philosopher: […].' Ibid., p. 73.

of the Modist is highly far-fetched.[17] In my research, I suggest a connection between Cavalcanti's linguistic experimentations and one—marginal— aspect of the theories of these grammarians; specifically, between the language of the minor rhymes and the notion of 'naturally signifying' signs, as we find it mentioned, among other texts, in the pages of Gentile da Cingoli, a philosopher with medical interests who studied in Paris around 1290 and then, in 1295, joined the circle of Taddeo Alderotti at the University of Bologna.[18]

In order to introduce the specific links that, I suggest, connect Cavalcanti's language to a subsection of the Modistic texts, I first look again at the lines of Sonnets VIII and XII, in which the inscribed heart of the lover is displayed. That moment, I claim, sets forth a crucial indication of the *Rime*'s linguistic procedures as it presents the reader with the possibility of a pre-conceptual language. While presenting his audience with the lover's heart bearing a wound that is a manifest sign of his blackout, Cavalcanti establishes a connection between sign and language. The inscribed cross in the lover's heart is displayed in order to convey a meaning: it tells readers of the lover's death. Calvalcanti however goes beyond the sign/language connection. By employing imprints as if they were words, he takes the introductory definition given by Aristotle in his *De interpretatione* and radicalizes it. The Aristotelian designation of words as affections of the soul is enacted literally by impressing in the lover's heart a cross that signifies death. Moreover, the engraved heart indicates that when the lover's mind collapses in the face of love, as happens in the section of the *Rime* I am considering here, then language coincides immediately with sensation; both are an 'impression.' The inscribed heart becomes the prototype for

---

[17] While Maria Corti claims a relation between Tuscan poets and Modists by indicating specific textual connections between Dante Alighieri and Boethius of Dacia (Corti, *Lingua universale e lingua poetica in Dante*, in: *Dante a un nuovo crocevia*, pp. 33-76) Alfonso Maierù excludes the possibility of indicating the derivation for the linguistic theories of both Guido and Dante ('Non sappiamo quali siano stati gli interlocutori di Dante nelle sue riflessioni sul linguaggio prima e dopo il 1295; non pare tuttavia ch'egli abbia adottato posizioni modiste piuttosto che genericamente aristoteliche; semmai gli interlocutori di Dante andrebbero forse cercati dalle parti del versante intenzionalista della grammatica speculativa piuttosto che sul versante modista. Per quel che sappiamo, non pare che la dottrina modista debba essere chiamata in causa per Cavalcanti.' Maierù, *La logica nell'età di Cavalcanti*, p. 43.) The issue is resumed by Ileana Pagani, who undermines Corti's findings by tracing a few divergences between Dante and Boethius, and concludes that the alleged relation is made, in fact, of 'concordanze di termini anche banali, non da concordanze concettuali.' (Pagani, p. 262).
[18] Siraisi, *Taddeo Alderotti*, pp. 42-45.

Cavalcanti's 'rhetoric of passion,' his most distinctive linguistic achievement. A decisive example of this rhetoric is in Sonnet VI. In it, Cavalcanti applies a figure of speech, the anaphora, to the sighs ('deh') released by the lover, thereby organizing the text according to a language of the body:[19]

> Deh, spiriti miei, quando mi vedete
> con tanta pena, come non mandate
> fuor della mente parole adornate
> di pianto, dolorose e sbigottite?
>
> Deh, voi vedete che 'l core ha ferite
> di sguardo e di piacer e d'umiltate:
> deh, i' vi priego che voi 'l consoliate
> che son da lui le sue vertù partite.
>
> I' veggo a lui spirito apparire
> alto e gentile e di tanto valore,
> che fa le sue vertù tutte fuggire.
>
> Deh, i' vi prego che deggiate dire
> a l'alma trista, che parl' in dolore,
> com'ella fu e fie sempre d'Amore.

> (Ah, my spirits, since you see me in such suffering, and because you do not send forth from my mind words embellished with tears, sorrowful and dismayed, alas, you see that my heart has wounds from looks and from beauty and from charity: alas, I beg you to give it consolation, for its powers have forsaken it. I see appear to it a spirit lofty and noble and of such strength that it makes all its powers flee. Alas, I beg you kindly to tell my saddened soul, that speaks in sorrow, how it was and always will be Love's.)

The anaphoric recurrence of the interjection *deh* that Cavalcanti employed in this sonnet to shape a language produced by the lover's physiological, not intellectual, capacities, is decisive. Not only does it exemplify the rhetorical rules at work in the *Rime*, but it also signals their

---

[19] The expression 'rhetoric of passion' is coined, and throughout elaborated, by Maria Luisa Ardizzone in her monograph about Guido Cavalcanti. Sonnet VI is specifically read from this rhetorical perspective: 'If we read Sonnet VI (*Deh, spiriti miei quando mi vedete* [Ah, my spirits, since you see me]), we may enter further into the rhetoric of passion and the method Cavalcanti employs. Here Cavalcanti introduces 'spirits' as a key word for his discourse of love. [...]. In this Sonnet, Cavalcanti's *inventio* is extraordinarily innovative. A central rhetorical role is played here by the pathetic exclamation *deh* [ah] repeated four times. If we connect the *deh* to the sigh, the *deh* appears here to be introduced as the rhetorical voice of a physical event: the actual sigh. [...]. The *deh* seems therefore to be a word-sigh that represents a physiological function as an instrument of responding to and resisting an emotional pressure.' Ardizzone, *Guido Cavalcanti. The Other Middle Ages*, pp. 21-23.

correspondence with a portion of the Modistic linguistic theories. With regard to the physiological language at work in the poems, the texts of the grammarians provide relevant material when they discuss the controversial topic of interjection, the involuntary and sudden utterance provoked by an emotion; Cavalcanti's rhetoric finds its place in this ambiguous corner of the debate on language.

The Modistae based their classification of *partes orationis* on two contrasting models: the first, that of Donatus, consisted of eight grammatical units, and the second, that of Priscian, of only seven, with interjection under the category of adverbs.[20] Discussion among the Modistae over the uncertain grammatical status of interjection led to the examination of other relevant issues, including the distinction between 'naturally' and 'rationally' signifying language (and the degrees of separation between the two); the function of instinct, will, and reason in the utterance of language; the two different modes, *per modum affectus* and *per modum conceptus*, governing linguistic productions. In brief, the problematic classification of interjections raised the equally problematic issue of verbal expressions considered 'unfinished,' not fully elaborated by human reason and will.

According to the Modistae, linguistic productions fall within categories characterized by different time intervals between impression and expression and, accordingly, different degrees of rational elaboration. When facing a painful event, for instance, the speaking subject can utter a cry; pronounce an interjection, *alas*; or, finally, formulate a sentence, 'I suffer.' In the *De signis*, Roger Bacon places the full range of human signs into a general semiological perspective. In his treatise, which organizes all the different types of signs included in the general category of *relationes*, he begins by citing the preliminary distinction taken from the realm of logic, between *signa naturalia* and *signa ordinata ab anima*. While the first serve as 'natural' signs, that is, without a meaning superimposed on them (such as *aurora est signum ortum solis*), the second, including verbal signs (*signum institutum an intellectu ut linguae et idiomata*),[21] signify 'by human convention' (*ex intentione animae*). In the course of his exposition Bacon further divides the *signa*

---

[20] The grammatical units consisted of, according to Donatus, four declinable parts (*nomen, pronomen, verbum, participium*) and four undeclinable ones (*adverbium, coniunctio, praepositio, interiectio*), or three, according to Priscian. Among the Modistae, in his commentary to Martin of Dacia's *Modi significandi*, for instance, Gentile of Cingoli departs from the scheme of Martin (and of Donatus) and classifies interjection under adverb, therefore listing seven *partes orationis*.

[21] Fredborg, p. 83.

ordinata ab anima into three categories: signs uttered by instinct (*quodam instinctu naturali et impetu naturae*) and signifying 'naturally' (such as cries or moans);[22] interjections; and, lastly, signs produced with the intervention of reason and will (*cum deliberatione rationis et electione voluntatis*).[23] In this threefold scheme, interjections occupy an intermediate position.[24] Even though they are released as an immediate reaction to and a sign of an affection, like naturally signifying signs, interjections are partially processed by the mind. Although quickly and imperfectly (*per privationem temporis sensibilis*) formed they result from rational elaboration: they signify an affection *per modum conceptus*.[25] Because of their property, therefore, interjections are transitional units between, on one hand, sounds that are immediate responses to passions and signify an affection *per modum affectus* and, on the other, words, or units, intellectually elaborated that likewise respond to affections but result from an act of deliberation and imposition, and thus signify a concept

---

[22] Bacon opts for the definition of cries and moans (among others) as signs naturally signifying rather than *signa naturalia* given the ambiguity of the notion of *natura*, (which means *substantia* but also *principium operationis*), therefore of the adjective *naturalis*: 'Si obiciatur quod voces significativas naturaliter debent dici signa naturalia et ita collocari sub signis naturalibus a principio dictis, dicendum est quod postquam voces significant naturaliter erunt signa naturalia. Sed signa naturalia sunt aequivoca secundum aequivocationem naturae. Ex libro enim Boethii *De duabus naturis* patet quattuor esse significationes "naturae," quarum unam est secundum intentionem Aristotelis II *Physicorum*, vel ut natura dicatur virtus agens sine deliberatione quae sit principium motus et quietis eius in quo est primo et per se et non secundum accidens; et a natura sic dicta dicuntur voces significativae naturaliter; talis enim natura in proposito est anima a cuius intentione datur ratio signi istis vocibus.' Ibid., pp. 85-86.

[23] 'Signum vero ordinatum ab anima et ex intentione animae recipiens rationem signi est duplex: unum sit ab anima cum deliberatione rationis et electione voluntatis, sive ad placitum, sive ex proposito, et huiusmodi est signum institutum ab intellectu ut linguae et idiomata et circulus vini et res expositae venditionis in fenestris venditorum positae pro signis, non solum ad repraesentandum alia, sed se ipsa, ut panis in fenestra [...]. Aliud signum ab anima datum est quod fit sine deliberatione rationis et sine electione voluntatis, nec ad placitum nec ex propositio sed quasi subito per privationem temporis sensibilis et quodam instinctu naturali et impetu naturae et virtutis naturaliter agentis.' Ibid., p. 83.

[24] 'Nota quod interiectiones omnes sunt mediae inter istas voces nunc dictas et inter voces plene significantes ad placitum, quae sunt scilicet aliae septem partes orationis.' Ibid., p. 84.

[25] In his *Communia naturalia*, on the other hand, Bacon combines interjections and natural signs, since both more strongly determined by an *affectus* rather than a *conceptus*: 'Dans le *De signis*, [...] Bacon distingue alors des signes naturels que sont le rires et le gémissements, toutes le parties du discours, qui ont en commun d'avoir une signification instituée volontairement. Contrairement à ce qu'il affirmait dans *Communia naturalium*, Bacon caractérise l'interjection, comme les autres parties du discours, par le fait que, précisément en tant que parties du discours, elles signifient sur le mode du concept (*per modum conceptus*), bien que la première signifie l'affect, la seconde le concept.' Rosier, p. 63.

per modum conceptus.²⁶ Passions affecting human souls produce linguistic reactions that are determined by the different degrees of deliberation involved in the process.²⁷

Sounds signifying an affection *per modum affectus* correspond to passions really affecting the soul, not just present in the form of an image.²⁸ Corresponding immediately to the soul's affections and grammatically unrefined, these sounds, which the Modistae acknowledged but did not include in their study, become the essential components of the pre-conceptual language of Cavalcanti's minor rhymes. Among the examples of these 'naturally signifying' signs, the grammarians indicate moans and sighs, as well as exclamations of surprise and pain: all dismissed as so much grammatical waste, like the *vox quam infirmi emittunt naturaliter* indicated by Gentile of Cingoli in his commentary to Martin of Dacia's *Modi significandi*;²⁹ or like the *vox significativa naturaliter* listed by Bacon, who went on to elaborate by listing what was included in this category: 'Ut omnes voces gemituum, dolorum et suspiriorum et admirationum et gaudiorum et ceteratum affectionum animi. Quando enim anima rationalis solum afficitur et sic affecta pronuntiat sine deliberatione, tunc vox prolata est significans naturaliter.' (Like all the sounds of moans, pains, and sighs and wonder and

---

²⁶ 'Interiectiones enim imperfecte significant ad placitum et parum significant per modum conceptus propter quod vicinantur vocibus illis quae solum per modum affectus subiecti significant cuiusmodi sunt gemitus et cetera quae tacta sunt.' Fredborg, p. 84. Martin of Dacia, on the ground of correspondence between *modi significandi* and meaning, claims that interjections signify a passion according to the mode of passion (Marmo, *Semiotica e linguaggio nella scolastica*, p. 252). In his commentary to Martin of Dacia's *Modi significandi*, Gentile da Cingoli concludes that interjection necessarily signifies *mentis conceptum* or it would not be treated by grammarians, who can not include among *partes orationis* sounds that signify *mentis affecta* (Alessio, p. 18).

²⁷ 'Quando enim anima rationalis solum afficitur et sic affecta pronuntiat sine deliberatione, tunc vox prolata est significans naturaliter. Quando autem non solum afficitur, sed ex deliberatione concipit huiusmodi passiones et profert voces easdem et significativas earundem passionum, sunt interiectiones. Voco autem affectum et animam affici, quando dolet et gaudet et miratur et huiusmodi, conceptum autem dico quando de passione afficiente vel non afficiente sive non existente deliberat, iudicat et cognoscit in tempore sensibili per modum plenae considerationis ex proposito.' Fredborg, pp. 84-85.

²⁸ 'Une chose peut être dans l'âme soit par son image, soit réellement. Dans le premier cas, elle y est sur le mode du concept, dans le second, sur le mode de l'affect.' Rosier, p. 66.

²⁹ 'Tunc, ad minorem, quoniam dicitur: "interiectio non significat mentis conceptum", certe dico, quod falsum est, quia dictio, que significat talem rem vel affectum qui est circa animam, non ut intelligatur ab anima et imponatur ad significandum ab anima, sed ut naturale illud significat, sicut vox quam infirmi emittunt naturaliter, non dicitur esse pars orationis [...] quia ista talis vox non est significativa ad placitum, sed naturaliter.' Alessio, p. 18.

happiness, and of all the other affections of the soul. In fact when the rational soul is simply affected and, while affected, it pronounces without consideration, then the emitted sound is naturally signifying).[30] These sounds are the rudimental, grammatically incomplete *voces* uttered, *sine deliberatione*, from a condition of 'being affected'; and, I claim, they constitute the theoretical grounds for the physiological language at work in the *Rime*, since they perform the special pre-abstraction functions required by Cavalcanti's love language. This language responds to the necessity of recounting a love venture whose protagonist is forced into darkness and deprived of his capacity to produce images. Interjections and sighs, cries and moans are considered by the grammarians as the unfinished and immediate linguistic expressions uttered by a subject impressed by passion. These sounds are *voces* bearing a meaning although they are not yet *dictiones* (in which the vocal expression is connected to a *ratio significandi*).[31] These are the voices of the body that, in the minor rhymes, function as the agents for poems narrating the obscuration of the mind.

In the next chapter, I will identify these voices of the body and show how the medical source interwoven in Cavalcanti's text not only bestows authority on the love theory he espouses, but also legitimates its rhetorical consequences. Acted upon by love, the *Rime* protagonist's body is inscribed by his affections, which are made visible, even legible, and capable therefore of creating a language regardless of his failed imagination.

III.2 Mapping the *Liber Canonis* in the *Rime*

Cavalcanti's rhetorical tools are forged in compliance with the theory his poetry conveys: since humans are limited in their sensorial capacities while

---

[30] Fredborg, pp. 84-85. Bacon includes among the *voces significantes naturaliter* also animals' noises, such as animal sounds. Incidentally, this would signal Bacon's extensive approach to linguistics and communication. To 'signify' concerns the relation between words and *res extra animam*, not the relation between words and concepts. Words signify reality and are simply symptoms of concepts, they attest that something occurred in the human soul: 'He [Bacon] studied physical utterances (be they sounds or other physical objects) as produced in order to refer to "res extra animam". Men emitting words or showing commodities, animal 'speaking' to each other, the infirms indicating by their wail the actual fact that they are suffering, all of them are, by some impulse, *denoting something*. It is exactly this extensional purpose that allows Bacon to put the voice of animals and the voice of men (along with visual sign such as the "circulus vini") all together.' Eco, Umberto, R. Lambertini, C. Marmo, A. Tabarroni, *On Animal Language in the Medieval Classification of Signs*, p. 23.
[31] Marmo, *Semiotica e linguaggio nella scolastica*, pp. 112-113.

experiencing love, they are unable to form abstract thought, which is instead expressed by the collective dimension of the possible intellect. This conclusion also concerns the actual recounting of the love experience; the fracture detaching individuals from intellectual processes bears important consequences on the sphere of language, since language depends heavily on abstraction. In order to tell of events whose protagonist is mired in matter and unable to complete the elaboration of his thoughts, Cavalcanti creates a language that, accordingly, does not result from an intellectual process but strictly from sensations. The signs found in Cavalcanti's language are peripheral to the coeval discussion on grammar: insofar as these signs are not produced by an act of reason and will, the grammarians relegate them to the margins. Cavalcanti's language is assembled by using either *voces mediae* only partially processed by the mind, such as interjections, or 'naturally signifying' signs, such as cries and moans, according to Roger Bacon's classification, which I mentioned in the previous pages. The *voces significativa naturaliter* employed in Cavalcanti's minor rhymes, which emphasize that the agent of communication is the body, find their classification in the grammatical schemes outlined by the Modistae and their scientific support and explanation in the medical sources.

The particular source I selected, Avicenna's *Canon*, provides an explanation of the love semeiotics of Cavalcanti's poems. In the course of this study I suggest a few instances in which the *Canon*'s contents function as the footnote apparatus of of the *Rime*. Further, this scientific source confers legitimacy on the *Rime*'s expressive mode, on the rhetorical laboratory in which the 'voices of the body' are forged and utilized. This study does not produce exact, complete parallels between the poetic content and the medical material; the poems are not the versification of a scientific treatise. Although the *Rime* and the *Canon* do frequently overlap, Cavalcanti often veers from the medical path. The discrepancies between the two texts, which have been explained in terms of dominant poetic imagery,[32] do not however render the poet's work arbitrary. The poetry's content is drawn

---

[32] 'Nobody of course believes that Italian poets were content with putting into verses the views of Averroist physicians. The often illuminating and satisfying results one can obtain by comparing physiological explanations and poetic figures of speech are not sufficient to explain the texts; and it is quite possible that with at least some poets the formulas borrowed from the natural science combined with a quite different philosophical outlook – Neoplatonism, or more eclectic and vague, made up of traditional beliefs, more or less successful adaptations, misunderstandings, and commonsense ideas, as is generally the case with any "verbal culture."' Klein, pp. 73-74.

from a complex and unfixed scenario, some tenets of which in fact lacked an established tradition, as exemplified by the elaboration in the *Rime* of the complex notion of 'spirit.' On the other hand, the language in the *Rime* corresponds to its content; as in a coherent whole, the writing process grounds itself in a theoretical assumption and brings it to its radical conclusion in the sphere of rhetoric. The process of language-forging is the ultimate ground on which to test Cavalcanti's faithfulness to his sources. My focus is to show that Cavalcanti obtains his most original results when he combines linguistic experimentation with the compositive method of weaving medical *auctoritates* into his text, in other words, when he allows the *auctoritates* in the text to alter the rules of rhetoric.

In particular I investigate a few instances in which the connections between the *Canon* and the *Rime* become visible. While engaged in developing a topic, Cavalcanti here deviates from the poetic tradition and embraces medical conventions as is the case with the spirits and their connections to sighs and the weeping. These terms are explained in the *Rime* through the meaning that the physicians have attributed to them. Their medical meaning, further, has crucial consequences on the sphere of language, since spirits, sighs and weeping become the voices, uttered by the body, that take the author's place. Sighs both talk (XXVI, 17-18): 'movonsi nell'anima sospiri/che dicon: «Guarda...»', (And in my soul are stirring sighs that say: "Look...") and reason (XV, 5-7): '...i miei sospiri,/che nascon della mente ov'è Amore/e vanno sol ragionando dolore/...' (My sighs, caused by anguished delights- [sighs] which are born of the mind where Love resides and go about expressing only sorrow), not simply as a result of the dramatization at work in the *Rime*, but, mainly, as the sign of a rhetorical experiment. The *Rime*'s cross-references to the *Canon* are not limited to the case of sighs and weeping. An expanded list of the terms connecting the two texts has produced the entries compiled in the *Appendix* of this study. It consists of a selection of passages from the *Canon* that correspond to, and explain, a list of terms relevant to the *Rime*. Utilizing Cavalcanti's vocabulary to read the physician's pages, I have outlined a lexical grid that acts as a tool in the interpretation of the poet's lines.

III.3 'Ché la 'ntenzione per ragione vale'

In the previous pages I presented an interpretation of Sonnet VI as a manifest example of the rhetoric of passion at work in the *Rime*. This reading is grounded in the fact that in applying a figure of speech, the anaphora, to the 'deh' emitted by the lover, Sonnet VI confers the status of linguistic sign on an interjection. Equally meaningful results stem from the inquiry into the *Rime*'s use of the 'naturally signifying' signs, that is, the utterances following the impulsive and unintended reactions to the soul's affections. These signs are widely employed in Cavalcanti's minor rhymes; in fact, the writing of the minor rhymes consists almost exclusively of the transcription of the body's automated responses to the passions impressed on it. In Sonnet VI, Cavalcanti himself provides his readers with the definition of this physiological language: his writing is a 'parlare in dolore' ('speaking in sorrow'). This language reflects the same truncation at work in the love process. While experiencing love, humans are detached from the sphere of intellection; likewise, the language of love is uttered before being filtered by reason. It is a language steadily produced *per modum affectus* and composed of the emission of unaltered sound reflecting the soul's passions. As such, it stands as the expression of an action rather than the result of an epistemological process.[33] As stated in line 33 of *Donna me prega*, human beings, when acted upon by love, are driven by 'intention' rather than guided by rationality: 'ché la 'ntenzione - per ragione - vale' ('since intention is operative in place of reason'). In medieval culture, 'intention' was endowed with multiple meanings: the notion of 'being attracted' towards the 'seen form' (*Donna me prega*, 21), the form itself,[34] and the process of change and adaptation occurring when perception is taking place. Exposed to

---

[33] This specific distinction regarding the two modes, *per affectus* and *per conceptus*, is illustrated by Irène Rosier: 'Dans tous les systèmes que nous allons brièvement évoquer, ces couples expriment une opposition entre une modalité visant la connaissance, et une modalité visant l'action. Cette opposition entre vrai et bon est située soit dans la distinction entre âme rationnelle et âme irrationnelle, soit à l'intérieur de l'âme rationnelle avec la distinction spéculatif/pratique, soit à l'intérieur de l'âme irrationnelle sensitive avec la distinction entre facultés cognitives ou appréhensives et facultés motrices.' Rosier, p. 67.

[34] 'Il desiderio ("intendanza" vale, nel linguaggio della poesia amorosa, sia "amore," sia, per metonimia, l'oggetto amato): cfr. *Conv*, III xv 8-9, dove a "desiderio naturale" corrisponde e equivale "intenzione naturale"; o anche l' "intentio formae", ossia la rappresentazione sensibile (cfr. 21) dell'oggetto amato (l'*intentio individui* di Averroè nel suo commento al *De anima*, II, t. c., 65), l'immagine che l'amante se ne fa. Ma il verso è evidentemente "ispirato" dalla clausola di Giovenale, *Sat.*, VI 223, "sit pro ratione voluntas" (Contini, *Lett. d. Or.*), del resto probabilmente presente anche a Guittone del son. *franchezza, segnoria* ... , 9, "ma franco è quei la cui voglia è ragione". *Per ragione vale*: sta per, si sostituisce alla ragione.' De Robertis, *Rime*, p. 102.

sensations as if they were blows wounding the heart,[35] the lover's body resonates with pain,[36] emitting responses resulting from the violence: the 'parole disfatte e paurose' ('my words, undone and fearful', XXXIV, 25) the 'voce sbigottita e deboletta' ('you, dismayed and frail voice', XXXV, 37).

The 'parlare in dolore' that Cavalcanti adopts in the most dramatic of his poems is articulated in distinct sounds. In my close reading I single out sighs and weeping. Both are referred to as tools of vocal communication: because of their being always intertwined with sighs, tears are given sounds. Tears and sighs are the immediate response of the mind 'awakened' by love,[37] the joint effect of love's attacks: 'I' sento pianger for li miei sospiri,/quando la mente di lei mi ragiona ' (I feel my sighs weeping forth, when my mind reasons to me about her, XXXI, 11-12).[38] These attacks strike at the lover's mind, which towers metaphorically over his body as its outpost; the 'cassero'—implied in the 'cassar de la mente' of Sonnet XXXVII—of a ship that is in the end 'disfatta' (XLIVb, 11); a citadel under siege, 'distretta' (XXXI, 2). Stormed by love, the mind is finally filled, like an empty container, with pain, in the opening lines of Sonnet VIII: 'Tu m'hai sì

---

[35] 'Deh, voi vedete che 'l core ha ferite/di sguardo e di piacer e d'umiltate:' (Alas, you see that my heart has wounds from looks and from beauty and from charity); 'Per li occhi venne la battaglia in pria,/che ruppe ogni valore immantenente' (Through the eyes came the first battering that at once routed all valor) VI, 5; VII, 9.

[36] 'Unlike "likeness," to which various categories of true and false can meaningfully be applied, intention is a matter of perception and point of view. Because of this, it is malleable and pliant, and "arbitrary" in the root sense of that word. In the *Tusculan Disputations*, Cicero sometimes used the word *intentio* almost as English uses the word "resonance." Indeed the root meaning of *intendo* is "tighten, make tense" as tightening the voice or the strings of an instrument makes it resonate in the first place and also causes different resonances as the tension changes. [...]. Intention is thus a matter of tone, of tension and of resonance.' Carruthers, p. 5.

[37] 'Voi che per li occhi mi passaste 'l core/e destaste la mente che dormia' (You who through my eyes penetrated my heart and wakened my sleeping mind), followed by: 'Lagrime ascendon de la mente mia/sì tosto come questa donna sente' (Tears rise up from my mind as soon as it senses this Lady). XIII, 1-2, and XIX, 18-19. See also XV.

[38] See also: 'L'anima mia dolente e paurosa/piange ne [l]i sospir' che nel cor trova,/sì che bagnati di pianto escon fòre' (My grieving and fearful soul weeps over the sighs it finds in my heart so that they come forth wet with tears, XVII, 9-11), and: 'd'angosciosi dilett' i miei sospiri,/che nascon dalla mente ov'è Amore/e vanno sol ragionando dolore/e non trovan persona che li miri,/giriano agli occhi con tanta vertute,/che 'l forte e 'l duro lagrimar ch'e' fanno/ritornerebbe in allegrezza e 'n gioia.' (My sighs, caused by anguishing delights, which are born of the mind where Love resides, and go about expressing only sorrow and find no one to look on them, would reach my eyes in such strenght that the hard and insistent weeping they perform would turn into cheerfulness and joy, XV, 5-11).

piena di dolor la mente/che la mente si briga di partire' (You have my mind so filled with sorrow/that the soul contrives to depart).

III.4 A World in Bewilderment

Sighs and tears are the most recurrent voices of the body echoing throughout the *Rime*. The text, however, bears multiple traces of the medical *auctoritas*: the *Rime*'s protagonist is characterized by features that find a medical explanation in the *Canon*. Struggling for his lost self-control, the lover is depicted by Cavalcanti in Sonnet VIII as 'fuor di vita' and barely capable of realizing how mechanical and lifeless his movements must seem to those observing him: '.../I' vo come colui ch'è fuor di vita,/ che pare, a chi lo sguarda, ch'omo sia/fatto di rame o di pietra o di legno,/che si conduca sol per maestria/' (I go like one who is outside of life/such that, to the onlooker, he seems a man/made of brass or stone or wood,/that can walk only by artifice). The symptoms of the loss of self-control are described by Avicenna when, for example, he discusses the *tremor*, which inhibits the *virtutes animales* and especially the *virtus motiva*: 'Tremor fit ex omnibus causis quibus virtutes animales contrahuntur. Tremor est morbus instrumentalis eveniens propter difectum virtutis motivae.' (Trembling is caused by a contraction of the vital powers. Trembling is a functional disease caused by an impairment of the motive power.)[39] Avicenna draws a connection between *tremor* and *stupor*, the two terms being strictly related, almost synonymous. When it strikes, the *tremor* Avicenna describes affects locomotion and tactility, which is impaired if the *tremor* is light or completely crippled, enervated, if it is strong:

> Usus huius dictionis stupor in libris est diversus: plurimum enim ponitur dictio stuporis synonyma dictioni *alrhase*, idest tremoris. Nos vero & plurimi hominum utuntur ea secundum hunc modum, & quidem stupor est morbus officialis faciens evenire in sensu tactuali nocumentum scilicet aut destructionem aut diminutionem cum tremore, si est debilis, aut mollificationem, si est confirmatus, quoniam virtus sensibilis non prohibetur a penetratione, nisi etiam motiva virtus prohibeatur, sicut exposui multoties, quamvis in quibusdam horis inveniatur stupor, absque difficultate motus, propter diversitatem nervorum, motus & sensus.[40]
>
> (The use of the notion 'astonishment' is different according to the sources: the notion of astonishment is especially conveyed by the synonym *alrhase*, that is, trembling. For the most

---

[39] *Tremor. Tremor fit ex omnibus causis quibus virtutes animales contrahuntur*, APPENDIX.
[40] *Stupor. De stupore*, APPENDIX.

part, we employ this expression according to this meaning, and certainly astonishment is a subordinate disease that causes damage to the sense of touch, that is, it is either destroyed or diminished because of trembling if it is feeble, or softened if it is confirmed, since the sensorial power is not impeded unless the motive power is also impeded, as I explained many times, although in certain hours astonishment becomes manifest without an impairment in movement, due to the imbalance of nerves, movements, and senses.)

If not diagnosed and promptly treated, *tremor* can also portend death, especially if the trembling affects the heart, the *tremor cordis*. The semeiotics used in the *Canon* to describe this strong *tremor* closely resembles the pathological phenomena represented in the *Rime*, where they too foreshadow death:

> Ille cui tremor cordis assidue acciderit de se ipso sit sollicitus, ne subita intercipiatur morte. [...]. Et similiter cum perduraverit, ut sensus sint turbidi, & motionum adsit debilitas cum repletione. Cum membra omnia stupida fuerint multum, [...]. Cum facies vehementer rubuerit & oculus & lachrymae fluxerint & lumen effugerit [...]. Cumque multa absque causa fuerit tristitia, & timor, regendus erit adusti humoris evacuatione, ne ad melancholiam deveniat [...]⁴¹

> (He who is affected by trembling must be prompt in treating it, so as to avoid death. [...]. And likewise, when it keeps manifesting itself, to the point that the senses are blurred, when a sense of weakness accompanies the movements, when all the members lack sensitivity, when the face reddens all at once, the eyes become full of tears, and vision slips...and when much happens, provoking sadness and fear, one will have to regulate the expulsion of the humors, in order not to fall into melancholy. [...]. And most of all, when every single thing changes its habitual condition, that is, one's desire increases, or decreases, or changes its quality, in that case a disease must be diagnosed.)

A pervasive and identifying feature Guido Cavalcanti builds into his *Rime* is also 'sbigotimento' ('dismay'). In some variants and derivatives ('sbigottito', 'sbigotire', 'sbigottitamente'), this condition serves as the medium for a syntactic and semantic democratization at work in the text, crucial to the activities of the writing agent. 'Dismay' successively affects different subjects that are made equal by this very shifting of the qualifier.

'Sbigottimento' is depicted on the lover's face after one of the destructive love encounters—'Amor, c'ha le bellezze sue vedute,/mi sbigottisce sì, che sofferire/non può lo cor sentendola venire,' (IX, 33-35) (Love, who sees her beauties, confounds me so that my heart cannot bear up on hearing her

---

[41] *Cor. Cordis tremor facit ut homines sint de eo soliciti*, APPENDIX.

approach)⁴²—and becomes a presage of death, in Canzone IX (55-56): '«Questi [gli spiriti] sono in figura/d'un che si more sbigottitamente»' ("These [spirits] are as a figure of one who is dying in dismay"). It is acknowledged by the Foresette in Ballad XXX (13-20)—'Elle con gli occhi lor si volser tanto/che vider come 'l cor era ferito/e come un spiritel nato di pianto/era per mezzo de lo colpo uscito./Poi che mi vider così sbigottito,/disse l'una, che rise:/«Guarda come conquise/forza d'amor costui!»' (They turned with their eyes just enough to see how my heart was wounded and how a little spirit born of tears had come out through the wound. When they saw me so dismayed one of them laughed and said: "Look how the violence of Love has laid him down!") The external symptom mirrors an internal condition, regarding both the lover's soul—'L'anima mia vilment' è sbigotita' (my soul is abjectly appalled, VII, 1)—and the expressions of the soul beginning with the lover's voice, which in Ballad XXXV is irregular and broken by his weeping following the fight of the spirits: 'Tu, voce sbigottita e deboletta/ch'esci piangendo de lo cor dolente' (You, dismayed and frail voice, who come weeping from the grieving heart, 37-38). The words themselves are affected and likewise in dismay: 'parole adornate/di pianto, dolorose e sbigottite' (Words embellished with tears, sorrowful and dismayed, VI, 3-4). In the enclosed scenario constructed by Cavalcanti, the symptomatology of love affects the soul, voice and writing, as well as the writing tools themselves, which in Sonnet XVIII are acted upon by the lover's dismay: 'Noi siàn le triste penne isbigotite,/le cesoiuzze e 'l coltellin dolente,/ch'avemo scritte dolorosamente/quelle parole che vo' avete udite.' (We are the poor bewildered quills, the little scissors and the grieving penknife, who have sorrowfully written those words that you have heard.)

The pattern shown by the occurrences of 'sbigottimento' exemplifies a fundamental rule at work in Cavalcanti's minor rhymes: the narrator of the love experience is also its protagonist and is, therefore, located in the same space as where the love semeiotics are happening. The dichotomy between the narrator and reality is compressed into one single sphere; the physiological events that signal love are taking place on a 'stage' that can be observed only from within, only by those who belong in it.

This very erosion of the boundary between the writer and the world being depicted (which contributed to the crowning of Guido as modern poet *ante*

---

[42] See also: 'E' trasse poi de li occhi tuo' sospiri,/i qua' me saettò nel cor sì forte,/ch'i' mi partì' sbigotito fuggendo.' (He [Love] then drew from your eyes the sighs that he shot into my heart so hard that I left dismayed in flight.) XXI, 9-11.

litteram in the essay by Italo Calvino)⁴³ determines the coinciding of narrator and protagonist in the lover's body. The content of the minor rhymes is a bodily dramaturgy to which the reader's attention is constantly directed. In order to ensure that the body is the only focus and indicate that it also functions as the agent of communication, the narrating voice is minimized and finally merged into the body itself. Cavalcanti's rhetorical technique aims precisely at diverting the reader's focus away from that voice through recurrent apostrophes to the personifications (Love, the soul, the spirits) present on the stage as, for example, in Canzone IX, in which the dialogue is measured by the sequence of 'dice' and 'mi disse.' Lausberg defined this rhetorical strategy as *sermocinatio*: by using direct speech to communicate the words of others, the speaker draws the attention away from himself.⁴⁴

The focus becomes the display of the passions altering the body under the effects of love. Lacking the ability to perform intellectually, the lover depicted by Guido Cavalcanti is defined by his sensitive powers and incorporated into matter, where his sensitive soul functions. Figuratively beheaded, the lover is muted. Accordingly, the narration consists in the exposition of the phenomenology of love: a chain of repeatedly staged, but verbally silent, events.

Throughout the *Rime*'s pages the readers also become participants, drawn to the scene by repeated appeals (emphasis mine)—'chi *vedesse*' , '*Vedete* ch'i son un che vo piangendo' (whoever saw, You see that I am one who goes weeping, VII, 7; X, 1)—and evoked through their impressions about what they are witnessing: 'I' vo come colui ch'è fuor di vita,/*che pare,* a chi lo sguarda.../' (I go like one who is outside of life, such that, to the onlooker, he *seems,* VIII, 9-10), '«Quest' ha dolore,/e già, *secondo che ne par de fòre,*/dovrebbe dentro aver novi martiri»' (This man has sorrow and now *from what appears outwardly* he must inwardly have fresh torments, X, 10-12).

---

⁴³ See n. 47, chapter I.
⁴⁴ '*Sermocinatio* is the fabrication – serving to characterize natural (historical or invented) persons – of statements, conversations and soliloques or unexpressed mental reflections of the persons concerned.' Lausberg, *Handbook of Literary Rhetoric,* p. 366. Some of the effects created by Cavalcanti fall also in the category that Lausberg define apostrophe: '*Apostrophe,* [...] is "turning away" from the normal audience, and the addressing of another, second audience, surpisingly chosen by the speaker. This practice has an emotive effect on the normal audience, since it is an expression, on the part of the speaker, of a pathos which cannot be kept within the normal channels between speaker and audience; apostrophe is, so to speak, an emotional move of despair on the part of the speaker. Possible second audiences for apostrophe are: the opponent in court; absent persons, living or dead; things (fatherland, laws, wounds, etc.).' Ibid., p. 338.

The inclusion of the audience in the scene finally turns the scene into a self-sufficient one, blurring the distinction between audience and actors. The roles are interchangeable and performed in turn by the hypostases called into play by love—the heart 'cut into a cross,' the spirits solicited for a pitying look in Sonnet VI, the *simulacra* triggered by the sight of the lover and converging on the scene, as in Sonnet XII, where (lines 5-8) the advent of the woman is followed by the appearance of the personifications of fear and the soul: 'Ch'una paura di novi tormenti/m'aparve allor, sì crudel e aguta,/che l'anima chiamò: «Donna, or ci aiuta...»' (For a fear of fresh torments appeared to me then, so cruel and sharp that [my] soul called out: "Lady, help us now..."). In the magnifying description of the bodily phenomena, the lover's body is in the end dramatically turned inside out: its interiority is sucked to the outside and the cavity holding the heart is laid bare in order to make the internal processes visible. The 'inside' is exposed as in a transparent case, through which on the internal organs, especially the heart, can be seen the sign of a cross which signifies the love encounter; the main witness is now the body itself, opened up and objectified as in the Ballad XIX (lines 4-7): 'Davante agli occhi miei vegg' io lo core/e l'anima dolente che s'ancide,/che mor d'un colpo che li diede Amore/ed in quel punto che madonna vide.'[45] (Before my eyes I see the heart and the grieving soul that are slain, that die from a blow that Love gave them, and at that point when they saw my lady.) The body is alone and separate from the observers in XV—'i miei sospiri,/.../e vanno sol ragionando dolore/e non trovan persona che li miri' (my sighs [...] go about expressing only sorrow and find no one to look on them, 5-8); and it even functions as a spectator of itself in Sonnet XVI: 'A me stesso di me pietate vène/per la dolente angoscia ch'i' mi veggio:/di molta debolezza quand' io seggio,/l'anima sento ricoprir di pene.' (Compassion comes from me to myself for the grievous anguish that I see in me: when out of great weakness I sit down, I feel my soul overcast with woes, 1-4.)

The inside of the lover's body is exposed because his empty eye sockets have been left unguarded by the spirits of the eyes, which have migrated towards the pained heart in Ballad X (lines 13-17): 'Questa pesanza ch'è nel cor discesa/ha certi spirite' già consumati,/i quali eran venuti per difesa/del cor dolente che gli avea chiamati./Questi lasciaro gli occhi abbandonati...'[46]

---

[45] Lines closely recalled in Dante's sonnet *A ciascun alma presa e gentil core*: 'Ostentazione di gusto cavalcantiano,' glosses Guglielmo Gorni in his commentary to the *Vita Nova*, p. 25.
[46] See also XII, 8-10.

(This affliction that has descended on the heart has already laid waste some little spirits that had come in defense of the grieving heart that had called them. They left the eyes deserted). In the same Ballad X, the eyes become the doors through which the inner death of the lover becomes visible to Beauty. This is the completion of the destructive sequence that, Cavalcanti cautions, must be observed without pity or compassion: '«Dentro, Biltà, ch'e' more;/ma guarda che Pietà non vi si miri!»' ("It is inwardly, Beauty, that he is dying; only take care that Compassion be not seen there!", 19-20.) In sharp contrast with the notion of companionship on which the Stilnovo grounds itself, Guido Cavalcanti makes an appeal for an indifferent observation of the lover's death. The 'chorus' of friends which played such an essential role in the foundation of the Tuscan poetic school is here reduced to a group of bystanders and fellow sufferers described in Sonnet V: 'gente/che ciascun si doleva d'Amor forte' (people each of whom was deeply sorrowing because of Love, 10-11), whose painful experiences do not lead to the creation of any ties between them. Cavalcanti's poetic achievement is a bodily venture and a displacing and isolating experience, an antisocial activity. Counter to the lover represented in the *Divine Comedy*, who is the subject of Christian meditation and a vector pointing at God, the *Rime*'s lover is entangled in matter and collapses into a condition of folly and blindness (since, as we shall see, his weeping is intended in its literal, mechanical sense). With his minor rhymes, the iconoclast Guido Cavalcanti strongly undermines the Dantesque theory that love is the unleashing of the highest imaginative capacity bestowed to humans, that of imagining God.

The stage on which the minor rhymes take place consists of the lover's inward space opened up, and visited by personifications that embody elements from nature and physiology. It is within this space that Avicenna's *auctoritas* finds room, mapping the sensible phenomena that agitate the lover's senses and, further, acting as a rhetorical tool, as with the sighs and weeping. The latter is the subject of the last chapter. In the following pages, I deal with the spirit, which, I claim, is connected in Cavalcanti's poetry to its biological, medical tradition and therefore treated in physical terms as puffs of air, connected with breathing. Together with sighs, breaths are included among Cavalcanti's voices of the body.

CHAPTER IV
Spirits in Storm

IV.1 The Debate about the Theory

The spirit is a tenet whose interpretation and gradual transformation brought about a cultural revolution.

The origin of this complex notion is located in ancient pneumatology and its development had wide influence in multiple spheres. The spirit runs inside the human body and outside of it (when the spirit is engaged in a cognitive act, it exits the body and models itself on the object of the perception), as well as inside the earth and the celestial bodies. As the thread connecting all the elements of the cosmos, the spirit is linked to a full spectrum of subjects. According to the reconstruction by Verbeke in his pivotal study, the spirit, or 'pneuma,' has influenced the study of theodicy, psychology, epistemology, doctrines of inspiration, medicine, magic and mysticism since the onset of its tradition.[1] The evolution of the meaning of spirit is therefore stratified, and its reconstruction casts a light on the history of ideas. The modification of this concept could in fact be accurately described as a revolution if observed in terms of the fundamental shift it underwent in the span of seven centuries, during which the penuma's *subtilitas*, bound to matter, disappeared into the incorporeality denoted by the term *spiritus*. Verbeke illustrates this process—whose beginning, in his view, coincides with an already 'double' pneumatology[2]—and indicates it as

---

[1] 'Quand donc nous parlons de la pneumatologie ancienne, cette expression ne désigne pas une doctrine nettement définie, mais elle recouvre une multiplicité de conceptions relevant de nombreux systèmes de pensée et ressortissant aux différent domaines de la recherche humaine: le pneuma nous a introduits au cœur même de la théodicée, de la psychologie, de l'épistémologie, de la doctrine de l'inspiration, de la médecine, de la magie et de la mystique.' Verbeke, *L'evolution de la doctrine du pneuma du stoicisme à S. Augustine*, p. 511.

[2] 'En somme, ce tableau synthétique montre qu'il existe dans la pensée ancienne deux pneumatologies nettement parallèles, mais dont les caractères s'opposent en un point important. Il y a, d'une part, une pneumatologie matérialiste: les significations essentielles du terme pneuma s'y ramènent à quatre: suivant qu'il désigne Dieu, l'âme, le principe de l'inspiration ou de la divination, ou enfin un don divin accordé à certains hommes. Il y a, d'autre part, une pneumatologie spiritualiste, dont les doctrines fondamentales peuvent se résumer également en ces quatre points. Un parallélisme fondamental apparaît donc entre ces deux pneumatologies. Ce qui les distingue avant tout, c'est que, d'une part, le pneuma est conçu comme un souffle *matériel*, tandis que, d'autre part, il est décrit comme une réalité *spirituelle*.' Ibid., p. 534.

originating with Zenon's pagan Stoicism, which conveyed a material conception of 'pneuma' but which also held the first hints of the forthcoming transformation of this element into spiritual terms, and culminating in Augustinian philosophy, which completed and fully expressed this process. Verbeke concludes that Biblical doctrine mainly determined the semantic remake of the spirit, followed in order of importance by the Platonic tradition.[3] It was an established method for Biblical doctrine to incorporate existing vocables by attaching new meanings to them, validated on the grounds of the sacred text's revealed truth. When finally the spirit was embraced by Judaic-Christian culture and applied to the sphere of transcendence, it became altogether incompatible with the sphere of materiality.[4]

The studies that attempt to map out this concept's gradual spiritualization comment on the difficulties encountered in this endeavor since all these influences made the process, and its description, erratic. For a long time, 'spirit' was a term that was not reducible to definite meanings. As has been suggested, it was the term's very instability and consequent 'glissement sémantique' it allowed that turned the spirit into a particularly attractive ground for thinkers, such as the twelfth- and thirteenth-century intellectuals, who placed symbolic and analogic connections at the core of their reasoning.[5] In Mediaeval Latin, the wide semantic oscillation of the

---

[3] Ibid., pp. 539-540.
[4] 'La religion judéo-chrétienne ne se présente pas comme un système philosophique qui s'appuie sur des évidences rationnelles et irrécusables; elle apparaît plutôt comme un système cohérent de vérités révélées qui toutes se rapportent à la destinée humaine et à la conduite de la vie. C'est ainsi qu'on trouve dans la Bible une certaine conception de Dieu et de l'âme humaine, conception qui n'est pas établie au moyen d'arguments rationnels, mais qui s'appuie uniquement sur la révélation divine. [...]. Nous croyons donc que la religion judéo-chrétienne doit être considérée comme le facteur déterminant de l'évolution du pneuma dans le sens du spiritualisme, parce qu'elle s'est servie de ce terme pour désigner la divinité *transcendante* et l'âme *immortelle*, ce qui devait conduire logiquement à la spiritualisation de la pneumatologie ancienne. En d'autres termes, la religion judéo-chrétienne a donné au pneuma un contenu qui le rendait incompatible avec la signification matérialiste que ce terme avait acquise dans la philosophie courante et dans les écoles médicales.' Ibid., pp. 541-542. Chenu reaches similar conclusions: 'Le vocabulaire biblique, nous l'avons vu, est la matière privilégiée de nos médiévaux; d'où ce premier nœud: les termes religieux rencontrent la langue profane, dans un concordisme candide et continu.' Chenu, *'Spiritus'*, p. 214.
[5] 'Il nous est possible maintenant de présenter avec une intelligence qui dépassera le classement matériel d'un catalogue, les divers sens de *spiritus* dans la langue latine médiévale. En signe de quoi, l'insistance sur le diversités de signification laissera intacte et légitime cette unité sémantique radicale des mots, qui si souvent déconcerte les traducteurs et les philosophes trop systématiques. Les médiévaux jouaient, eux, sans scrupule, de ce glissement sémantique, que

term *spiritus* included a range of different and interacting meanings that described the spirit as an astral substance connected to magic in religious and philosophical doctrines, as well as a result of the 'combustion' of food in medical theories.[6] Since the beginning of the thirteenth century, the physiological conclusions drawn by Galen that had given the 'pneuma' a material quality were combined with other learnings: new questions arose from complex cosmogonical issues,[7] as well as from the theological program animating thirteenth-century culture.[8]

---

renforçait en outre leur goût pour les liaisons analogico-symbolique irréductibles à la logique linéaire des mots et des concepts.' Ibid., p. 223.

[6] '*Spiritus* a d'abord un sens physique. C'est le souffle, le souffle de l'air, du vent, de la respiration. En langue vulgaire, en langue biblique, en langue scientifique. Les théologiens ne se feront pas faute de se servir, et de multiples manières, jusqu'à l'allégorie, de l'analogie si suggestive du souffle vital pour décrire le plus hautes inspirations (*spiritus*) de l'âme. Puis vient le sens biologique. Là la théorie scientifique donne bientôt au mot une consistance technique. Le *spiritus* est, pour le physiologue, le principe même de la vie: *spiritus vitae*, appelé aussi *spiritus animalis*, *spiritus physicus*. Élément corporel, mais dégagé de la pesanteur et de l'immobilité de la matière, de nature subtile par conséquent, apparenté au feu, il est l'instrument des énergies de l'âme végétative, et dessert les force motrices et appréhensives de l'âme.' Ibid., pp. 223-224.

[7] Despite the fact that the spirit went through an undeniable dissolution of its material components, Chenu insists on the material quality retained by the spirit, traditionally bound to perceptions and imagination, and distinct from the *nous-mens* that, instead, are employed as an organ of mystical intuition: '*Nous-mens* est un terme typique de la philosophie hellénique, au point où se rejoignent, dans son développement historique, son intellectualisme et son aspiration mystique. Or c'est précisément à ce point de jonction, dans les œuvres néoplatoniciennes, directement ou indirectement connues, que les Latins du moyen âge reçoivent avec empressement, le mot *mens*. Ce *nous* grec est un organe d'intuition mystique; et il le faut traduire non par *spiritus*, qui relève d'une tradition différente, «pneumatique», mais par *intellectus*, ou par *mens*. [...]. La concurrence *mens-spiritus* se poursuivit parfois cependant, du fait que *spiritus* conserve sa référence au souffle vital, donc à un psychisme inférieur par rapport au *mens*, tout «spirituel». De là une classification courante, dans la seconde moitié du xiie siècle et au delà: *anima*, *spiritus*, *mens*, où *spiritus* couvre les activités psychologiques liées aux perceptions sensibles et imaginatives.' Ibid., pp. 217-218.

[8] James J. Bono describes the 'theological program' of the thirteenth-century Christian thinkers in terms of the assembling of a language in which existing vocables are given wider meaning, including the spheres of theology and natural philosophy: 'Speaking in a current fashionable idiom we might say that behind the "text" of Galenic theoretical medicine stood the more privileged 'text' of biblical exegesis and theological commentaries.' The semantic complexity of the spirit made the process possible: 'My argument thus far has been that the problem of the precise relationship between the medical notion of *spiritus* and the philosophical notion of *anima* raised by such a text as Costa ben Luca's *De Differentia Animae et Spiritus* was met in the Christian West with an attempt to construct a language joining pneumatology with a psychology rooted in a universal theological language. As far as the specific notion of *spiritus* is concerned, twelfth-century tracts like that of Hugh of Saint Victor provided the exegetical basis for such a language. By transforming various Biblical images into metaphors capable of

This study shall not presume to take a definitive stand regarding a notion whose definition has been produced by interference from such disparate fields. It mainly observes this composite landscape from the point of view of its object, that is, the notions of natural philosophy incorporated in Guido Cavalcanti's *Rime*. In this field of natural philosophy the spirit is defined as a subtle and barely corporeal substance consisting of the vapor produced by the evaporation of hot bodily fluids; it circulates throughout the human body and performs the duties of maintaining and transmitting life. The spirit transmits the powers of the soul: through the spirit, the soul performs its physiological and psychological activities. This close connection triggered an active debate in the borderland between physiology and psychology, aimed at formulating a definition of the relation between *spiritus* and *anima*. A decisive contribution to the generative power contained in the spirit is provided by the *De generatione animalium*, in which Aristotle illustrates the distinction of the vegetative, sensitive and intellective souls starting from semen, which presides over the generation process.

Aristotle describes semen as the residual of a final digestion of the blood. Once it has concluded its nutritive functions and reaches the *membra radicalia* (heart and brain), the blood leaves behind a surplus that is digested in the seminal vessels and transformed into semen. This corporeal semen contains *in nuce* the powers of the soul that express themselves through bodily organs, which are the powers pertaining to the vegetative and sensitive souls. The powers pertaining to the intellective soul, which are not locatable in any body part, come from the outside.[9] In Aristotle's words, the semen carries the vegetative and sensitive powers precisely because it is

---

informing a philosophical language of theology, *spiritus* could be conceived as a *medium* between soul and body. In turn, this formulation focused the more generalized problem of the relationship between *spiritus* and soul upon the specific problem of interpreting how *spiritus* is a medium.' Bono, p. 118. With regards to the traces of a lively debate concerning the pair *spiritus/anima* in the School of Salerno, see: Ch. Burnett. *The chapter on the spirits in the Pantegni of Constantine the African*. In: *Constantine the African and Ali Ibn Al-Abbas Al-Magusi*. E. Brill. New York, 1994, pp. 99-120.

[9] 'Quod quidem igitur non possibile est omnes preexistere, manifestum est ex talibus. Quorumcumque enim principiorum est operatio corporalis, palam quia haec sine corpore impossibile existere, ut ambulare sine pedibus; quare et deforis ingredi impossibile: neque enim ipsas secundum ipsas ingredi possibile inseparabiles existentes, neque in corpore ingredi: sperma enim superfluum permutati alimenti est. Relinquitur autem intellectum solum deforis advenire et divinum esse solum: nichil enim ipsius operationi communicat corporalis operatio.' Aristoteles latinus, *De generatione animalium*, II, 736b 22-29.

enriched with the spirit, an element that resembles what the celestial bodies are made of and bears the *virtus informativa*.[10]

The spirit, as explained by Aristotle, does not perform an intermediary role between the incorporeal quality of the soul and the material substance of the body: the hylomorphism at the basis of the Stagirite's thought did not give rise to the necessity for a connecting element between the two. A section of the medical learning, such as Alfred of Sareshel's *De motu cordis*, did establish a current grounded on the opposite conclusion,[11] but Aristotelian thought, especially the *De anima* with the commentaries that made it an active force in twelfth- and thirteenth-century culture, provided most of the material for the theory of the spirits elaborated by the thinkers of these decades. Among them was Albert the Great. Rooting his theories in the Aristotelian source, he defines the spirit as the instrument permitting the soul to operate throughout the body.[12] It performs tasks indicated by distinct designation that, however, do not cause the spirit to multiply into many spirits. According to Albert the Great the spirit is undoubtedly one, like the one blacksmith with his one hammer creating many works:

---

[10] 'Omnis quidem igitur anime virtus altero corpore visa est participare, et diviniore vocatis elementis: ut autem differunt honorabilitate anime et vilitate invicem, sic et talis differt natura; omnium quidem enim in spermate inexistit quod facit gonima esse spermata, vocatum calidum. Hoc autem non ignis neque talis virtus est, sed interceptus in spermate et in spumoso spiritus aliquis et in spiritu natura, proportionalis existens astrorum ordinationi.' Aristoteles latinus, *De generatione animalium*, II, 736b 30-737a2.

[11] 'His abitis, intuendum diligentius quod corpus, cuius hebes et solida naturaliter essentia est, et anima, quae quidem ob subtilissimam incorporeae essentiae naturam vix cuiusquam providetur ingenio, medium aliquid vincire oportuit, quod in neutrius componentium termino, utriusque tamen naturae participatione aliqua, tam absonae dissidentia in unius eiusdemque essentiae foedus uniret.' Bauemker, X, 1. Some scholars concluded that in the course of the thirteenth century the theory of the spirit's mediating role was generally agreed on: 'Principe de la vie animale, le *spiritus* est donc l'intermédiaire entre le corps et l'âme; il fait le lien et l'unité du composé humain. Il se dissout ainsi à la dissolution du corps. Telle est la doctrine philosophico-scientifique communément enseignée. Le *De motu cordis* d'Alfred de Sareshel en fournit, au début du xiiie siècle, une expression autorisée et généralement acceptée.' Chenu, '*Spiritus*', p. 225.

[12] 'Aliqui enim fuerunt, qui dixerunt omnino incorporeum et omnino grossum corporeum coniungi non posse sine medio quod conveniat cum utroque: et hoc dicunt spiritum esse, qui subtilitate sua convenit cum anima, et corporeis dimensionibus convenit cum corpore. Haec autem sententia nulla prorsus habet veritatem, et est contra omnia dicta Peripateticorum: quoniam spiritus non est medium quo anima coniungatur corpori: eo quod sine medio unita est ei sicut omnis perfectio suo perfectibili sine omni unitur medio, sed potius spiritus est, per quem anima operatur in corpore opera vitae.' Albertus Magnus, *De spiritu et respiratione*, I, i, p. 225. For a synthesis of Alberto Magno's conclusions about *spiritus*, see Bertola.

> [...] sicut enim unum instrumentum quod est malleus, habet faber ferrarius, per quod omnes inducat in ferrum formas artis suae: ita hoc unum instrumentum iunctum est animae, per quod in toto corpore inducit omnes universaliter formas et operationes vitae: et sicut in arte fabrili est unus artifex et una ars et unum instrumentum, sed multae formae artis et multi motus instrumenti, et per consequens multa artificiata:[...].[13]
>
> ([...] like the blacksmith has one instrument, which is the hammer, through which he creates in the iron all the forms of his art, in the same way just one instrument is linked to the soul, through which [the soul] produces in general in the whole body all the life's forms and operations: and, as in the craft of blacksmith, there is one artisan, one art, and one tool, but many forms of art and many movements of the tool, and, consequently, many artifacts.)

The radical spirit is a vapor produced in the semen by virtue of the semen's heat; it penetrates the viscous skin of the seed and through its pulsing activates the *virtus formativa* presiding over the formation of the body.[14] Once the organism is shaped, the Galenic tradition describes a threefold division of the spirit, determined by the specific organ where the spirit is lodged and by the distinct operation it carries out. The vital spirit is generated in the left ventricule of the heart by the exhalation of the blood's vapor; it is multiplied and expelled through the heartbeat, and circulates in the arteries in order to activate the senses and transmit movement. The natural spirit is formed in the liver and, as the instrument of the nutritive soul, nourishes the body. Lastly, the animal spirit resides in the brain, where it rises 'digested' from the heart, and presides over the elaboration of the sensorial data. By means of multiple purifications that make it progressively more pure and subtle, the animal spirit runs through the brain's three chambers, in which it presides over the post-sensationary faculties: the internal senses, whose treatment was greatly influenced by the Arabic philosophical tradition, as I mentioned in chapter II.[15]

Aristotle's theory of the spirit is taken up again by Avicenna, who, by rethinking visual perception and internal senses, made Aristotle's conclusions more 'spiritual' and his commentary especially compatible with

---

[13] Ibid., p. 220. Translation is mine.

[14] 'Et hic spiritus est, qui primo per virtutem formativa quae in semine est, calido seminali excitatus et loci spirat in semine, et post ante hoc in viscositate ipsius seminis continetur retentus. Cum autem humidum seminis formari a virtute formativa incipit exterius, id quod formatur, pelle circumducitur viscosa, intra quam spirans spiritus ille primo pulsare incipit, vehens artificem formantem, qui est virtus formativa, et virtus eius in omnium membrorum formationem.' Ibid., p. 221.

[15] See II.4.

the Western world.[16] From the psychological perspective of the *De anima*, Avicenna describes the spirit as the *vehiculum* of the powers—the spirit's different *complexiones* correspond to different powers.[17] The 'spiritualization' carried out by Avicenna consisted in attributing to the spirit the function of being the site of perceptions, rather than simply their instrument, as becomes clear in the sections discussing sight.[18] From the physiological perspective of the *Canon*, the spirit is a translucent and subtle substance similar to that composing the celestial bodies and generated in the left ventricle of the heart; its stream is induced by the movements of dilatation and compression of the arteries:

> Et ista quidem dispositio in humano spiritu reperitur. Et spiritus quidem in summa est res nata ex comistione elementorum vergens in similitudinem celestium corporum. Et propterea indicatur de spiritu quod fit substantia luminosa seu lucida.

> (This disposition is found in the human spirit. And, in one word, the spirit is a substance generated from the mixture of elements coming together, like the celestial bodies. Therefore, we know about the spirit that it is a substance luminous or lucid.)

> Creavit deus ex concavitatibus cordis sinistram ut esset armarium spiritus et minera generationis illius.

> (God created the left hollow of the heart so that it could be the case of the spirit and the mine of its generation.)

> Et post ligamenta sunt arteriae quae sunt corpora, quae a corde nascuntur, concava in longitudinem extensa, nervosa, & in sui substantia ligamentalia habentia motiones, dilatando se & constringendo, quae ex quietibus discernuntur: quae quidem ad hoc fuerunt creatae,

---

[16] 'Le résultat global est évidemment un «Aristote nouveau», une psychologie repensée, enrichie et restructurée; cet enrichissement se remarque surtout dans l'étude consacrée aux sens internes et à la perception visuelle. L'image de l'homme telle qu'elle ressort du traité d'Avicenne est indéniablement plus spiritualiste que celle du Stagirite; s'est pourquoi elle sera accueillie avec sympathie, dès le treizième siècle, par l'Occident chrétien.' Verbeke, *Introduction sur la doctrine psychologique d'Avicenne*, p. 1.

[17] 'Primo igitur dicemus quod virtutum animalium corporalium vehiculum est corpus subtile, spirituale, diffusum in concavitatibus, quod est spiritus. Si enim virtutes animae pendentes ex corpore diffunderentur non evectae corpore, oppilatio viarum non prohiberet diffundi virtutes motivas et sentientes et etiam imaginabiles: sed prohibet manifeste secundum eum qui cognovit experimenta physica. [...]. Habet autem complexionem propriam, quae mutatur etiam prout necesse est in ea esse diversitatem propter quam fit vehens virtutes diversas: complexio enim qua concupiscitur non est apta ut per eam sentiatur, nec complexio quae est apta visibili spiritui est apta spiritui moventi; [...]' Avicenna latinus, *Liber de Anima seu Sextus de Naturalibus*, V, viii R 263 49-63.

[18] Verbeke, *Introduction sur la doctrine psychologique d'Avicenne*, pp. 86-90.

> ut cor eventetur, & fumosus vapor ab eo expellatur & spiritus membris corporis distribuatur.[19]

(And after the ligaments are the arteries, bodies originating in the heart, concave, long, strong, whose ligamental nature produces movement of dilatation and contraction, which are visible in the inactive bodies: they [the arteries] were created in order to come out of the heart, so that the smoky vapor could be carried away from it, and the spirit could be distributed to the members of the body.)

A fluent and uninterrupted circulation of the spirit is a necessary preliminary for good health and full effectiveness of the body; an interruption of the spirital circulation can provoke paralysis:

> Causa vero retentionis est oppilatio, aut separatio pororum & transitum perducentium ad membra cum sectione. Oppilatio autem aut est secundum semitam contrictionis pororum aut secundum semitam prohibitionis ex humore oppilante: aut secundum semitam rei aggregantis ambas res, & est apostema, quare causa mollificationis & paralysis faciens abscissionem spiritus a membris est contrictio pororum.[20]

(The cause of the retention [of the spirit] is congestion, or the separation of the channels reaching the members with a cut. A congestion arises either following the compression of the channels, or following their impenetrability due to an obstructing humor: or following what combines the two, that is, a lump; since this produces a detachment of the spirit from the members due to the softening and paralysis, a compression of the channels results.)

The vital spirit presides over all the *virtutes*, the soul's powers, and stands as a sign of life of a body organ even when these powers have disappeared; the task of the vital spirit is to activate the *operationes virtutum*, the performances of the organs, by interacting with the individual *complexio*, the balance among the four primary qualities—wet, dry, hot, cold:

> Virtutes enim animales in spiritu quidem & in membris non proveniunt, nisi postquam haec vitalis provenit virtus. Ideoque licet virtutes animales alicuius membri destruantur. Vivum tamen membrum adhuc existit, nisi haec virtus in eo fuerit destructa. [...] Restat ergo ut sit praeparans alia res, quae propriam sequantur complexionem, quae vocatur virtus vitalis. Et ipsa quidem est prima virtus, quae in spiritu provenit, cum spiritus ex subtilitate humorum procedit. Deinde spiritus secundum philosophum Aristotelem per eam recipit principium primum & animam primam, ex qua aliae profluunt virtutes. [...] Cum ergo pars spiritus in ventriculum pervenerit, cerebri complexionem recipiet & erit conveniens ut ex eo

---

[19] *Spiritus. Spiritus diffinitio; Spiritus armarium est sinistra concavitas cordis; Spiritus distribuitur per arterias membris corporis*, APPENDIX.
[20] *Spiritus. Spiritus spiritus retentio fit ex oppilatione*, APPENDIX.

proveniant virtutum operationes, quae in eo primo repertae sunt, & similiter in hepate & similiter in testiculis.[21]

(The animal powers are not found in spirit and members before the vital power intervenes. Therefore, it might happen that the animal powers of a member are destroyed. However, a member stays alive, unless the vital power in it is destroyed. [...] What is left, is [a power], called the vital power, that predisposes other things, which follow their complexion. This is certainly the first power that comes into the spirit, when the spirit comes out of the subtlety of the humors. Then, according to the philosopher Aristotle, the spirit via the vital power receives the first vital principle, from which all the other powers derive. Then, when a part of the spirit arrives in the hollow [of the brain] it receives the brain's complexion and, consequently, the powers' operations originate in it, and the same happens in the liver, and in the testicles.)

Natural, vital, and animal spirits are also differentiated according to their qualities: the natural spirit, residing in the liver, is thicker and hot, almost ebullient as it has a nourishing function; the vital spirits are cooler and drier, and they bring coolness to the heart; the animal spirits are the subtlest (because sublimed), brightest (because susceptive to the forms produced by the senses), and coolest (because heat would confuse the animal operations while their coolness helps them retain the forms).[22]

This bodily vapor, running inside the human body and activating the soul's power, became a literary topic widely popular among thirteenth- and fourteenth-century poets pondering the effects of love and the knowledge stemming from it. At the beginning of the *Vita Nova*, Dante depicts an animated dialogue among the author's vital, animal, and natural spirits,

---

[21] *Spiritus. Spiritus generatur ex humorum subtilitate secundum aliquam complexionem*, APPENDIX.

[22] 'Spiritus enim naturalis turbidus est et grossus et calidus quasi calore bulliente: [...]. Hi autem qui dicuntur vitae spiritus, oportet esse temperatiores et frigidiores et magis tenues et sicciores, et quasi semper expulsos, ita quod idem numero non retrahitur, sed alius similis sibi, et sunt magis albi spiritus isti, habentes tamen modicum tenuissimi sanguinis admixtum: sunt tamen temperatiores et frigidiores propter hoc quod refrigerium quoddam cordi dederunt. Tenues autem et subtiles sunt, ut undique cum vita quam advehunt, possint penetrare: sicciores autem sunt, ut sint velocioris motus: [...]. Animales autem subtilissimi, clarissimi, et frigidiores omnibus sunt, et multiplices magis aliis, et diversi inter se huiusmodi qui vocantur spiritus animales. Subtilissimi autem sunt, ideo quia ad altiorem locum sunt sublimati. Clarissimi autem sunt, ut susceptibiliores sint formarum et intentionum quae recipiuntur sensus ex quibus perficiuntur operationes animales: et ut non commisceant rationes et formas, ablata est ab eis caliditas: quia si essent calidi, resolverent substantiam cerebri et permiscerent formas, et operationes confunderent animales. Sunt autem adhuc etiam alia de causa frigidi, ut scilicet in se habeant aliquod retentivum formarum apprehensionis, quas in se vehunt: multiplices deserviunt virtutibus animalibus, de quibus in libro de *Anima* satis dictum est.' Albertus Magnus, *De spiritu et respiratione*, I, ii, p. 239.

stirred at the sight of Beatrice.[23] An established interpretation indicates Albert the Great as the source of this scene, specifically his *De spiritu et respiratione* and *De somno et vigilia*. The scholarship suggesting him as Dante's source for this specific passage emphasized the fact that the poet imported this topic from the scientific text into his own virtually without rhetorical elaboration. The personification of the spirits had in fact already been the work of natural philosophers, who described this vapor running through the bodily vessels as having an independent and animated life.[24] While those who supported this conclusion suggested the strictly physiological nature of the spirits circulating in thirteenth-century Italian lyrics, others professed that the spirit is also active in the Stilnovo in its divinatory functions: the idea of the *spiritus peregrinus* leaving the body addressed not only the question of the soul's life outside of the body but, also, that of human imaginative powers. One specific wing of the 'spiritual' tradition, in fact, interpreted the 'luminous pneuma,' the radical spirit produced by the semen and presiding over the body's development, as the means for the human soul's supernatural contacts. Based on his reading of the *Vita Nova* Sonnet, *Oltre la spera*, Robert Klein demonstrates how the Stilnovo successfully merged the different traditions regarding the spirit on original, syncretic grounds.[25]

---

[23] 'In quel puncto dico veracemente che lo spirito della vita, lo quale dimora nella secretissima camera del cuore, cominciò a tremare sì fortemente, che apparia nelli menomi polsi orribilmente; e tremando disse queste parole: "Ecce Deus fortior me, qui veniens dominabitur michi!". In quel puncto lo spirito animale, lo quale dimora nell'alta camera nella quale tutti li spiriti sensitivi portano le loro perceptioni, si cominciò a maravigliare molto, e parlando spetialmente alli spiriti del viso, disse queste parole: "Apparuit iam beatitudo vestra!". In quel puncto lo spirito naturale, lo quale dimora in quella parte ove si ministra lo nutrimento nostro, cominciò a piangere, e piangendo disse queste parole: "Heu, miser, quia frequenter impeditus ero deinceps!" ' *Vita Nova* 1. 5-7. As is well known, Dante again addresses the issue of the spirit, in relation to the more general question of the origin of the individual soul, in *Purgatorio* XXV. In this canto, Dante presents a real lesson in embryology through the words of Statius, establishing that, of the three spiritual powers of the soul, vegetative, sensitive and rational, the last is infused into the human brain by divine intervention. With this 'spirito novo, di virtù repleto' (line 72), Dante takes a stand against radical Aristotelianism, declaring that the possible intellect adds the universal forms to the individual soul, thereby connecting, within the individual soul, the rational soul to the sensitive and vegetative ones. A detailed exposition of Dante's positions on this issue is in Nardi, *Origine dell'anima umana secondo Dante*. In: *Studi di filosofia medievale*, pp. 1-68.

[24] 'Non si è badato che lo spirito non aveva bisogno d'essere personificato dai poeti per aver moto e vita. I naturalisti, ad un voce, lo additavano palpitante di vitalità.' Vitale, p. 172.

[25] 'In fact, the scientific or philosophical theory of the spirits was never monopolized by naturalists to the extent of obliterating its original link with the themes of purification and ecstasy—hence the possibility of reintroducing all these aspects, including "Platonism", into the

IV.2 Spirits Leaving the Body, Sighs, and the Poet's Craft

Against the background of the stratification affecting the meaning of the word spirit in thirteenth-century culture, Guido Cavalcanti made his ideological stand and turned this notion into the trademark of his poetry. The condensed manifesto of the spiritual quality of the *Rime* is Sonnet XXVIII, which records the obsessive recurrence of this term in each line. In the following pages I will present a close reading of this sonnet. Counter to a prevailing definition that has labeled the sonnet a 'self parody,'[26] I claim that the repetition of the term 'spirito' produced throughout the fourteen lines does not undermine the import of the mot but, conversely, emphasizes its meaningfulness in connection with the scientific sources. Sonnet XXVIII heralds Cavalcanti's treatment of the spirit in a medical key; moreover, it stands as a model of the interference between grammar and physiology, the mark of Cavalcanti's language. In the minor rhymes, language and body are enclosed within the same physical boundaries. As a result, language is affected by features that apply to bodies and to their elements. The feature shaping the language I investigate here is the main quality of the spirit, namely, this fluid's subtle materiality.

Subtlety links Cavalcanti's *Rime* to the coeval debate about vernacular poetry. *Subtilitas*, the specific property that Cavalcanti, via medical literature,

---

repertory of "naturalistic metaphor". The *spirito* of the poets was, much oftener than that of the physicians, *peregrino*—chased away by Love, sent as a messenger to the Lady, attracted or fascinated by her. [...]. The sonnet 'Oltre la spera' from the *Vita Nuova* is in that respect the sum of all these elements: we find in it medical mechanistic theories (*spirito=sospiro*), a rational or allegorical explanation (*spirito=pensiero*) and 'shamanic ecstasy' (the ascent to heaven of the wandering spirit, whose vision will be explained, as the reader is invited to conjecture, in the *Divina Commedia*).' Klein, p. 82.

[26] This is the definition proposed by Gianfranco Contini in his introduction to this sonnet: 'Il Sonetto può considerarsi, e per l'iterazione del vocabolo, e per il diminuitivo (il quale cade in posizioni viscerali, a chiusura di quartina, 4, 7-8, e della prima terzina, 12, cfr. in chiusa XXXIII 14, altrimenti X 4 e XXX 15) un'elegante autoparodia della nozione di *spirito*. Il vocabolo è preso sia nell'accezione tecnica di ipostasi di pensiero o di immagine, sia in quella di sinonimo di *anima* (5, cfr. XXV 14-5).' Contini, *Poeti del Duecento*, t. II, p. 530. Robert Klein reaches similar conclusions, downsizing the scientific substratum of the Stilnovo's theories about love to a façade: 'In Dante's times, it would have been almost impossible to think of love with any degree of psychological precision without referring to models furnished by magic. It is not coincidental that the migratory *spiritus* was chosen, in the playful form of the *spiritelli*, as a poetic fiction, proper for rendering the effects of love in the terms of a pseudomedical scientific façade; behind it we can see the outline of a psychology of ecstasy and fascination, and the entire range from sorcery to poetic grace, which we cover by the word "charm".' Klein, pp. 69-70.

attributes to the spirit and to his language, was in fact also a literary feature discussed by thirteenth-century Italian poets who identified with 'sottiglianza,' the feature of a new poetic practice. The development, fraught with consequences, was imparted by the poets who initiated the inclusion of philosophical material in their verses. Poetic subtlety[27] was especially one of the charges leveled at Guinizzelli's groundbreaking canzone, *Al cor gentil rempaira sempre amore*, whose philosophical basis was at once decried as exceeding the traditional purpose and balance of a poetic composition. A direct accuser of the canzone was Bonagiunta Orbicciani who through his Sonnet *Voi ch'avete mutata la maniera* condemned Guinizzelli and his text, lamenting its undecipherable meaning and derogatorily tagging it as too subtle, that is, imbued with academic learning.[28] In the well-known lines of *Purgatorio* XXIV Bonagiunta is ultimately the one who bestows a name on this literary revolution, which he addresses by acknowledging a methodological 'knot' that distances himself, and the other vernacular poets adhering to the old 'maniera,' from the 'stil novo' embodied by the pilgrim: 'O frate, issa vegg'io- diss'elli-il nodo/che il Notaro e Guittone e me ritenne/di qua dal dolce stil novo ch'i' odo.'[29]

The polemic raised by the originality of the new poetry had a wide resonance. It also expanded into rhetorical issues, as supported by a few documents directly concerning Cavalcanti's work. Among them, chapter 16 of the *Vita Nova*,[30] which focuses on the effect on language of the newly employed philosophical content. In this chapter, Dante makes a digression concerning the figures of speech. He begins by resuming the prosopopeia he employed in one of his sonnets, *Io mi senti' svegliar dentro allo core*, in which he made Love talk, as if it were *'sustantia corporale.'* Figures of speech that are not verisimilar such as this one are allowed, Dante claims, when the lines have a content that the author is able to explain; such is the case of the few

---

[27] Francesco Bruni traces the debate about the actual capacity of the vernacular to express intellectually sopisticated concepts. Bruni, *Semantica della sottigliezza*.
[28] 'Voi ch'avete mutata la maniera/de li piagenti ditti de l'amore/de la forma dell'esser là dov'era,/per avansare ogn'altro trovatore,/avete fatto como la lumera,/ch'a le scure partite dà sprendore,/ma non quine ove luce l'alta spera,/la quale avansa e passa di chiarore./Così passate voi di sottigliansa,/e non si può trovar chi ben ispogna,/cotant'è iscura vostra parlatura./Ed è tenuta grave 'nsomilliansa,/ancor che 'l senno vegna da Bologna,/traier canson per forsa di scritura.'
[29] ' "O brother, now I see" he said "the knot that kept the Notary, Guittone, and me short of the sweet new manner that I hear" ' *Purgatorio*, XXIV, 55-57.
[30] According to the division of Guglielmo Gorni's critical edition that I have used for all my references to Dante's *prosimetrum*. It corresponds to 24 of the previous division.

vernacular poets who are not 'grossi,' that is, those who can unveil the meaning hidden behind the 'colore rectorico' of their verses (these include Dante and his 'primo amico' Cavalcanti).[31] Dante states here that if the poetry's content is subtle, that is, grounded in philosophical sources, language likewise becomes subtle by extending its poetic license. The science interwoven in the verse implies a rhetorical disenthrallment.

The same topic of the linguistic repercussion of the content's scientific nature is tackled in the literary quarrel between Guido Cavalcanti and Guido Orlandi, the latter reproaching the former for his excessive 'sottiglianza' in the Sonnet *Per troppa sottiglianza il fil si rompe*. In parallel with the passage from the *Vita Nova*, in his text Orlandi exemplifies his conclusion by citing a line in which Cavalcanti describes Love as capable of weeping—'...se non fosse che 'l morir m'è gioco,/fare'ne di pietà pianger Amor' (And, if it were not that dying for me is joy, I would make Love, out of pity, weep over it, XI, 8)—an image that spoils the text because of its rhetorical straining. 'Amor sincero,' Orlandi makes clear in his sonnet, 'non piange né ride.' Forced to lower himself to the rough argumentation of his correspondent, in the Sonnet *Di vil matera mi conven parlare* Cavalcanti rebuts by contrasting the 'base matters' in Orlandi's text with the material of his own lines: the teachings of Love, which speaks 'sottile e piano,/di sua manera dire e di suo stato' to those empowered to understand it. By qualifying Love's mode of communication, a speaking mode, with the attribute 'sottile,' Cavalcanti says that Love speaks to the initiated, and that in its speaking, content shapes language. The poet's work is described as the transliteration of Love's exposition on philosophical matters into a language accordingly forged.

In the minor rhymes, this forging process by which the medical sources affect the poet's language is carried out through the notion of subtlety, which creates an active interface between body and language. In compliance with the medical literature, the feature of *subtilitas*, is explained in pneumatic terms as the subtle materiality of the spirits running through the body. The subtle materiality of the spirits touches upon the rhetorical sphere when Cavalcanti not only employs the lover's sighs as linguistic units but also, as

---

[31] 'Però che grande vergogna sarebbe a colui che rimasse cose sotto vesta di figura o di colore rettorico, e poscia, domandato, non sapesse denudare le sue parole da cotale vesta, in guisa che avessero verace intendimento. E questo mio primo amico e io ne sapemo bene di quelli che così rimano stoltamente.' (For, if any one should dress his poem in images and rhetorical coloring and then, being asked to strip his poem of such dress in order to reveal its true meaning, would not be able to do so-this would be a veritable cause for shame. And my best friend and I are well acquainted with some who compose so clumsily.) *Vita Nova*, XXV, 10.

we will see for Sonnet XVIII, makes the rhetorical structure of the text reflect the spirits' physiological functions. The lover is not allowed to express himself through words because the sensorial scenario containing the love experience also dictates the corporeal tools of its delivery, as described in Sonnet IV (emphasis mine): 'Chi è questa che vèn, ch'ogn'om la mira,/che fa tremar di chiaritate l'âre/e mena seco Amor, *sì che parlare/null'omo pote, ma ciascun sospira?*' (Who is she who comes, that everyone looks at her, who makes the air tremble with clarity and brings Love with her so that no one can speak, though everybody sighs?) Therefore, as Cavalcanti declares in the above quoted Sonnet to Orlandi *Di vil matera mi conven parlare*, the poet is called upon to make this physiological language conveyable, that is, to polish ('file,' literally) the sighs produced by the lover's body in the throes of his love venture: 'Amore ha fabricato ciò ch'io limo' (Love has fashioned what I am polishing).

The voices of the body, the rough material crafted by the poet, are legitimized by the medical *auctoritas*. As outlined above, natural philosophers describe the spirit as a subtle, almost immaterial substance resulting from the evaporation of the body's humors. The spirit interacts with the complexion of an organ and charges that organ with its distinct power. The three spirits presiding over the main functions of the organism are vital, animal and natural. The first and foremost is the spirit generated in the left ventricule of the heart as vital spirit, whence it imparts the *virtus vitalis*. The vital spirit is diversified according to the distinct functions it performs through the body parts: from the *virtus vitalis* all the other *virtutes* derive. These are the indications that Cavalcanti incorporates into his lines. The threefold distinction of vital, animal and natural spirit enters the *Rime* in a twofold form: the vital and the animal spirit. The animal spirit, which rises to the brain where it acts in the post-sensationary capacities, is not an unusual choice for a poet, given its crucial function in the course of image production.[32] In Cavalcanti, the animal spirit surfaces the text in all those occurrences that employ the term 'spirit' tout-court as image. The image addressed as 'spirito' is the woman's phantasm that the lover produces but is not able to elaborate further because the turmoil of his bodily reactions shuts down his mind. As theorized in *Donna me prega* (lines 63-68), and

---

[32] 'For the poetry of love, it is naturally the *spiritus animalis* of the brain, instrument of the outward senses, of imagination and memory, that has pride of place together with the *spiritus* of the heart in which the vital force is found.' Klein, p. 72. Following the tradition of the *spiritus peregrinus*, in poem IX Cavalcanti describes the spirits leaving the lover's body and accompanied by the canzone in front of the Lady, as a sign ('figura') that he is dead.

staged in XIV, the image of the Lady is doomed to darkness, it 'dies': 'Amor mi dona - un spirito 'n su' stato,/che - figurato, - more" (XIV, 7-8) (Love grants me a spirit of his own dignity which, once it is figured forth, dies).

Given the fatal outcome of the love encounter, the 'spirit of love' is fearful, because its appearance signifies death as stated in Sonnet XXII: 'lo qual sòl apparir quand'om si more,/e 'n altra guisa non si vede mai.' (That fearful spirit of love that is wont to appear when one is dying, and otherwise is never seen). 'Spirito pauroso' also defines the phantasms of Love: both the Lady's and Love's phantasms bring about the near obliteration of the lover's vital capacities. The two images blur and almost overlap, as suggested in the Ballad XIX, in which, in the original language, the 'gentile spirito' could be either Love's or the Lady's:

> Davante agli occhi mei vegg' io lo core
> e l'anima dolente che s' ancide,
>   che mor d'un colpo che li diede Amore
> ed in quel punto che madonna vide.
>   Lo su' gentile spirito che ride,
> questi è colui che mi si fa sentire,
> lo qual mi dice: «E' ti convien morire».[33]

(Before my eyes I see the heart and the grieving soul that are slain, that die from a blow that Love gave them, and at that point when they saw my lady, his noble spirit that laughs is the very one that makes itself heard by me, that tells me: 'You will have to die'.)

The use of spirit as image critical to my investigation is found in Sonnet VI. In this poem, the term spirit is employed simultaneously to mean both image and sigh. I will return to this later, to demonstrate how the latter meaning overshadows the former.

The second spirit, in addition to the animal one, that Cavalcanti imported from the medical literature is the vital spirit. The animal spirit presides over the process of mental elaborations, while the vital spirit carries life. In Sonnet XIII, when Love strikes, it targets precisely the spirit's *armarium*,[34] the left cavity of the heart where the vital spirit is generated: 'Sì giunse ritto 'l colpo al primo tratto,/che l'anima tremando si riscosse/veggendo morto 'l cor nel lato manco.' (The blow came so straight at the first draw, that [my] soul, trembling, was startled at seeing my heart struck dead on my left side,

---

[33] XIX, 4-10. This ambiguous construction has been noted by De Robertis, in his critical apparatus (De Robertis, *Rime*, p. 63).
[34] See n.19 in this chapter.

12-14.) If the animal spirit is fearful, the vital spirit is grieving.[35] Its pain is prescriptive: in *S'io fosse quelli che d'Amor fu degno*, Cavalcanti displays the suffering of the vital spirit in reply to Dante's celebrated invitation to embark on the enchanted vessel (*Guido, io vorrei che tu e Lippo ed io*). Guido must turn down the offer because he is aware, in contrast with his friend, that love's potential to produce an unperturbed and intellectually refined state of mind is nothing but a dreamful memory: 'S'i fosse quelli che d'amor fu degno,/del qual non trovo che rimembranza/...' (If I were he who was worthy of love, of which I find only the memory, XXXVIII[b] 1-2). Unlike his friend, Guido knows that Love is a merciless dominator whose arrows bring pain and erase will: 'E tu, che se' de l'amoroso regno/là onde di merzé nasce speranza,/riguarda se 'l mi' spirito ha pesanza:/ch'un prest' arcier di lui ha fatto segno/e tragge l'arco, che li tese Amore,/sì lietamente, che la sua persona/par che di gioco porti signoria.' (And you, who are of the amorous realm where hope is born of favor, consider whether my spirit has grievance: for a swift archer has taken aim at it and draws the bow that Love strung for him, so cheerfully that he himself seems to have lordship over joy.) In the *Rime*, in contrast with Dante's sonnet, Love does not empower the lover with an imagination that overcomes reality; rather, it makes the lover relapse into reality. Love is the swift archer who rages in the heart, targeted as the vital spirit's source and turned into a designated battlefield in XI: 'e 'l cor che tanto ha guerra e vita poco;' (my heart has much war and little life). The heart trembles and is frightened,[36] 'diviso' by the love wound,[37] finally consuming itself like the wick of a lantern. In the final act of the love dramaturgy staged in the *Rime* the darkened scene is brightened only by the burning heart of the lover lighting up his corpse, like the fire of a sinking ship in Sonnet XLIV[b]: 'Avegna che la doglia i' porti grave/per lo sospiro, ché di me fa lume/lo core ardendo in la disfatta nave.' (Though I bear a heavy sorrow for the sigh, since my heart in burning makes me a light in the ruined ship.)[38]

The attacks of Love that reach inside the lover's heart also affect the spirits into which the vital spirit divides itself in order to perform the soul's many powers. As one learns from the medical literature, a rich and smooth

---

[35] 'Pieno d'angoscia, in loco di paura,/lo spirito del cor dolente giace/per la Fortuna che di me non cura/' XXXIV, 18-20.
[36] V, 8.
[37] IX, 39.
[38] For the metaphor of the lover's body like a sinking ship, see the examples quoted from the Sicilian School in V.2, especially in Giacomo da Lentini's *Membrando ciò ch'Amore*.

circulation of the spirits, which also explains the larger and braver heart of the young,[39] signals well being, the good functionality of the organs and, in short, life. The spirits' quality and quantity was also believed to affect personality.[40] The abundant spirit circulating in the healthy young heart and organism progressively thins out after a condition of stress manifests itself, or when death approaches:

> Et spiritui quidem visibili quandoque accidit ut inspissetur & ut subtilietur & accidit ei ut ingrossetur & accidit ei ut multiplicetur. Et accidit ei ut minoretur. Multiplicatio autem est melior res & magis iuvativa. Et subtilitas quidem plurimum accidit ex siccitate, [...] Et paucitas quidem quandoque est a principio creationis & quandoque est propter vehementiam siccitatis [...] & propinquitatem mortis quando resolvit spiritum.[41]

> (And it happens to the visual spirit, that it is made thicker, or subtler, or grows and multiplies itself. And it happens also that it is diminished. Its multiplication is a better and more helpful thing. And its subtlety is due to dryness, [...] and its scarcity is at times from its creation, and at times from the excessive dryness [...] and when death approaches and the spirit dissolves.)

In the *Rime*, in Ballad X, when Love strikes, spirits rush to the help of the targeted heart struck by Love only to be depleted: 'Questa pesanza ch' è nel cor discesa/ha certi spirite' già consumati,/i quali eran venuti per difesa/del cor dolente che gli avea chiamati.' (This affliction that has descended on the heart has already wasted some little spirits that had come in defense of the grieving heart that had called them, 13-16). Cavalcanti describes this depletion as the spirits' departure from the body as it suffers Love's blows in Canzone IX: 'La mia virtù si partìo sconsolata/poi che lassò lo core/a la battaglia ove madonna è stata:/la qual degli occhi suoi venne a ferire/in tal guisa, ch'Amore/ruppe tutti miei spiriti a fuggire.'[42] (My vitality departed disconsolate after it surrendered my heart to the battering where my lady was: she who with her eyes came to strike in such a way that Love put to rout all my spirits, 9-14).

This sapping of the spirits' force is not only described by the poet, but also enacted by the lover, who intensifies his breathing and releases sighs,

---

[39] 'Juvenes, propter caliditatem naturae, habent multos spiritus, et ita in eis cor ampliatur; ex amplitudine cordis est quod aliquis ad ardua tendat.' S. Thomas, *Summa Th*, I^a II^{ae}, q. 40, a. 6. The passage is quoted by Chenu, *'Spiritus'*, p. 225 n.
[40] Albertus Magnus, *De motibus animalium*, I, ii, p. 277.
[41] *Spiritus. Spiritus grossitudo fit propter humiditate*, APPENDIX.
[42] See also: 'Qualunqu' è quei che più allegrezza sente,/se vedesse li spirti fuggir via,/di grande sua pietate piangeria.' VII, 12-15.

under the effects of love. Natural philosophers explain that breathing causes the pneuma circulating in the body to mix with the inhaled air. They also explain the connection between spiritual circulation and breathing in instrumental terms: the inhaled air improves the spirits' quality and functionality. The function of inhaling is to temper the spirit, by purifying and ventilating it;[43] further, inhaling tempers the overheating of the heart, counterbalanced by the intake of air.[44] Deep breaths, or sighs, are the body's response to a situation of stress, such as when intense mental concentration causes one to hold his breath, which is compensated for by the sighs.[45] Since they have the essential function of cooling down the thermic upsurges provoked by the change in blood and spirit circulations in the body and are the body's response to obsessive mental concentration, the medical sources include sighs among love symptoms.[46]

---

[43] 'Aer est elementum nostrorum corporum & spirituum & praeter hoc, quod est elementum nostrorum corporum & spirtuum, est etiam quid successive nostris adveniens spiritibus, & est causa meliorationis eorum, non tantum sicut elementum, sed etiam sicut faciens, scilicet temperans. [...]. Et hoc quidem temperamentum, quod ex aere nostris advenit spiritibus, ex duabus pendet operationibus, quae sunt mundificatio & eventatio. Eventatio vero est temperamentum complexionis spiritus calidi, cum superfluit propter coarctationem secundum plurimum & alteratur, & per temperamentum intelligimus temperamentum comparativum, quod scivisti. [...]. Cumque aer ad ipsum pervenit, impellit ipsum & miscetur cum eo, & prohibet ipsum ne ad igneitatem convertatur coarctativam vel suffocativam, ex qua ipse ad malitiam pervenit complexionis, per quam removetur a preparatione recipiendi impressiones animales in eo, qui est causa vitae & prohibet ne resolvatur ipsiusmet substantia vaporalis humida. Mundificatio vero fit apud reversionem vel egressionem anhelitus, propter associationem eius quod ei attribuit virtus separativa ex vapore fumoso, cuius comparatio ad spiritum est comparatio humoris superflui ad corpus. Temperamentum ergo eius est propterea quod spiritui advenit aer cum attrahitur, & mundificatio est propter eius exitum cum expellitur.' *Spiritus. Spiritus mundificatio sit respiratione & egressione anhelitus*, APPENDIX.

[44] 'Primum igitur principium non quidem movens, sed desideratum a movente est refrigerium cordis et spiritualium quae circa pectus sunt, quae calore cordis et hepatis nimium laedarentur et consummarentur si non eventarentur per huiusmodi inspirationem et respirationem.' Alberti Magni, *De spiritu et respiratione*, II, ii, p. 247.

[45] 'Suspirium enim nihil aliud est nisi quidam magnus haustus attracti aeris propter aequalis anhelitus intercepti restaurum: anhelitus autem aequalis vocatur quando secundum proportionem aequalitatis inter superfluum et diminutum habuerit aerem, et intumescere facit pectus, et caecat membra anhelitus. Contingit enim talis anhelitus interceptio propter tres causas praecipue, scilicet propter mentis in aliquo fortem fixionem: tunc enim extrahitur homo ab intentione eaqualiter aerem hauriendi: et ideo postea oportet suspirare.' Ibid., p. 250.

[46] Among the possible sources, I quote here from Alessandro of Afrodisia *Problemata*: '*Cur moeretes et amatores, et irati multum ac saepe suspirant?* Quod moerentes quidem in moerore animam habeant consternatam amatores autem in cupidine excandescentes vero in iram qua feruntur. Anima igitur consternata ad se movendum et exusitandum negligit, ac quasi obliviscitur vim motabilem pectoris musculis suggerere. Proinde cor neque diductione pectoris aerem suscipiens

In the *Rime*, sighs and spirits are connected, their distinction constantly shifting. Sighs, like spirits, are generated in the heart (Sonnet XXXIII): 'De la gran doglia che l'anima sente/si parte da lo core uno sospiro/che va dicendo: «Spiriti, fuggite».' (Out of the great grief that the soul feels, a sigh issues from the heart that keeps saying: "Spirits, you are fleeing.", 9-11). Both are employed as self-portraits in Canzone IX: '«Questi sono in figura/d'un che si more sbigottitamente»' ("These are as a figure of one who is dying in dismay", 55-56) and Sonnet XVIII: 'cose dubbiose nel core apparite;/le quali hanno destrutto sì costui/ed hannol posto sì presso a la morte,/ch'altro non n'è rimaso che sospiri' (Dreadful things that have appeared in the heart which have so undone him and brought him so close to death that nothing else is left of him but sighs, 8-11). Like the spirits, the sigh speaks and reasons.[47] Further, as if they were spirits, in the sense of images, sighs are employed to indicate the phantasm of the woman penetrating the lover's eyes and wounding his heart in Sonnet XXI: 'E' fu Amore.../E' trasse poi del li occhi tuo' sospiri,/i qua' me saettò nel cor sì forte,/ch'i' mi partì' sbigotito fuggendo.' (It was Love who drew from your eyes the sighs that he shot into my heart so hard that I left dismayed in flight, 1-11).

The shading of one term into the other supports my claim that the sighs released by the lover in the *Rime* not only describe a physiological reaction but also stand as the phenomenological representation of the fleeing spirits. Here I briefly recall Sonnet VI. The poem epitomizes the incapability of verbal expression and is particularly relevant to my investigation. Besides

---

et sufflatum et frigefactum neque correptionem efflans sordidas superfluitates, quas ex sanguine genuit exustio. Anhelitum nullum faciat necesse est inde sub comminiscendo cogitur plurimum musculis motum mistrare et maiorem sufflationem ac efflationem efficere ad multitudinem frigidi aeris capiendam et superfluitatum copiam extrudendam, ut quod exiguas ac iuges respirationes facere oportuit ampla una efficiat idque apud veteres datur suspirare iuxta cordis angustiam etiam aliquandiu valde suspirant idque saepenumero faciunt quod anima adversus ipsam movente semper sit aversa.' *Alexandri Aphrodisei e graeco in latinum traducta per Georgium Valla et Aristotelis Problemata Theodoro interprete, et Plutarchi Problemata*, p. not numbered, registro b5recto, And from Arnaldo da Villanova: 'Macerantur igitur hiis de causis corporis membra, precipue rariora et molliora et ea quae magis sunt resolutioni subiecta, quamobrem facies extenuatur et oculi concavantur et efficiuntur solito sicciores – nisi contingat eos in lacrimas emanare ex concepta tristitia, utpote cum elongationem rei desiderate percipiunt aut eiusdem repudium. [...]. Tale etiam in absentia desiderate rei tristantur, et cum ad compressum diu cordis recreationes copiosius aer attractus forti spiritu cum vaporibus diu prefocatis interius expellatur, oritur in eisdem alta suspiriorum emissio; [...].' Arnaldi de Villanova, *Tractatus de amore heroico*, pp. 5-15.
[47] XXXIII, 10; XXXV, 31-39.

demonstrating the rhetorics of passion at work in the *Rime*—as previously noted, in the sonnet sighs become the language of the poetry while their releasing creates the prosody, cadenced by the sequence of 'Deh,...Deh,...deh,....'—[48] the sonnet also establishes the semantic correspondence of spirits and breaths that signals the crucial disconnection of Cavalcanti from the tradition that embraced a dematerialized spirit. In Sonnet VI, the poet makes a plea for the releasing from his mind of 'parole adornate di pianto'—in compliance with the rhetoric of passion, the language's *ornatus* is made of tears, a topic I will expand on in the last chapter. The result is the breathing of sighs that starts, and produces, the lines. This chain of sighs is the physiological result of the altered condition in which the lover finds himself under the effects of the woman's gaze. Cavalcanti incorporates the indications of natural philosophy as well as turning the exhalations into a rhetorical agency: they correspond to the 'words' which the poet invoked and emitted through the spirits. But sighs here are also the representation of the spirits leaving the body of the lover. These sighs, that is, embody the 'vertù partite' from the heart because of its 'ferite/di sguardo e di piacer e d'umiltate' (wounds from looks and from beauty and from charity). A similar choice of words indicating the laceration of the heart followed by the spirits fleeing is in Sonnet XIII: 'E' [Love] vèn tagliando di sì gran valore,/che' deboletti spiriti van via' (He comes slashing with such great force that the frail spirits depart). The collapsing of the spiritual circulation concurs with the formation of the woman's image (the spirit 'alto e gentile e di tanto valore' of Sonnet VI) because the very image provokes that collapsing, by altering the balance of the body's circulatory pressure and, as a result, by making all the vital powers flee ('fa le sue [of the heart] vertù fuggire'). The sighs themselves convey this very meaning, that of the spirits fleeing while death approaches in Canzone IX (emphasis mine):

> Canzon, tu sai che de' libri d'Amore
> io t'asemplai quando madonna vidi:
> ora ti piaccia ch'io di te mi fidi
> e vadi 'n guis' a lei, ch'ella t'ascolti;
>   e prego umilemente a lei tu guidi
> *li spiriti fuggiti del mio core*,
> che per soverchio de lo su' valore
> eran distrutti, se non fosser vòlti,
> [...].

---

[48] See III.1. n.19.

> Però li mena per fidata via
>   e poi le di', quando le se' presente:
> «*Questi sono in figura*
> d'un che si more sbigottitamente».

(Song, you know that when I saw my lady I copied you from the books of Love: now may it please you that in you I put my trust, and go to her thus that she may listen to you; and I pray humbly that you lead to her the spirits that have fled from my heart, which would have been destroyed by her excess of power if they had not turned in flight; and they go lonely, without company, and are full of fear. So lead them in a safe way and then say to her, when in her presence: 'These are as a figure of one who is dying in dismay'.)

In the short circuit sparked by the sonnet, spirits, sighs and words overlap. It is the dominant, pneumatic use of the term spirit in the text that semantically weakens the notion of spirit as image, repeated in lines 9-11 of Sonnet VI—'I' veggo a lui spirito apparire/alto e gentile e di tanto valore,/che fa tutte le sue vertù fuggire'—but caught in the same pneumatic circulation agitating the lover's body while producing the sonnets' lines.

By selecting medical *auctoritates*, I claim that Guido Cavalcanti employs the spirit mainly in its physical meaning of a breath of air. As a result, spirits and sighs interact in his poetry and share functions in the poems. The interaction of spirits and sighs is legitimized by the medical source, which explains deep exhalations as a physiological reaction to the altered circulation of the spirits provoked by pain. Besides drawing the spirit's pneumatic conception from his medical *auctoritates*, Cavalcanti treats sighs as linguistic carriers. He stages a phenomenology of the spirit in which the poetic imagination, maimed by the very occurrence of love, is replaced by the display of a physiological process. The elements drawn from the medical literature also play a dramaturgical role since sighs are turned into actors impersonating the spirits. More specifically, the spirits represented by sighs are the vital spirit fleeing the lover's heart when death approaches.[49] In connection with the tradition that associates asthma to the *meditatio mortis*,[50] sighs ultimately represent the lover's last breath. Love's powers destroy the lover's imaginative capacities and obliterate his senses. The sound of his

---

[49] See the 'spiriti fuggiti dal mio cuore' of IX, 47, as well as the fleeting 'spirti' in VII, 13, and the 'deboletti spiriti' in XIII, 6.

[50] 'Identifying the spirit escaping from the wounded heart with the lover's sigh might seem the gratuitous invention of a *concettiste avant la lettre* if it did not have such a well-established tradition. With the "last sigh" one "surrenders the spirit"; Seneca tells us that physicians call asthma *meditatio mortis*, because "faciet [...] aliquando spiritus ille [the breath] quod saepe conatus est;" ' Klein, p. 76.

sighs that signal the fleeing vital spirits is all that is left to indicate his presence and define his identity in Sonnet XVIII: '.../le quali [dreadful things] hanno destrutto sì costui/.../ch'altro non n'è rimaso che sospiri.'[51]

IV.3 Pneumatic Circulation and Syntax in Sonnet XXVIII

Pegli occhi fere un spirito sottile,
che fa 'n la mente spirito destare,
dal qual si move spirito d'amare,
ch'ogn'altro spiritel fa[ce] gentile.

Sentir non pò di lu' spirito vile,
di cotanta vertù spirito appare:
quest' è lo spiritel che fa tremare,
lo spiritel che fa la donna umìle.

E poi da questo spirito si move
un altro dolce spirito soave,
che siegue un spiritello di mercede:

lo quale spiritel spiriti piove,
ché di ciascuno spirit' ha la chiave,
per forza d'uno spirito che 'l vede.

(Through the eyes strikes a delicate spirit that awakens a spirit in the mind, from which stirs the spirit of loving that ennobles every other little spirit. A lowly spirit can have no feeling of it, as spirit of such great strength does it appear: this is the little spirit that makes one tremble, the little spirit that makes the lady charitable. Then from this spirit comes another sweet gentle spirit which is followed by a little spirit of favor: this little spirit rains spirits, for it has the key to each spirit by virtue of a spirit that sees.)

In the text of the *Rime* the term spirit is employed mainly with three meanings: as the subtle matter circulating in the human body, as sigh, and as image. The term conveys all of the above through the spirit's pneumatic nature. When employed as sigh, it corresponds to one of the non-verbal signs of communication composing Cavalcanti's special language.

The spirit is of outmost importance in Cavalcanti's work and is the lexical foundation of Sonnet XXVIII, which unfolds the cluster of the spirit's meanings and at the same time produces the ultimate synthesis of the *Rime*'s rhetorical law. In this sonnet Cavalcanti enacts the interference between language and body at the core of his poetry by conferring a double

---

[51] See also XVIII and XIII.

function on the term spirit: the spirit is the fluid that enlivens the bodily organs and members guaranteeing the vital functions, as well as the lexeme that joins the syntax of the text. In both modes, physiological and linguistic, the emphasis is on the spirit's connecting ability. The result is a text in which body and language are made specular to each other and which serves as a model for Cavalcanti's procedure: to give rhetorical agency to the content of his scientific sources. In my reading, I claim that in composing Sonnet XXVIII Cavalcanti manufactured a telling piece of evidence of his linguistic devices, eluding not only the polemic created by his own contemporaries about poems that look like 'sporte piene di spirti'[52] but, also, the posthumous definition of 'elegant self-parody' that Gianfranco Contini dismissively attributed to this text.

The striking stylistic mark of Sonnet XXVIII is the repetition of the word spirit. Including the morphologic variant 'spiritello' it recurs fifteen times (once per line, with a double occurrence in line 12). This rhetorical device is a figure of speech included by Lausberg among the *figurae per adiectionem*. Repetitions determine an emotional and intellectual reinforcement[53] as well as a rhythmic and thematic strengthening.[54] The rhetorical awareness of Guido Cavalcanti is well documented. According to what we learn in chapter 16 of the *Vita Nova*,[55] Guido Cavalcanti is among the poets who did not indulge in the coloring of their language for the mere sake of varnishing it; he employed rhetorical adornments to hide a meaning underneath. The *figura per adiectionem* of Sonnet XXVIII is therefore a linguistic color that calls for careful consideration.

In this sonnet the repetition illustrates a causative chain of physiological facts triggered by the sight of the woman. More specifically, it dramatizes the awakening of the spiritual circulation in the lover's body after another and external 'spirito sottile,' the image detaching itself from the woman, penetrates through the lover's eyes. The flow of spirits stirred by the woman's image is qualified mainly according to the vocabulary established

---

[52] I am referring here to the sonnet by Onesto da Bologna (*"Mente" ed "umìle" e più di mille sporte*) directly addressed to Cino da Pistoia, but, as suggested by de Robertis in his introduction to Cavalcanti's Sonnet XXVIII, presumably also to Guido (De Robertis, *Rime*, p. 108).

[53] 'Repetition is for reinforcement, generally with emotional emphasis, but it is also exploited intellectually.' Lausberg, *Handbook of Literary Rhetoric*, p. 274.

[54] 'Letterariamente gli effetti sono molteplici (e, ovviamente, non esauribili). Come costituente e al tempo stesso emanazione dell'enfasi, questa specie di anadiplosi agisce da rinforzo tematico e ritmico. […]; in prosa come in poesia scandisce gli intervalli e la durata delle unità ritmiche.' Mortara Garavelli, p. 192.

[55] See IV.2.

in Guido Guinizzelli's *Al cor gentil rempaira sempre amore*, in as much as the spirits are given the attributes, among others, of 'gentile' and 'vile.' The sonnet, however, treats the matter of the heart's 'gentilezza' and poetry from an inner, corporeal perspective. As happens in the entire text of the *Rime*, in Sonnet XXVIII Cavalcanti incorporates the notions of natural philosophy and suitably treats the spirit mainly as a pneumatic element: the spirit performs different tasks in the poem and assumes different meanings, but it keeps its feature of subtle materiality throughout. The spirit is a subtle matter not only when the term refers to the spiritual circulation but also, as happens in the opening lines, when it indicates image. Lines 1 and 2 deal with the source of the forthcoming spiritual awakening, visual perception: 'Pegli occhi fere un spirito sottile,/che fa 'n la mente spirito destare.' The 'spirito sottile' and the 'spirito' that awakens in the mind indicate the form of the seen object and its correspondent mental image, respectively. Cavalcanti draws his description of how sight operates from Aristotelian optics as elaborated by Avicenna in the *De Anima* as well as in the *Liber Canonis* (although the latter mainly treats ophtalmological issues); however, he departs from Avicenna by emphasizing the materialization of the visual process.[56] Cavalcanti defines the image striking the observer's eyes 'spirito sottile' and, in doing so, he connects spirit in the sense of image to the feature of the spirit running through the human body: a *substantia subtilis*, in the definition of the *Canon*. To underline the subtle materiality attached to the term spirit, Cavalcanti uses the verb 'fere' to describe the penetration of the image into the observer's eyes; the image literally 'wounds' the eyes. The word choice not only creates a lexical anticipation of the upcoming battle provoked by love, but also points at the susbtantiality of the image that pierces the eyes.

In his *De anima*, Book III, Avicenna describes visual perception. By arguing that a direct contact between real things and the organs of perception must be excluded, Avicenna claims that 'seeing' means that the sensory organ receives a *simulacrum* of the object generated in the

---

[56] 'Au terme de cet exposé, il importe de mesurer à sa juste valeur la contribution avicennienne à la théorie de la vision. De façon générale, Avicenne a 'spiritualisé' la perception visuelle dans le sens de la psychologie aristotélicienne et sous l'influence de la philosophie néoplatonicienne. Notons d'abord qu'il ne considère pas la lumière comme une réalité corporelle; rejetant toute théorie corpusculaire, il conçoit la lumière comme l'acte du diaphane en tant que tel et comme l'acte des couleurs. Celle-ci existent réellement dans les choses, mais elles y sont seulement en puissance: c'est grâce à la lumière que les couleurs sont actualisées.' Verbeke, *Introduction sur la doctrine psychologique d'Avicenne*, p. 90.

transparent medium when the diaphanous is transformed into an actuality. The *simulacrum*, a form resembling the object, is first impressed in the *humor crystalleidos*. This *humor*, actually, bears two *simulacra* that are subsequently impressed in the *spiritus visibilis*, the very seat of the visual faculty, running through the two hollow nerves connecting the eyes to the brain. At the point of intersection (*in modo crucis*) between the two nerves, the *simulacra* are reduced to one and further transmitted: the *simulacrum* is impressed in the pneuma of common sense and then in the pneuma of the *virtus imaginativa*. While common sense receives the form, the *virtus imaginativa* retains it, that is, it ultimately creates a form independent of the original object.[57]

Avicenna describes sight as the handing down of the form's impression, via pneuma, from one faculty to another. In a subsequent section of his *De anima*, after having listed the four causes that explain why the *simulacrum* is double, Avicenna explains the transmission of the *simulacrum* through the faculties on the grounds of the fact that each perceptive faculty is naturally pushed towards its object, almost as if it were entertained by it (*ita ut quasi delectetur cum illo*). The effect Avicenna depicts is the dynamic flowing of the substance of the spirit carrying the mold of the sensorial datum.[58]

---

[57] 'Verum est autem quod simulacrum visi redditur, mediante translucente, membro receptibili apto leni illuminato, ita ut non recipiat illud substantia translucentis aliquo modo secundum quod est ipsa forma, sed cadit in illud secundum oppositionem non in tempore. Primum autem cui imprimitur simulacrum visi est humor crystalleidos, penes quem non constistit certe videre; alioquin unum videtur duo: duo enim simulacra sunt in crystalleidis, sicut cum tangitur aliquid utraque manu sunt duo tactus. Sed hoc simulacrum redditur a duobus nervis concavis ubi coniunguntur in modo crucis, qui sunt duo nervi, quorum dispositionem assignabimus cum loquemur de chirurgia. […]. Deinde quod est post hoc, est spiritus reddens quod videtur, non apprehendens iterum; sin autem, divideretur iterum apprehensio propter divisionem nervorum; et iste reddens est de substantia videntis, et penetrat in spiritum qui est repositus in primo ventriculo cerebri, et imprimitur iterum forma visa in ipso spiritu qui est gerens virtutem sensus communis, et sensus communis recipit illam formam, et haec est perfectio videndi. […]. Deinde haec virtus quae est sensus communis reddit formam alii parti spiritus, quae est continua cum parte spiritus quae vehit ipsum, et imprimit in illam formam ipsam, et reponit eam ibi apud virtutem formalem, quae est imaginativa, sicut postea scies, quae recipit formam et conservat eam. Sensus enim communis est recipiens formam, sed non retinens; imaginativa vero retinet quod recipit illa.' Avicenna latinus. *Liber de Anima seu Sextus de Naturalibus*, III, viii, R 151 35-66. See also from the *Canon*: 'Virtus visuum & materia spiritus visibilis penetrat ad oculum per viam duorum nervorum concavorum, quos novisti per anatomiam..' *Spiritus. De anatomia oculi*, APPENDIX.

[58] 'Debes autem scire quod praeter has causas est ibi alia causa materialis adiuvans illas, quae est haec scilicet quod substantia spiritus est substantia ultimae subtilitatis et velocis oboedientiae ad recipiendum motum, ita ut, cum contingerit in eo causa propter quam debeat mutari simulacrum de una parte ad aliam, sequatur moveri substantia spiritus aliquo motu in directum illius partis, quamvis sit parvissumus ille motus. Causa autem huius est quoniam unaquaeque

The same uninterrupted stream animates Cavalcanti's lines. After the image has been impressed on the eye's surface, line 2 ('che fa 'n la mente spirito destare') describes the consequent phase. Through the *spiritus visibilis* the object's form is transmitted to the pneuma of common sense, which resides in the anterior ventricle of the brain where it receives and assembles the data produced by the different senses, as we learn from the *Canon*:

> Sensus enim communis est illa quae omnia sensu percepta recipit & ab eorum formis patitur, quae in ipsa coniunguntur. Phantasia vero est illa quae eas custodit postquam coniunguntur & retinet eas post sensus absentiam. Et quae harum duarum est recipiens, alia est a custodiente. Hoc autem certificare est philosophi. Sed qualitercunque fuerit eius sedes & operationis eius principium est anterior cerebri ventriculus.'[59]

> (Common sense is what receives all the data of the sense, and is impressed by their forms, which are connected in it. Imagination is what keeps the forms after they have been connected, and holds them after in the absence of perception. Of these two things, one receives the impressions, the other keeps them. This is certified by the philosopher. Regardless of the seat and the function, the principle is in the anterior hollow of the brain.)

From the pneuma of common sense, the image is transferred to the additional hollows of the brain where the rational and memorial processes take place. The mental activity aroused by and around the abstract form is compressed in the 'spirito d'amare' described in line 3 and 4: 'dal qual si move spirito d'amare,/ch'ogn'altro spiritel face gentile.' The persistence of the image in the chambers of the brain corresponds to the main symptom of the lover's condition: it is the 'excessive meditation upon the beauty of the opposite sex' that Andreas Cappellanus introduced at the beginning of his treatise *De amore*.[60] According to the equation established by Guido Guinizzelli in his *Al cor gentil rempaira sempre amore*, being able to love means being 'gentili.' In Sonnet XXVIII, the obsessive meditation that signals love

---

virtutum apprehendentium impellitur naturaliter ad suum comprehensibile, ita ut quasi delectetur cum illo; cum vero pellitur ad illud, inclinatur eius gerulus ad illud aut inclinatur cum gerulo suo ad illud; et propter hoc spiritus visibilis totus impellitur ad lucem et retrahitur a tenebris naturaliter. Cum autem simulacrum inclinatur ad unam partem spiritus et non ad aliam, virtus quasi impellitur cum suo instrumento ad partem inclinationis simulacri: instrumentum etenim oboedit illi ad partem quam petit virtus, et propter hoc contingit in spiritu motio ad illam partem, subtilitate sui et sua velocitate ad recipiendum motum, tamquam sequatur motum simulacri.' Avicenna latinus, *Liber de Anima seu Sextus de Naturalibus*, III, viii, R 157 82-98.

[59] *Cerebrum. Cerebri pars anterior est sedes sensus communis*, APPENDIX.

[60] 'Amor est passio quaedam innata procedens ex visione et immoderata cogitatione formae alterius sexus, ob quam aliquis super omnia cupit alterius potiri amplexibus et omnia de utriusque voluntate in ipsius amplexu amoris praecepta compleri.'

ultimately influences the entire organism; it is the spiritual circulation as a whole that is 'gentile.' Accordingly, the sentient subject incapable of being impressed by the sight of the woman is discriminated, on the grounds of his 'vile' spirit: 'Sentir non pò di lu' spirito vile,/di cotanta vertù spirito appare.' The gentle heart, 'gentilezza,' is identified via its ability to experience love, which Cavalcanti proceeds to describe as a condition of altered physiology. In Cavalcanti's terms, experiencing love means being shaken by the reaction of the sensorial system when it is overstimulated by the form perceived through the eyes. The source of the agitated response of the body is the very woman. By entering the field of vision of the lover, she produces a form that penetrates the lover's eyes and is the main cause of his body's disquiet, that is, she almost 'creates' the spirit that makes him tremble:[61] 'quest' è lo spiritel che fa tremare,/lo spiritel che fa la donna umìle.' The trembling lover is what triggers the woman's sweetness and mercy: 'E poi da questo spirito si move/un altro dolce spirito soave,/che sieg[u]e un spiritello di mercede.'

A similar process is described in Sonnet XXII,[62] which I presented in II.4 with regard to imagination as the *prima perfectio hominis*. The sonnet's first quatrain introduces the predetermined mechanics of love: the appearance of the 'pauroso spirito d'amore,' that is, of the image of the woman, is a herald of proximate death. Although the production of that image fills the lover's heart with a momentary 'dolcezza' (since it represents the lover's supreme achievement), what follows is the galvanization of the spirits running through the lover's body, and his consequent death, i.e., the inability to complete the process of abstraction of the image. The collapse of the mind in the opening lines of Sonnet XXII is announced by the stirring up of the spirits at the conclusion of Sonnet XXVIII. The last tercet records the frenzied downpour of spirits caused by the merciful glance of the woman: 'lo quale spiritel [un spiritello di mercede] spiriti piove,/ché di ciascuno

---

[61] I consider 'donna' as the subject of the verb 'fa'. She is the source of the whole process and, logically, a feasible subject, according to the norm recorded by Domenico De Robertis in the footnotes of his edition (although a norm he does not apply in the case of line 8): 'La posposizione del soggetto e in genere l'*ordo artificialis* è caratteristico delle proposizioni dei primi tre versi, nonché dei versi 5-6, 9-10, 11.' De Robertis, *Rime*, p. 109.

[62] 'You could see, when I encountered you, /that fearful spirit of love/that is wont to appear when one is dying,/and otherwise is never seen./It was so near me that I thought/that it might kill my grieving heart:/my soul then took on the color of death,/wretched from the moans that it would heave;/but then it held back when it saw issuing/from your eyes a gleam of favor/that infused into my heart unusual sweetness;/and that delicate spirit of sight/rescued the others that thought they were dying,/burdened by anguishing weakness.'

spirit' ha la chiave,/per forza d'uno spirito che 'l vede.' Exposed to a cascade of spirits, as well as shaken by sighs,[63] the lover's body is flooded with a tumultuous circulation that impedes the completion of the process of abstraction.

The language of Sonnet XXVIII, and its organization, replicate the physiological stream of the pneumatic vessel, as well as the violent spiritual alteration that ensues if the object of the vision is the woman. In order to express the overflowing movement of the pneuma, Cavalcanti employs a linguistic adornment that disseminates the term spirit in each line (the *repetitio*) as well as a structure modeled after the spiritual flow, which he creates by inserting the word spirit at a specific point of each line. The position of the repeated word in the sentence or in the verse establishes a cycle and is a further channel of meaning, as claimed by Lausberg in his classification of the *figurae per adiectionem*. In order to prove his conclusion, Lausberg collects a few examples, such as the effect of a coming back, of an established reoccurrence, conveyed by the location of the word at the extremes of the syntactic component.[64] In Sonnet XXVIII Cavalcanti almost unfailingly (except for four verses: 5, 6, 8, and 12) creates hendecasyllables *a maiore* in which the secondary stress of the 6th syllable coincides with the tonic stress of the key word 'spirito.' By making the spirit both mark and connect the hemistichs, Cavalcanti creates a metric and prosodic structure that mimics the assembling function performed by the spirit's circulation inside the human body. The central position in the line stands for the circulatory apparatus of the text. The text mirrors the human body it describes.

Far from being a self-parody, Sonnet XXVIII is the accurate assemblage of all the different meanings borne by the word spirit in the *Rime*: penuma, image, sigh; and it demonstrates a strict adherence to the medical source by employing the spirit in its different meanings, all of which maintain the spirit's subtle materiality. This sonnet stands as the perfected model of the mutual affection between language and physiology which is at the root of Guido Cavalcanti's poetry.

---

[63] See De Robertis' footnote for line 12: '*spiriti*: da intendere verosimilmente come "sospiri", quasi "spiriti di sospiri" (ossia per sineddoche) alla luce di XXXIII 10-11.' De Robertis, *Rime* p. 110.

[64] 'Le generale funzione semantica di questa figura è l'*amplificatio* emozionale, all'interno della quale trova posto l'espressione del ritorno di reciprocità, della consequenza immanente al destino, della relazione ciclica tra finito, infinito (*come subiecto rationis*) e finito.' Lausberg, *Elementi di retorica*, p 142.

CHAPTER V
Blinding Tears

V.1 Experimental Colors: the *Ornatus* is Made of Tears

Sonnet XVIII contains an image that I introduced as a portrait of Cavalcanti. The tools on his desk, the quills, penknife, and scissors, take over the telling since, as the readers are told in the second quatrain, the dreadful events of the heart have reduced the lover to his sighs, that is, to the bundle of spirits leaving his body. The sonnet indicates, on one hand, the aftermath of the events repeatedly staged in the *Rime*; on the other, that the lover's sighs also replace his words. As an effect of the rhetorical reshaping laid out in the *Rime*, language and its organization are affected by pain, like the body. The painful 'being acted upon' inflicted on the lover's body in fact alters, or drastically impedes, the formation of images. As a consequence, since imagination is necessary to language production, the signs that convey meaning are not verbal; they consist of the body's immediate responses to the affections provoked by love. As with a short circuit, pain connects body and language. The final result narrows the expressive potential of the *Rime*'s tongue down to pain: the language speaks in sorrow ('l'alma trista che parl' in dolore,' VI, 12-13) and speaks sorrow ('voce alquanta, che parla dolore,' XIII, 8).

Sonnet VI is especially relevant with regard to the forging of a language ruled by the body's pain. The invocation of the spirits opening the sonnet is the invocation of a rhetoric capable of organizing physiological communication, the only kind left. The 'dismayed and sorrowful words' consist, in fact, of sighs that set in motion the sonnet's lines. Those sighs dramatize the spirits fleeing the lover's heart through the many wounds opened there. The spirits leaving the lover's body as sighs are given the mandate to 'speak', and they convey that the lover is about to die. This physiological language is ultimately mirrored in the agent of its utterance. Sighs speak to the very soul, as it shares their language: 'Deh, I' vi priego che deggiate dire/a l'alma trista, che parl' in dolore,/com'ella fu e fie sempre d'Amore.' On these grounds, I believe that the definition of 'linguaggio analitico drammatico' suggested by Domenico de Robertis in his footnotes for Sonnet VI is incomplete. De Robertis claims that Cavalcanti creates a language that aims at making the pain 'visibile anche là dove non arrivano gli occhi.' Cavalcanti's language, however, does not simply dramatize and mimic an emotional condition as set forth by Brunetto Latini in his *Rettorica*: 'parlando in dolore sia la testa inclinata, il viso triste e gli occhi pieni di lacrime e tutte sue parole e viste dolorose...'[1] Cavalcanti lets the affection, and the body's response to that affection, radically modify the rhetorical rules of the language employed to recount it. These are not just words portraying pain as if they were actors, but words whose basic features and organization are changed because of love. Love's appearance immediately determines the resetting of a mode of expression, which, without mediation, turns words into sighs.[2]

In Sonnet VI, as has been pointed out, a physical expression of pain becomes a rhetorical figure: the sequence of sighs signaling the affection is organized into an anaphora.[3] In the first quatrain of the same sonnet Cavalcanti inserts a further indication. In order to alleviate the 'tanta pena' that afflicts him, the poet invokes the spirits and urges them to release from his mind 'parole adornate/di pianto, dolorose e sbigottite.' With these two lines, Cavalcanti announces that in his writing he has employed tears as a tool for *ornatus*, the stylistic tool of language embellishment.[4] A familiar manifestation of pain, weeping, thus determines the expression of language's most important, because most effective, virtue.[5]

As we shall see in the next pages, this special *ornatus* is also relevant with regard to the textual connections between Cavalcanti's poems and Avicenna's *Canon*. In treating the topic of tears Cavalcanti drastically departs from the existing poetic tradition and connects, instead, with the medical source. Consequently, instead of explaining weeping through the conventional metaphor of weight release, he interprets it as a physical

---

[1] 'Guido sembra attenersi al precetto di Brunetto, Rett., 32, 5: «parlando in dolore (cfr. 13!) sia la testa inclinata, il viso triste e gli occhi pieni di lagrime e tutte sue parole e viste dolorose...». Ma col conforto della retorica, si ha qui, a partire dai complementi 'con tanta pena' e 'fuor della mente', anzi da 'vedete', il primo e cospicuo esempio di linguaggio analitico drammatico per cui la pena è visibile anche là dove non arrivano gli occhi, la sua manifestazione è un'uscita di parole fuor dalla mente, e queste sono atteggiate a pianto, a dolore e sbigottimento.' De Robertis, *Rime*, p. 23.
[2] '.../e mena seco Amor, sì che parlare/null'omo pote, ma ciascun sospira?' (IV, 3-4.)
[3] See III.1.
[4] Ardizzone, *Guido Cavalcanti. The Other Middle Ages*, p. 23.
[5] '*Ornatus* [...] is the most sought-after virtue because it is the most brilliant and most effective *virtus*, transcending linguistic correctness and intellectual comprehensibility of expression [...]: an audience likes to hear an embellished speech [...] and will listen with receptive attentiveness [...].' Lausberg, *Handbook of Literary Rhetoric*, pp. 242-243.

phenomenon of obstruction. In the *Rime* tears do not make the lover's heart lighter, but make the lover unable to perceive colors. This reversal of the function tears are attributed in the coeval poetic repertory operates as well on the ground of their rhetorical import. Cavalcanti employs weeping, of which he emphasizes the shading effect, as a tool for *ornatus*, which by definition consists of the addition of colors to words. By displaying tears among his rhetorical tools Cavalcanti presents tears as a perfect synthesis of linguistic elaboration and pain phenomenology. By overturning the traditional function of *ornatus*, Cavalcanti solves the problems arising from the necessity of embellishing a language that stems from the lover's collapse into darkness.

V.2 Weeping Lovers in the Sicilian School

The mutation introduced by Cavalcanti on the topic of tears becomes evident when the *Rime* are countered with the tradition to which they belong. By tradition I mean here the group of Sicilian notaries introduced by Dante in the *De vulgari eloquentia* as the predecessors of the vernacular poets.[6] Among the Sicilian poets, whom Bruno Panvini promoted as forming a literary group by assembling their verses in his pivotal edition, weeping is a widely treated topic. It is treated in accordance with a few recurrent typologies and is often constructed as an antitheton. Tears are contrasted with the lover's anguish, which is compared to a fire burning in his heart. Tears do not quench the internal bonfire but have the main purpose of signaling the pain to the outside world.[7] More frequently, weeping is contrasted with laughter. The oscillation between the two opposite signs is presented as the hypostasis of the condition of folly into which love drags the lover.[8] The unrestrainable succession of alternating moods is mirrored by the weather conditions:

---

[6] '[…] et quia regale solium erat Sicilia, factum est ut quicquid nostri predecessores vulgariter protulerunt, sicilianum vocetur: quod quidem retinemus et nos, nec posteri nostri permutare valebunt.' Dante, *De vulgari eloquentia*, I, xii, 2-3.

[7] 'Membrando cio c'Amore/mi fa soffrire, e sento/dismarrimento, - und'eo son al morir;/...]/ca tuttor ardo e 'ncendo/sospirando e piangendo,/c'Amor mi fa languire/per quella cui m'arrendo,/di me merzè cherendo,/e non mi degna audire.' *Membrando ciò ch'Amore*, 1-12, dalla sezione XLIII *Poesie di dubbia attribuzione*, Panvini, p. 446.

[8] Cavalcanti's folly, on the other hand, does not correspond to an oscillation but to the certitude about the destiny of death preying on the lover: therefore 'folli' are the eyes opened on that destiny, and 'folle' is the time going by while in the lover's heart the war of spirits rages: V, 1-4 ('Li mie' foll'occhi, che prima guardaro/vostra figura piena di valore,/fuor quei che di

II
[...]
con tut<t>i folli vo' tener congilio
e de l'amor no *saccio* dir ragione
[...]
V
Ed agio gra[n] letiza e vo ridendo,
com'om che non si puote rallegrare,
e tu<t>or mi lamento e vo piagnendo
com'omo c'à gran voglia di cantare :
e ciò ch'io sapo tut<t>o 'l vo dicendo
com'om ch'è mutolo e non può parlare.
Truona e piove e l'aira sta serena
e l'aqua corre in giuso e su mi mena,
e sto in sollazo e vivo in gran[de] pena,
laonde rido e piango e sto gaudente.[9]

(I want to be part of all the mad ones, and I have no explanation for love [...]. And I have a good time and I laugh, like a man who can not rejoice, and I always lament and cry, like a man who feels like singing, and I say everything I know, like a mute who can not speak. It thunders and rains and the air is serene, and water falls and lifts me, and I am happy and I am in pain, so that I laugh and cry and stay happy.)

In the Sicilian repertory, laughter and tears are entwined. Together, they create a network for the arduos initiation of the lover, described in terms of metal refinement:

Così af<f>ino ad amarvi
com'auro a la fornace,
c'af<f>ina pur ardendo.
Senza veder guarda[r]vi,
donna, già non vi piace
lo mio affannar piangendo;
bagnandomi lo viso,
pianger mi torna riso
e d'ira mi discorda:

---

voi, donna, m'acusaro/nel fero loco ove tien corte Amore,/...'); XI, 5-12 ('E dico che' miei spiriti son morti,/e 'l cor che tanto ha guerra e vita poco;/e se non fosse che 'l morir m'è gioco,/fare'ne di pietà pianger Amore./Ma, per lo folle tempo che m'ha giunto,/mi cangio di mia ferma oppinione,/in altrui condizione,/sì ch'io non mostro quant'io sento affanno:/...'). On the topic of the links of love to folly and melancholy, therefore to a pathological condition, see Fontaine, Marie-Madeleine, *La lignée des commentaires à la chanson et Guido Cavalcanti 'Donna me prega': évolution des relations entre philosophie, médecine et littérature dans le débat sur la nature d'Amour*. In: Ceard, pp. 159-178.

[9] *Già mai null'om non à sì gran ricchezze*, 14-15; 41-50, sezione XLIV, *Poesie anonime*, in Panvini, p. 486. Translations are mine.

la dolz'agua m'ac<c>orda - piange[r] ridendo.[10]

(This way I am purified, like gold in a furnace, which is refined while it burns. I look at you without seeing, lady, and you are not pleased with my anxious crying; while I cry, weeping is made into laughter and I forget my wrath; the sweet water allows me to cry, while I laugh.)

With the blending of tears and laughter, hidden accesses to the experience of love are revealed and the lover, like a phoenix, is regenerated. Trying everything in his power, he aims at reaching the woman ('le vie d'Amore ch'io saccio – tutte provo').[11]

This well-established combination of weeping and laughter is undone by the Notary. In Giacomo da Lentini's lines, weeping is the only symptom left of the condition of love, and is further articulated. In *Dal core mi vene*, in contrast with the copious shedding of tears represented by other authors, the Notary transforms tears into the slow and quiet descending of dew ('rosata') that the lover suddenly perceives on his visage:

I
    Dal core mi vene
che gli occhi mi tene - rosata;
    spesso m'adivene
che la ciera ò bene - bagnata,
    quando mi sovene
di mia bona spene, - c'ho data
II
in voi, amorosa,
bonaventurosa;[12]

(From the heart comes a dew held by the eyes; often I realize that my face is wet, when I remember on what I have pinned my hopes: on you, lovely, and fortunate creature.)

In the same text, the manifestation of what signals the anguish of love is accompanied by voluntary isolation from the others. The lover escapes the glances of the passersby and aims for a solitary space where he can meditate, 'pensivo,' on the love venture:

XVII
[...]

---

[10] *Così affino ad amarvi*, 1-10, sezione XLIV, *Poesie anonime*, ibid., pp. 511-512.
[11] 'E sì com'omo dice/de la fenicie - che si rinovella,/in foco, eo così faccio,/chè 'n fiamma e 'n pena e 'n ghiaccio - mi rinovo;/di gioia canto e poi taccio,/le vie d'Amore ch'io saccio - tutte provo.' Guilglielmo Beoroardi, *Gravosa dimoranza*, 35-40, ibid., p. 284.
[12] Giacomo da Lentini, *Dal core mi vene*, 1-8, ibid., p. 36.

> cantanto in gioia vivo,
> or vivo pur pensivo
> e tutta gente *ischivo*,
> sì ch'io vo fugendo,
> [...]
>
> XVIII
> pur cherendo - ond'io m'ascond;:[13]
> [...]
>
> (While singing I am joyous, but also pensive, and I avoid all the people, so that I run away, and I search for a place where I can hide.)

Giacomo da Lentini is especially relevant with regard to Cavalcanti because of an amplification of the theme—the consequential connection between weeping and pain release.[14] In the Notary's lines, the shedding of tears is clearly explained in terms of the lifting of a weight burdening the heart of the lover. The metaphor is introduced in the Canzone *Membrando ciò ch'Amore*. In this text, the lover is tormented by sighs and tears. His being in 'sospiri ed in pianto' corresponds to the discharging of a load that weighs him down. Despite the lover's release of sighs and tears, the conclusion is his wreckage: the lover is like a broken ship 'che pere per lo canto/che fanno tanto dolze le serene.' The same image is in one stanza of Giacomo da Lentini's *Madonna dir vo voglio*, where it is further elaborated; the metaphorical range is expanded, and meanings shifted. The ship does not stand for the lover but for the woman's love, the 'nave' that drags the lover 'in mare tempestoso'; the lover's sighs and tears stand for the ballast that needs to be thrown overboard in order to avoid sinking:

> IV
> Lo vostr'amor, che m'ave
> in mare tempestoso,

---

[13] Ibid., p. 42. Rustico Filippi makes a different case, since he asks his own tears to help him hiding from Love, and the Love's 'erore' in which he fell: 'Tutto lo giorno intorno vò fugiendo,/credendo mi camoare davanti Amore;/e, s'io trovo nesuno, fortte piangiendo/lo prego che mi c[i]eli al mio sengnore.' *Concordanze della lingua poetica delle origini* vol. I, V837, p. 526.

[14] Although the texts of the Notary present the greatest number of occurrences of this interpretation of tears, it can also be found in other authors' texts, such as Guglielmo Beroardi's *Gravosa Dimoranza* (1-13): 'Gravosa dimoranza/ch'eo faccio lungiamente,/mi fa sovente - lo core dolere,/ed aggione pesanza,/ca lo viso piagente/de l'avenente - non posso vedere./Gioia par mi s' asconda,/temmo non mi confonda - lo pensare,/und'a gli occhi m'abonda/le lagrime com'onda - delo mare.' Panvini, p. 283.

è sì como la nave
c'a la fortuna getta ogni pesanti,
[...];
similemente eo getto
a voi, bella, li miei sospiri e pianti;
chè, s'eo no li gittasse,
parria che soffondasse;
e bene soffondara,
lo cor tanto gravara - in suo disio!
Chè tanto frange a terra
tempesta, che s'atterra;
ed eo così rinfrango:
quando sospiro e piango, - posar crio.[15]

(Your love, which keeps me in a stormy sea, is like the ship that throws away its weight, [...]; likewise, I give to you, lady, my sighs and cries; because, if I did not give them, I feel I would sink, and I actually would, since my heart is so weighed down by its desire! Like the tempest breaks over the ground, I break: and when I sigh and cry, I feel I can rest.)

Using these precedents for comparison, I evaluate Cavalcanti's *Rime* on the specific topic of tears, to demonstrate his disengagement from the existing poetic repertory. Cavalcanti treats tears from a radically different angle, that of his scientific sources. As a result, tears are attributed a different, literal function in his lines. This literal function alters his rhetoric as well. Cavalcanti connects the Rime to a few motifs in Giacomo da Lentini's repertory, but only in order to elaborate them medically. As happens in the lines of *Dal core mi vene*, Cavalcanti includes tears among the causes of the lover's isolation. In Ballad X, he describes weeping as a screen that alters the lover's vision of the outside world and, reciprocally, makes the lover almost invisible to that world: 'Vedete ch'i' son un che vo piangendo/.../e già non trovo sì pietoso core/che, me guardando, una volta sospiri.' (You see that I am one who goes weeping [...] and I find no heart so compassionate that, looking at me, would ever sigh once, 1-4). The isolation of the lover is, however, in the case of Cavalcanti, the result of the incommunicableness of the lover's language of the body. In the previous pages I introduced the self-contained language of the *Rime*: in Sonnet VI, the sighs are exhaled from the heart only to turn back and address the soul. In Sonnet XV, the lover is likewise doomed to solitude because of a physiological mode of communication he can not share: 'd'angosciosi dilett' i miei sospiri,/che nascon della mente ov'è Amore/e vanno sol ragionando

---

[15] Giacomo da Lentini, *Madonna dir voglio*, 49-64, ibid., p. 6.

dolore/e non trovan persona che li miri.' (My sighs, caused by anguishing delights, [sighs] which are born of the mind where Love resides and go about expressing only sorrow and find no one to look on them, 5-8). The correspondences between the *Rime* and the existing tradition are altered because Cavalcanti draws from different sources and therefore elaborates the topics on a different tangent. In particular, in the *Rime* weeping is interpreted not as a release of pain, but, according to the medical indications, as an ophtalmic issue. Tears are literal; they provoke an obstruction in the eyes that impedes clear perception, namely, clear perception of the object of love. As we shall see, by blinding the lover, tears become the empirical demonstration that the appearance of the object of love inevitably interrupts the habitual course of visual perception at its very source. In other occurrences perceptions are damaged by an irregular and unbalanced flow of the spirits; when instead tears are shed, the senses are unable to function properly because the spirits do not flow. An exemplary sequence of verses that describes tears as the chief cause of a visual inability arising in connection with love is in Ballad XIX. In this poem, the encounter with the woman moves the lover to shed tears. As a consequence, the lover's sight is partially impaired. He is unable to fully possess the vision of the woman, blurred as it is by the tears, as signaled by the 'spirito dolente' which strenuously, and feebly, finds its way through the eyes of the observer:

> Lagrime ascendon de la mente mia,
> sì tosto come questa donna sente,
> che van faccendo per li occhi una via
> per la qual passa spirito dolente,
> che[d] entra per li miei sì debilmente
> ch'oltra non puote color discovrire
> che 'l 'maginar vi si possa finire.[16]

(Tears rise up from my mind as soon as it senses this lady; they make, through the eyes, a conduit through which passes the grieving spirit that enters through my eyes so weakly that it cannot reveal any color beyond that which imagining could be completed with it.)

---

[16] Gianfranco Contini explains these verses in terms of an imperfect vision impeding knowledge: 'La figurazione della donna, penetrando per gli occhi dell'uomo, li trova ostruiti dalle lacrime: di conseguenza non può accompagnarsi alla visualizzazione del colore, e l'immagine resta generica e inadeguata per il contemplante. Di *colore* in quanto allusivo alla piena conoscibilità, si discorre in termini concordanti in XXV 9 e XXVII 67.' Contini, *Poeti del Duecento*, t. II, p. 513.

The explanation of tears in terms of an obstruction that, by impeding the formation of a clearly perceived image as well as its movement through the channels connecting the eyes to the chambers of the brain, threatens the entire imaginative process is directly drawn from the scientific source with which this study deals. Avicenna's *Canon* treats tears from an ophtalmologic perspective, and addresses them not as the external sign of psychological pain but mainly as an *aegritudo*, as a disease.[17] This disease is explained in terms of a congestion of the channels through which images gain access to the brain. Avicenna employs the specific term of *aegritudo oppilativa* which prevents the forms from penetrating the eyes.[18] *Oppilatio*, in other passages of his *Canon*, indicates in general an unhealthy malfunctioning of the spiritual flowing system.[19]

The general principle is that an unobstructed and balanced spiritual flow is at the basis of a well functioning organism. The consequences of a poorly functioning spirit on sight are described, among others, by Averroes. He treats the phenomenon in his *Epitome* to the *Parva naturalia*. In this text, he explains visual perturbance as a consequence of the heat aroused by a condition of emotional agitation, which causes the visual pneuma to exhale fumes. Since this pneuma is feverish, limpid vision is not possible.[20]

The alteration of sight described by Cavalcanti happens for mechanical reasons as well. The inability of the spirits to circulate freely because tears are obstructing the channels impedes the formation of the image. It is an occlusion in the human vessels, provoking an immediate unbalance, that causes this condition. Tears, one of the signs that the lover manifests at once when facing the woman, are explained in compliance with the medical

---

[17] 'Haec aegritudo est ut sint oculi semper humidi humiditate aquosa. Et quandoque currunt lachrymae. Et earum quidem aliae sunt nativae, aliae accidentales. Et de accidentalibus sunt quae sunt inseparabiles in sanitate & sunt aliae sequentes aegritudinem, quae removentur si removeatur aegritudo, sicut fit in febribus.' *Lachrymae. De lachrymis*, APPENDIX.

[18] 'Descensus aquae est aegritudo oppilativa, & est humiditas extranea stans in foramine vueae, inter humorem albugineum, & siphac corneae, aut siphac corneum, quare prohibet penetrare formas ad visum.' *Lachrymae. De aqua*, APPENDIX.

[19] *Spiritus retentio fit ex oppilatione*. APPENDIX.

[20] 'Et manifestum est quod istud instrumentum est necessarium in comprehensione istarum virtutum. Istud autem instrumentum non agit nisi quando fuerit in sua complexione naturali, nullo adveniente turbante ipsum. Et ideo iracundus in hora ire et habens calorem ascendentem recipiet inde corruptionem sui visus, et forte videbit unum pro duo propter motum contingentem spiritui apud iram, quoniam, quando pars recipiens formam movetur et venerit ad suum locum ex alia parte, describitur forma in secunda parte; et adhuc non abscisa est a prima parte: et sic una forma apparebit forme due, sicut forma solis cadens super aquam correntem apparebit due.' Averroes, *Compendia Librorum Aristotelis qui Parva Naturalia vocantur*, 191vb 45-55.

tradition. They are accounted for as excessive moisture in the eyes that impedes what should be a smooth flow and alters vision because the channels through which the *spiritus visibilis* runs are occluded. Again drawing from the *Canon*, Cavalcanti indicates the source of the emanation of tears. Since the content of the text of the *Rime* is physiological, it is not the heart that is weighed down by tears, but the brain. The 'dew' that the Notary describes as coming from the heart ('Dal core mi vene/che gli occhi mi tene - rosata'), or the 'aqua' moving 'dal core' of Rinaldo d'Aquino[21] changes origin in the *Rime*, as Cavalcanti describes weeping as a production of the mind in Ballad XIX (line18): 'Lagrime ascendon de la mente mia' following the indications of Avicenna, who in the paragraph dealing with the *aegritudo aquosa* and the different types of *lachrymae*, *accidentales* and *nativae* specifies that tears are a byproduct of the moisture in the brain, which is discharged because of the brain's inability to retain it.[22]

Elaborating the topic of tears in a medical key, Cavalcanti infers that visual perception will inevitably be compromised when the glance falls on an object of love. This is what determines the inclusion of tears among the demonstrations of the laws that, according to Guido Cavalcanti, rule human love. The conclusion is drawn in Ballad X. It its first stanza, the lover weeps and, while doing so, he gives a demonstration: 'Vedete ch'i' son un che vo piangendo/e dimostrando - il giudicio d'Amore,/...' (You see that I am one who goes weeping and showing outwardly Love's judgment.) In the context of the *Rime* the term 'dimostramento' has a specific meaning, established by lines 5-10 of *Donna me prega*.[23] Cavalcanti, who is a logician, uses 'dimostramento' in connection with the vocabulary of Aristotle's logic.[24] Therefore the line of Ballad X 'dimostrando il giudicio d'Amore' does not simply indicate that, through his tears, the lover shows that he is serving the sentence inflicted on him by the court of Love. By shedding tears that make him blind, the lover produces one of the demonstrations of love connecting logic and physics. Ballad X holds proof that love is an 'accidente fero,' a

---

[21] Giacomo da Lentini, XIII, *Dal core mi vene*, Panvini, pp. 35-36; Rinaldo d'Aquino, *Un oseletto che canta d'amore*, ibid., p. 118.

[22] 'Causa autem in accidentalibus est debilitas retentivae [...]. Et principium quidem illius humiditatis est cerebrum & cursus eius ad oculum in una duarum viarum praedictarum multoties.' *Lachrymae. De lachrymis.* APPENDIX.

[23] 'Ed a presente – conoscente – chero,/perch'io no spero – ch'omo di basso core/a tal ragione porti canoscenza:/ché senza - natural dimostramento/non ho talento di voler provare/là ove posa, e chi lo fa creare.'

[24] Ardizzone, *Guido Cavalcanti. The Other Middle Ages*, pp. 50-51.

potentiality whose transformation into an actuality consists of darkness. In the following stanza, the lover presents his own phenomenology of love to the 'persone accorte,' an equivalent of the 'presente – conoscente' summoned in *Donna me prega*. However, although the poet suggests creating a bond with them based on a shared sensitivity on the model of the Stilnovistic community, Cavalcanti's lover finds no compassion. As I mentioned earlier, quoting from the same Ballad X, the physiological communication the lover must resort to is not a collective language: 'e già non trovo sì pietoso core/che, me guardando, - una volta sospiri' (and I find no heart so compassionate that, looking at me, would ever sigh once). The lines that follow are in clear contrast with the example quoted above from Giacomo da Lentini's *Madonna dir vo voglio*. Rather than working as a release of pressure on the heart, the tears in Ballad X augment the sense of compression and leave the heart with an affliction that Cavalcanti renders as a weight descended on the heart, a 'pesanza': 'Questa pesanza ch'è nel cor discesa...' The lover's spiritual circulation is altered and weakened. Finally, 'già consumati,' the spirits, including the visual spirits, leave his body. In the conclusive lines of the ballad, the lover's body serves as the stage for the final dramatization of love I pointed out in III.4. The stage is occupied by two personifications that act upon the body of the lover. The perception still active is the auditive one, and it consists of the threatening sound of a 'noise' ('romore'), which is an off-stage voice making sure that Pity deserts the scene. The lover's gaze must not look for Pity. Or, as the voice warns in Cavalcanti's even more drastic depiction of the lover's spiritless and abandoned body, Pity mustn't stare at herself in his eyes: '«ma guarda che Pietà non vi si miri!»' ('only take care that Compassion be not seen there!').

Sonnet XVII starts with an entreaty for the unattainable intervention of Pity. Cavalcanti reintroduces the 'nova donna' who first appeared in the preceding Sonnet XVI[25] and stages a scene in which the lover acknowledges his merciless destiny. The 'nova donna' is associated with 'nova crudeltate,' ill hidden behind her apparent gentleness: 'Onde ti vien sì nova crudeltate?/Già risomigli, a chi ti vede, umile,/saggia e adorna e accorta e sottile/e fatta a modo di soavitate!' (Whence does such unusual cruelty come to you? And yet you seem, to one who sees you, charitable, wise and lovely and aware and subtle and created in the guise of gentleness, 5-8). The lack of a merciful and amorous correspondence causes the lover's pain and

---

[25] 'Tutto mi struggo, perch'io sento bene/che d'ogni angoscia la mia vita è peggio;/la nova donna cu' merzede cheggio/questa battaglia di dolor' mantene.' XVI, 5-8.

fear. His spiritual circulation is finally upset, and the collapse is announced by the spirits that leave his body as sighs drenched in tears (one of the occurrences in which the two voices of the body overlap): 'L'anima mia dolente e paurosa/piange ne[l]i sospir' che nel cor trova,/sì che bagnati di pianto escon fòre.' (My grieving and fearful soul weeps over the sighs it finds in my heart so that the come forth wet with tears.) Since the lover is crying, tears obstruct the channels of the visual spirit and he is at once blinded. The very moment in which his sight is impaired coincides with the moment in which the phantasm originates from the woman. The image is formed and immediately disconnected from the viewer since it cannot penetrate his eyes. This disconnection seals the end of Sonnet XVII. The two tercets describe the two facts as almost synchronical, yet they also produce a fracture, visualized by the gap between the strophes. The 'allora' of the last tercet ensures that the formation of a barrier of tears over the lover's eyes, described in the lines quoted above, happens at the same time as the formation of the woman's image: '*Allora* [emphasis mine] par che ne la mente piova/una figura di donna pensosa/che vegna per veder morir lo core.' (It then seems that into my mind rains a figure of a lady deep in thought who comes to see my heart die.) But the two facts also immediately mark a division, which foretells the lover's death. In fact, in the last tercet the subject can only intuit the image ('par') because his sense is impaired. The lack of visual perception is presented as an imminent collapse of the heart, to which the newly formed image of the woman is witness. Overwhelmed by his reactions, the lover becomes detached from the phantasm, which joins the possible intellect.

In one instance, the presence of the woman is connected to blindness to such an extent that the action is not described so much as seeing but as sensing. The text I am referring to is the ballad I employed to introduce the topic of this chapter. Ballad XIX starts off with Cavalcanti's appeal to the traditional community of fellow poets. Guido addresses them in the first line of the poem, calling them 'you who speak of sorrow'—'I' prego voi che di dolor parlate'—and calling their attention to the venture of love he is about to share. In fact, the account of his 'pena' is a hallucination, delivered in darkness, describing the outcome of his gaze at the woman and the consequent striking of the soul by Love. The lover pronounces that he sees ('veggio') his own heart displayed before his eyes, together with his soul, which kills itself: 'Davante agli occhi miei vegg' io lo core/e l'anima dolente che s' ancide,/che mor d'un colpo che li diede Amore/ed in quel punto che madonna vide.' (Before my eyes I see the heart and the grieving soul that are slain, that die from a blow that Love gave them and at that point when they saw my lady, 4-6). The evidence that this description is delivered after the ability to see has been damaged, and therefore in the dark, lies, I claim, in the fact that the verb 'vedere' is conjugated in the present when referring to the hallucinatory display of the heart, but in the preterit when referring to the observation of the woman: 'in quel punto che madonna vide.' In other words, the actual capacity to see dates back to the phase preceding the moment in which amorous glance and blindness coincide chronologically ('in quel punto'), and anticipate the failing of the imaginative process. Once the bodily functions of the lover have collapsed, the lexical choice changes, and the lover doesn't 'see' any longer, he can only 'sense': 'Lo su' gentil spirito che ride,/questi è colui che mi si fa sentire,/lo qual mi dice: «E' ti convien morire».' (Her noble spirit that laughs is the very one that makes itself heard by me, that tells me: 'You will have to die'.) The geography of the ballad is strictly limited to the inside of the body. The desire for the other poets' compassion regards a condition that, likewise, is not visible from the outside: 'Se voi *sentiste* [emphasis mine] come 'l cor si dole,/dentro dal vostro cor voi tremereste:/...' (If you could sense how the heart grieves, within your hearts you would tremble.) The same emphasis on 'sentire,' vs. 'vedere,' is found in the last stanza, which is also crucial to my conclusion—weeping in Cavalcanti's *Rime* consists, as the physician concludes, of a mechanical phenomenon of sight impairment. In his *Canon* Avicenna begins the paragraph by discussing the causes underlying the imaginative faculty, the *imaginationum causae*, and employs the terms *colores* and *sentiuntur*, which Cavalcanti includes in his stanza ('sì tosto come questa donna sente,'; 'ch'oltra non puote color discovrire').[26] In Cavalcanti's description, the tears produced by the brain make a conduit ('fanno una via'); pushing their way through the channels of the *spiritus visivus*, they obstruct the flow of the *spirit*, and therefore the conveyance of the image. The image carried by the *spiritus visivus* is 'dolente' and, struggling, enters the lover's eyes 'debilmente.' Ballad XIX concludes with the final effect of the hindered flow of the visual spirit through the eyes' channels. Colors are not visible, and the production of the image is interrupted: 'ch'oltre non puote color discovrire/che 'l 'maginar vi

---

[26] 'Sunt colores qui sentiuntur coram visu ac ipsi sint misti in aere, & causa in eis est statio rei non perviae inter glacialem [the adjective 'glacialis' indicates here the state of coagulation of the ocular membrane] & inter ea quae vident' *Imaginativa (virtus). Imaginationum causae sunt colores quibus sentiuntur coram visu*, APPENDIX.

si possa finire' (it can not reveal any color beyond that which imaging could complete from it.).

By impeding the process of imagination, the mechanical dimming of the eyes impairs language production. Maimed in his ability to retain images, at times even in his ability to receive them, the lover is incapable of producing abstractions, therefore concepts, and is left with a pre-rational language. This language defers to the body's affections and is overturned. More specifically, Cavalcanti alters rhetorical rules by subjecting them to the same darkness into which the love experience plummets. In order to demonstrate this radical change, Cavalcanti transforms *ornatus* into darkness, that is, into tears which disable vision. By definition *ornatus* consists of the embellishment of the text through colors, as explained at the beginning of the chapter dealing with *ornatus* of Boncompagno's *Rhetorica Novissima*.[27] The outcome of the 'accidente fero,' explained in *Donna me prega* through the metaphor of the diaphanous as the predestined inability to have access to an intellectual activity, has consequences upon language, and on the same metaphoric ground: the potentiality of the diaphanous that, when transformed into actuality, necessarily becomes darkness, corresponds to the *ornatus* made of tears in the *Rime*. The colors of language are turned into blindness. Language is affected by the body in as much as the body is acted upon by Love.

Cavalcanti experiments with suggestions drawn from the tradition, whose import he broadens and radicalizes. The dispatch of 'saluti e dolze pianto' that Giacomo da Lentini describes in his canzone *Dal core mi vene*—'e mandovi infratanto/saluti e dolze pianto:/[eo] piango per usagio:/già mai non rideragio/mentre non vederagio/lo vostro bel visagio'[28]—portends a bolder endeavor on the part of Cavalcanti, as if the voice expressed by the Notary were awaiting perfected results, to wit, a language whose expressive tools lie tout-court in the physiological manifestations of pain. Cavalcanti takes the 'saluti' that in the same line the Notary had combined with the 'dolze pianto' and fully expands the linguistic potential of that allusion. By taking to its extreme consequences Giacomo da Lentini's indication, he founds a poetic language entirely made of tears, sighs and trembling, with which the body speaks.

---

[27] 'De adornationibus. Incipit prologus. Ea quae serenant et clarificant dictamina oratorum merito debent adornationes vel colores ab omnibus appellari; quia discolorata est oratio quam adornatio aliqua non colorat.' Boncompagni, vol. II, pp. 251-297.
[28] Giacomo da Lentini, *Dal core mi vene*, Panvini, p. 40.

I conclude my inquiry into the tradition anticipating Cavalcanti's rhetoric of the body with a text that might announce the 'dolenti' writing tools on Guido's desk. It is the Sonnet by Rinaldo d'Aquino, *Un oseletto che canta d'amore*, in which once more the focus is on the tears descending from the heart, but whose final effect allows a wide net of references to the repertory of Guido to surface:

> Un oseletto che canta d'amore,
> sento la not<t>e far sì dulzi versi,
> che me fa mover un'aqua dal core
> e ven a gl[i] ogli, nè pò ritenersi
> che no sparga fora cum tal furore,
> che di corrente vena par che versi;
> et i' pensando che cosa è l'amore,
> si *zeto* fora suspiri diversi.
>
> Considerando la vita amorosa
> di l'oselet<t>o che cantar no fina,
> la mia gravosa pena porto in pace:
> fera pos<s>anza ne l'amor reposa,
> c'ogn'amador[e] la dot<t>a e[d] inclina,
> e dona canto e planto a cui li place.[29]

(I hear in the night a little bird singing of love, and making verses so sweet, that he makes water move from my heart, which comes to my eyes and I can not hold inside, so that it spreads out furiously, almost as if it came out of a vein, and I, thinking about what love is, give diverse sighs. Pondering the love life of the little bird, that does not stop singing, my anguish is pacified: the fierce power of love rests, [the power] which guides any lover, and donates song and cry to those who like it.)

These fourteen lines suggest the possibility for a more fully developed rhetoric of passion. Here the voices of the body on which Cavalcanti's poems bestow a new poetic status make their first appearance. The first reference is in line 1: 'l'oseletto che canta d'amore' in the incipit resembles the 'cantar d'augelli e ragionar d'amore' included in the Plazer listed in Cavalcanti's Sonnet III. Further, 'versi' (line 2) are attributed to the 'oseletto.' In addition to the implied simile of the poet/'oseletto', lines 1 and 2 suggest a correspondence between the inarticulated voice of the animal and the poet's work, and point the way to a new rhetoric. The voices of the body also surface—not only 'l'aqua dal core' which signals and speaks of the condition of love, but, also and foremost, the rising from the heart of the

---

[29] Ibid., p. 118.

'suspiri diversi,' whose being 'diversi' indicates the possibility for a morphology of the body's expressions. The emphasis on these new expressive tools significantly concludes the sonnet, with the recalling of tears this time in close *junctura* with 'canto:' 'e dona canto e planto a cui li place.' Rinaldo d'Aquino accords both terms, the 'pianto' as well as the 'canto,' a new poetic value, the surmounting of a customary expressive horizon in poetic language.

Cavalcanti takes these anticipations to their extreme consequences. The lover's weeping does not simply anticipate the following lines; it virtually replaces those lines, and becomes the privileged message of the communication of love together with the other signs of the passion upsetting the lover's body.[30] All of them symbolize, 'in figura,' the essence of the venture of 'one who is dying in dismay.'[31] This venture does not spare the words of poetry themselves. Even when they seem to be resurrected as a dominant message in the envoi of Ballad XXXIV, they are at once clothed on the grounds of the characteristics of the same symptoms of love distressing the lover's body.[32]

V.3 Guido and Dante

Vernacular Italian poetry—according to Gianfranco Contini's conclusive argumentation in his *Introduction* to Dante's *Rime*—originates in the literary project whose *raison d'etre* was built around the idea of friendship.[33] At the

---

[30] Tears and sighs are often combined in the *Rime*: 'L'anima mia dolente e paurosa/piange ne[l]i sospir' che nel cor trova,/sì che bagnati di pianto escon fòre.' (XVII); 'Lagrime ascendon de la mente mia,/sì tosto come questa donna sente,/che van faccendo per li occhi una via/per la qual passa spirito dolente,/...' (XIX); '[Era in penser d'amor quand'i' trovai/due foresette nove.]/.../Elle con gli occhi lor si volser tanto/che vider come 'l cor era ferito/e come un spiritel nato di pianto/era per mezzo de lo colpo uscito.' (XXX); 'I' sento pianger for li miei sospiri,/quando la mente di lei mi ragiona;/e veggio piover per l'aere martiri/che struggon di dolor la mia persona,/...' (XXXI).
[31] 'Questi sono in figura/d'un che si more sbigottitamente.' IX, 43-56.
[32] XXXIV, 25-31.
[33] 'Il dolce stile è la scuola che contiene con maggior consapevolezza e buona grazia il senso della collaborazione a un'opera di poesia oggettiva, e insomma la scuola che più ha il senso della scuola. [...]. Il sonetto *Guido, i' vorrei che tu Lapo ed io* giustamente s'interpreta per solito come prodotto tipico del gusto stilnovistico, non però in quanto si estragga da questa lirica il motivo dell'evasione fatata verso esotiche lontananze, [...], ma in quanto quella fuga verso un mondo irreale si dovrebbe compiere affettuosamente fra amici stretti, con le loro belle, e in questa vicinanza, fatta più calda dalla sua natura immaginativa, i desideri sarebbero gli stessi, e la voglia di stare insieme crescerebbe. Assoluta separazione dal reale che si converte in amicizia,

same time the tradition that evolves from this school finds its origin in a dispute. The dispute that on board of the imaginary vessel Dante longs for in his celebrated sonnet—'Guido, i' vorrei che tu e Lapo ed io/fossimo presi per incantamento,/e messi in un vasel ch'ad ogni vento/per mare andasse al voler vostro e mio'—destroys the fellowship of the two most renowned companions of that select community, Guido Cavalcanti and Dante Alighieri. Their pledge is clearly stated in the *Vita Nova*, where Dante repeatedly identifies Guido as his 'primo amico,' making the initial intensity of the bond unmistakable. The development of their dispute, like much of the cultural scene of those decades for modern readers, is, however, blurry and largely conjectural.

The 'prima amicizia' of Italian literature ('prima' both chronologically speaking and for the entity of its consequences, which reverberate throughout the entire Italian literary tradition) is shaken by a crisis that is difficult to reconstruct fully. Following the deterioration of their fellowship, the modes of communication between Guido and Dante are set down by the latter in *Inferno* X. The only canto in the *Commedia* where Guido Cavalcanti is directly evoked in reference to the emotional climate produced by the Stilnovistic friendship[34] is constructed around a lacuna. The infernal conversation in which Dante engages Guido's father, Cavalcante, barely begins before it is interrupted by the ruthless Farinata and fogged by reticences and silences that generate crucial misunderstandings (not only among the characters speaking on the scene, but also between the text and its readers). As John Freccero has observed,[35] the pilgrim and his former

---

questo è il contenuto autentico della lirica; e l'amicizia è l'elemento patetico definitorio di stil nuovo.' Contini, *Introduzione*, in Dante Alighieri, *Rime*, p. LVIII.

[34] In *Purgatorio* XI, (97-99) Guido's evocation is linked to a literary frame: 'Così ha tolto l'uno a l'altro Guido/la gloria della lingua; e forse è nato/chi l'uno e l'altro caccerà del nido.'

[35] 'Il tempo è essenza per un aristotelico, accidente per il cristiano, poiché essi differiscono profondamente nella loro concezione dell'effetto del tempo sul soggetto, cioè sull'anima. [...]. Cavalcante, presumibilmente un aristotelico radicale come suo figlio, crede che l'anima muoia con il corpo, ragione per cui egli è qui, dopotutto, con i seguaci di Epicuro: "che l'anima col corpo morta fanno". Il tempo perfetto si presta ad entrambe le polarità: un aoristo in un verbo di aspetto imperfetto, usato in relazione ad un soggetto ora morto, od un semplice passato in un verbo di aspetto perfetto. Nel secondo caso il verbo è completo e finito; nel primo, è Guido stesso.' Freccero, *Ironia e mimesi: il disdegno di Guido*, p. 51. In her study, Ardizzone resumes the debated lines to decisively pin down how, via their grammatical tools, Guido and Dante define their opposite views: 'Both Dante and Cavalcanti seek the ontological implications of their tools. For Cavalcanti, the absolute is located in the field of accidentality and matter, of which the human soul is part; for Dante, the absolute and the human soul are related to the

friend's father, in their tortured communication, face a temporal misconception which ultimately produces disruptive gaps in the text. The evocation of Guido, the main, albeit absent, character, stands out against the background of a torn web of references. Scholars inquiring into the break-up of Guido and Dante are forced to look for reasons in the indirect dialogue between the two poets who, with the exception of the *Vita Nova* and a few sonnets of correspondence,[36] fulfill the Stilnovistic pledge by keeping their debate active even as they cease to confront one another directly. I reconstruct a portion of that lacunose dialogue by citing Cavalcanti's *Rime* and a few excerpts from the *Vita Nova* and *Inferno* VIII. In my reading, I arrange the texts in order to reproduce a 'ragionar d'amore' between the two poets around a specific theme, namely the use of the symptoms of Love, and especially tears, as tools for poetic communication.

In the *Vita Nova* the most critical references to Guido Cavalcanti are found in chapters 15 and 16. In chapter 15 Dante mentions Guido through the telling of a dream, an 'ymaginatione,' the protagonist of which, together with Love and Beatrice, is the 'gentil donna, la quale era di famosa bieltade e fue già molto donna di questo mio primo amico' (a gentle lady, who was famously beautiful and was the much beloved lady of this foremost of my friends), Giovanna. In the dream, Love points the two women out to Dante and explains the reason for their order of appearance (Giovanna first, then Beatrice) through an etymology: Guido (whom Love inspires to bestow names) has given Giovanna the name of 'Primavera' not because of her beauty, 'secondo che altri crede' (as people believe), but because she anticipates ('Prima-verrà') the true apparition of Beatrice. Without much effort, the reader can infer a similar relation for the two women's lovers, reading Guido as performing the allegorical function of John the Baptist, since, like John the Baptist, Guido is a precursor of the major figure, Dante. In chapter 16, which I have recalled in IV.2, Dante makes a stylistic digression which serves to justify his decision to use images apparently risible, specifically the personification of Love who laughs and talks in the dream he just recounted. Those images, Dante explains, stand out as an example of rhetorical color (that which 'colors' the text through figures of

---

permanent world of substance and form.' Ardizzone, *Guido Cavalcanti. The Other Middle Ages*, p. 70.

[36] With regard to the literary correspondence between the two, Dante is the receiver of six sonnets by Guido Cavalcanti: XXXVI; XXXVII; XXXVIII; XXXIX; XL; XLI, and the author of *A ciascun alma presa*, and *Guido, i'vorrei che tu Lapo ed io*.

speech), and they are sanctioned by the models he finds in classical poets. However, Dante adds, the embellishment of the text through figures of speech is allowed only to those vernacular poets who are able to unveil the meaning of the figures with which they color their texts, such as Guido and himself. To support his statement that select vernacular poets are allowed a wider stylistic license than prose writers, Dante concludes with a few illustrious quotes taken from various *auctoritates* that are mainly relevant to the prosopopeia, the figure of speech which was the starting point for his digression (Love walking, laughing and talking during the 'ymaginatione' of chapter 15).

My investigation here into the two authors' texts is conducted around the subject that Dante indicates as decisive in his relationship with Guido: the employment of figures of speech. Among the figures of speech, I consider the use of love's *signa ex parte corporis*, its external symptoms, as signs of poetic language. In particular, I focus here on tears and their expressive function in the *Vita Nova*—although the motif is just as important in the *Divine Comedy*, where Francesca da Rimini, Cavalcante Cavalcanti, and Count Ugolino are introduced by the syntagma 'dire piangendo.' I claim that the topic of tears speaking in the poet's stead is one of the marks of the exclusive pact binding together Guido and Dante in the *Vita Nova*. However, it is also a crucial cause of the later rupture in the two poets' communication. The subject matter strikes me as notable not only given its vast relevance as regards the early *corpus* of Dante's work, but also thanks to a further reference in the *Commedia*.

Following the statement he makes in the *Vita Nova*, Dante reinforces in the *Commedia* the mastery of figures of speech as one of the cruxes of his dialogue with Guido, thereby providing the reader with more information about the development of that querelle. I am referring here to the episode in *Inferno* VIII. Whilst crossing the Stygian fifth circle, Dante faces, among the wrathful, Filippo Argenti's weeping spirit. This episode has long engaged scholars mainly in tracing the possible biographical reasons behind Dante's unusually violent reaction. Leaving aside the hypotheses arising from the excessive verbal response of the pilgrim, who almost sounds like one of the damned,[37] I am interested in the literary echoes of the episode. The dialogue

---

[37] Daniel Donno recapitulates the critical contributions that investigate Dante's unusual lost of temper, especially after the dialogue: 'E io: "Maestro, molto sarei vago/di vederlo attuffare in questa broda,/prima che noi uscissimo dal lago." ' *Inferno*, VIII, 52-54. Dante is generally

between Dante and the spirit is fairly dry, with Filippo sharply uttering less than a hendecasyllable, which is enough to recall, *in absentia*, the presence of Guido Cavalcanti. 'Chi se' tu che vieni anzi ora?' Filippo asks. To which Dante replies: 'S'i vegno, non rimango; ma tu chi se', che sì se' fatto brutto?' Filippo's answer and closing of the dialogue: 'Vedi che son un che piango.' (And while we steered across the stagnant channel, before me stood a sinner thick with mud, saying: "Who are you, come before your time?" And I to him: "I've come, but I don't stay; but who are you, who have become so ugly?" He answered: "You can see—I'm one who weeps.) I have singled out Filippo's lines to point to their echoing of two of Cavalcanti's *incipit*, respectively from Sonnet IV: 'Chi è questa che vèn ch'ogn om la mira/.../?' (Filippo: 'Chi se' tu che vieni anzi ora?') and from Ballad X: 'Vedete ch'i' son un che vo piangendo.' (Filippo: 'Vedi che son un che piango.'). The surfacing of Guido's voice in the wrathful spirit's words suggests a correspondence between Cavalcanti's *Rime* and *Inferno* VIII, and indicates weeping as on of the issues around which the Guido and Dante debate revolves.

    The point I wish to make here is that by echoing Cavalcanti's voice behind Filippo's muddy face, Dante equates the figure of the wrathful and weeping spirit to that of Guido. Dante's labeling of Filippo as 'one who weeps' does not refer exclusively to the tears induced by the smoke pouring from the Stygian marsh—an easily decipherable metaphor of the fumes fogging the mind of the wrathful and the melancholic according to the medical indications of the times.[38] More precisely, Filippo's tears in the *Commedia* reveal the intersection of Love—according to Cavalcanti's theory—and wrath. In other words, Filippo's lines reinforce Dante's

---

rehabilitated by recalling the distinction he makes in *Purgatorio* (XVII 68-69) between good and bad wrath. Donno, *Dante's Argenti: episode and function*.
[38] The connection between melancholy and wrath is indicated in one of the pseudo-Aristotelian *Problemata*, XXX 1, which portrays men affected by *calida* melancholy as intellectually outstanding as well as easily moved to anger and desire ('[...] si autem fuit [colera nigra] multa et calida, fiunt maniaci et boni ingenii ad discendum, amorosi et cito mobiles ad iram et ad alios anime affectus.') The same section of the *Problemata* points at the 'fumosity' or 'smokeness' of black bile, which is what darkens and saddens moods of the melancholic (see: Wack, pp. 12-13.) Medical literature often associates 'ira' (wrath) with heat: 'Ira namque vehementer calefacit & tristitia multum exiccat' (*Ira. Ira calefacit*, APPENDIX); 'Sanguis autem grossus & turbidus & additae caliditatis disponit ad tristitiam & ad iram etiam perdurantem. Ad tristitiam quidem quia generatur ex eo spiritus turbidus, ad iram vero quia velociter inflammatur propter caliditatem suam; quod autem efficit perdurantem est spissitudo eius.' (*Ira. Ira est modus ad expellendum*, APPENDIX.)

perspective: in *Donna me prega* Cavalcanti theorizes Love in its pathological version, as the *amor hereos* that medical literature included in its case histories and treated as the expression of a pathological lack of measure.[39] It is Love as degeneration, a steady and irrepressible *cogitatio* fixed upon a mental image, explained through an alteration of the virtues operating within the ventricles of the brain, in particular that of the *virtus estimativa* and (because of its contiguity to it) of the *virtus imaginativa*.[40] Dante depicts Cavalcanti as a natural philosopher whose conclusions about love are that it is a psychological deterioration assimilated to melancholy and, precisely, wrath, on the grounds of similar symptoms, weeping among them.

In *Inferno* VIII, Filippo Argenti's tears therefore bring together two pathologies, wrath and love. The connection is made clear by Cavalcanti himself. In the fourth stanza of *Donna me prega*,[41] following the indications of his scientific sources, he cites wrath as one of the consequences of Love, when Love is 'oltra misura – di natura':

> La nova - qualità move sospiri,
> e vol ch'omo miri – 'n non formato loco,
> destandos' ira la qual manda foco
>   (imaginar nol pote om che nol prova),
> [...]
>
> (The new quality provokes sighs, and it obliges man to gaze at an unformed place, arousing one's anger that gives off fire.)

I want to suggest here that the wrathful and weeping spirit of Filippo Argenti whom the pilgrim meets in the *Commedia* is the figura of Guido Cavalcanti. The infernal character not only emphasizes Cavalcanti's conception that love corresponds to wrath. The infernal Filippo Argenti also embodies another important indication: it is through the rhetorical procedure of employing tears as a metaphor of poetic production that Dante distances himself from Guido. Both poets, in the excerpts that I've

---

[39] Massimo Peri summarizes the medical tradition around this topic in his chapter *Amor hereos* (Peri, pp. 23-41).
[40] The source is Arnaldo da Villanova: *De Amore Heroico*. Massimo Peri quotes the passages where Villanova indicates the psychological (as opposed to humoral) nature of love sickness. Ibid., pp. 31-32.
[41] In relation with the triangulation wrath/melancholy/love see Tonelli, pp. 63-117. Tonelli recalls De Robertis' glosses to the first tercet of *Guata, Manetto* (where 'niquità' has to be read as 'wrath') and widens medical sources including Hildegard of Bingen, to whom she attributes new relevance among Dante's sources.

compared here, identify tears as a symptom of the psychological condition which is a prerequisite to poetry: love. Both poets employ tears tout-court as poetic locution; however, the conclusions they draw on the relation of weeping and poetry are very different. While Guido treats weeping as a sign of congestion, as we have seen in the previous pages, for Dante tears are a sign of melting, or fluidification. The 'speaking tears' in Cavalcanti's poetry cause a mechanical phenomenon of obstruction, which, following the Averroistic ideology that lies beneath the lines, compromises the visual process and disconnects it from the intellectual elaboration of the image. In the end it is this obstruction that threatens the author's rhetorical capacity. In Dante's text, on the contrary, tears are a phenomenon of fludification, as I will demonstrate in the following examples. It is in that capacity that tears are related to poetry making. I am referring here to a specific passage, when the pilgrim is at the end of his ascent to the top of the mountain of Purgatory, and he describes the painful melting of his own icy heart in the presence of Beatrice (the pilgrim's heart stands on the top of Purgatory as the counterpart of the infernal frozen heart of the Earth: the latter is eternal, the former is open to a transformation and to a different destiny). The thawing of the heart[42] triggers the topos of the sequence of sighs and tears, the 'ragionar d'amore' before a true object of praise, Beatrice. Here follow the lines from canto XXX which conclude the second cantica and foretell of love as the path of knowledge it will become in the *Paradiso*:

> Sì come neve tra le vive travi
> per lo dosso d'Italia si congela,
> soffiata e stretta da li venti schiavi,
>
> poi, liquefatta, in sé stessa trapela,
> pur che la terra che perde ombra spiri,
> sì che par foco fonder la candela;
>
> così fui sanza lagrime e sospiri
> anzi 'l cantar di quei che notan sempre
> dietro a le note de li etterni giri;
>
> ma poi che 'ntesi ne le dolci tempre
> lor compatire a me, più che se detto

---

[42] The Dantesque 'melting' of the heart relates to the mystical metaphor of the *liquatio cordis*, which has, among its sources, the Book of Psalms 21, 15: 'Sicut aqua effussus sum [...]. Factus est cor meum tamquam cera liquescens.' For the 'liquid' metaphors produced around this topic see: Pozzi, pp. 190-226.

avesser : «Donna, perché sì lo stempre?»,

lo gel che m'era intorno al cor ristretto,
spirito e acqua fessi, e con angoscia
de la bocca e de li occhi uscì del petto.[43]

(Even as snow, among the sap-filled trees along the spine of Italy will freeze when gripped by gusts of the Slavonian winds, then, as it melts, will trickle through itself—that is, if winds breathe north from shade-less lands—just as, beneath the flame, the candle melts; so I, before I'd heard the song of those whose notes always accompany the notes of the eternal spheres, was without tears and sighs; but when I heard the sympathy for me within their gentle harmonies, as if they'd said: "Lady, why shame him so?"—then did the ice that had restrained my heart become water and breath; and from my breast and through my lips and eyes they issued—anguished.)

The same theme of poetic production performed through tears and sighs has extraordinary recurrences in the pages of the *Vita Nova*. Tears, in particular, are mentioned or directly described in 15 out of the 31 poems,[44] and the protagonist is portrayed as crying in 10 of the 31 chapters.[45] Dante is not the only weeping character. The natural spirit cries in chapter 1, in the surrender of the spirits at the first appearance of Beatrice. Love cries when he appears in three of Dante's 'ymaginationes': chapter 1, in the dream which gives rise to the first sonnet, *A ciascun alma presa e gentil core;* chapter 5, since Dante cannot yet partake in the perfect circularity which distinguishes Love: 'Ego tamquam centrum circuli, cui simili modo se habent circumferentie partis; tu autem non sic;' and in the canzone *Donna pietosa e di novella etate* (chapter 14), crying with Dante at the premonitory vision of Beatrice's death. The chorus of women cries when the young companion of Beatrice dies (chapter 3); Beatrice cries at her father's death (chapter 13); the chorus of women, bemoaning the 'lady, young and gentle,' cries around Dante who is painfully dreaming of Beatrice's death, as do the sun and the stars, reddened by tears as if they were eyes: 'le stelle si mostravano di colore ch'elli mi facea giudicare che piangessero;' (the stars appeared of a color that made me think that they wept, chapter 14); the canzone, finally, cries in the envoi of *Gli occhi dolenti* (chapter 20).

---

[43] *Purgatorio* XXX, 85-99.
[44] *A ciascun alma presa è gentil core; O voi che per la via d'Amor passaste; Piangete, amanti, poiché piange Amore; Tutti li miei pensier' parlano d'Amore; Voi che portate la sembianza umile; Se' tu colui che ch'ài tractato sovente; Donna pietosa e di novella etate; Gli occhi dolenti per pietà del core; Venite a 'ntender li sospiri miei; Era venuta nella mente mia; Videro gli occhi miei quanta pietate; Color d'amor e di pietà sembianti; L'amaro lagrimar che voi faceste; Lasso, per forza di molti sospiri; Deh, peregrini, che pensosi andate.*
[45] Chapters 3, 5, 7, 13, 14, 19, 20, 24, 25, 28.

In its frequent appearance, weeping is directly related in many passages of the *Vita Nova* to poetic production. The text combines tears falling and lines assembling as events bound by a tight chronological sequence or by a causative relationship that is made as immanent as one of direct assimilation—not only do tears pre-figure poetry, they become poetry. The characteristics of this phenomenon and the frequency of its occurrence indicate that tears are what make the assembly of the prosimetrum possible; they are the crucial tool that in the laboratory of the *Vita Nova* gives rise to the text. The speaking function of tears is highlighted in a few passages where, as mentioned above, tears are not only the prerequisite for love poetry but also, tout-court, its expression. In chapter 25 Dante sets forth his encounter with the Pietosa (the 'compassionate Lady') revealing the relation of contiguity and causality by pairing tears and poetry:

> E certo molte volte non potendo lagrimare né disfogare la mia tristitia, io andava per vedere questa pietosa donna, la quale pareva che tirasse le lagrime fuori delli miei occhi per la sua vista. E però mi venne volontà di dire anche parole parlando a llei, e dissi questo sonetto, lo quale comincia *Colore d'amore*; ed è piano, senza dividerlo, per la sua precedente ragione.
>
> (And certainly often, unable to weep or relieve my sadness, I went to see this compassionate lady, who seemed to draw tear from my eyes by her sight. And so I felt the desire to write some words, addressing her, and I wrote this sonnet, which begins *Colore d'amore*; and it is clear without dividing it, because of the previous account.)

Three passages make it explicit that Dante articulates his resolution to construct the 'libello' precisely while he is crying. The first passage is in chapter 3, on the occasion of the death of Beatrice's young companion, when the women are weeping and Dante, while not restraining himself, conceives a literary project: 'anzi piangendo mi propuosi di dicere alquante parole della sua morte' (rather, weeping, I resolved to write some words about her death). After the episode of the mockery in chapter 7, Dante takes shelter in the 'room of tears' and while there he resolves to write: 'E in questo pianto stando propuosi di dire parole, nelle quali parlando a llei significassi la cagione del mio trasfiguramento.' (And in my weeping, I resolved to write words in which, addressing her, I would express the cause of my transfiguration). Finally in chapter 20, with the background of the city mourning for the death of Beatrice, Dante raises his private lament, which anticipates a canzone: 'Poi che li miei occhi ebbero per alquanto tempo lagrimato, e tanto affaticati erano che non poteano disfogare la mia tristitia, pensai di voler disfogarla con alquante parole dolorose. E però propuosi di fare una canzone, nella quale piangendo ragionassi di lei, per cui tanto dolore distruggitore era fatto di vita mia;' (After my eyes had for some time wept, and were so tired that they could not relieve my sorrow, I thought I would relieve it with some sorrowful verses; so I resolved to write a canzone in which, weeping, I would speak about her because of whom so much pain had become the destroyer of my soul).[46]

The 'sorrowful verses' to which Dante alludes in the last quoted passage are the first lines of the canzone that follows, *Gli occhi dolenti per la pietà del core* (chapter 20), which opens with a double preterition, both physiological and rhetorical: if tears perform the function of elocution their nonappearance also threatens the appearance of the text. In the opening lines of the canzone, Dante announces his inability to weep and give vent to his pain since his eyes have been drained by their long shedding of tears: 'Gli occhi dolenti per pietà del core/ànno di lagrimar sofferta pena,/sì che vinti son rimasi omai.' (The eyes grieving for the heart's pity have from weeping suffered pain so that overwhelmed they desist in the end). His eyes are left 'per vinti di lagrimar' (that is, as Gorni glosses *ad locum,* 'han cessato ormai di piangere'). However, this preliminary warning is overcome by the tears that do eventually appear. In fact, the text following the onset of weeping is imbued with tears since weeping is the condition naturally ascribed to gentle hearts, and is, furthermore, their mark of distinction amidst the historical circumstances of Beatrice's death—'e dicerò di lei piangendo' (and I will write of her as I weep) Dante says—since 'Chi no la piange, quando ne ragiona,/core à di pietra sì malvagio e vile,/ch'entrar no i puote spirito benigno' (Who weeps not for her, when speaking of her, has a heart of stone so wicked and base that no good spirit can enter it). To complete the action of weeping in the process of verse making, tears finally influence the canzone itself, which cries, while it is dismissed in the envoi in lines mentioned above: 'Pietosa mia canzone, or va piangendo,/e ritruova le donne e le donzelle/a cui le tue sorelle/erano usate di portar letitia/e tu, che se' figliuola di Tristitia,/vatten disconsolata a star con elle.' (My rueful canzone, now go, weeping; and find again the ladies and the maidens to

---

[46] A similar connection between tears and literary construction is worded in chapter 13, although tears and poetry are bound in it only indirectly. In that chapter Dante is weeping for Beatrice's father's death: 'Onde io poi pensando propuosi di dire parole, acciò che degnamente avea cagione di dire: nelle quali parole io conchiudesse tutto ciò che inteso avea da queste donne.' (Hence I later, thinking, resolved to write words, since I had a worthy reason to speak, in which I would include all I had heard from these ladies.)

whom your sisters were accustomed to offering delight; and you, who are a child of sadness,/go disconsolate to stay with them).

As we have seen earlier in this chapter, tears are included among the *signa ex parte corporis* engaged in their rhetorical capacities in Cavalcanti's *Rime*. Tears are largely employed in connection with the weeping lover, a topic which Cavalcanti inherits from the tradition of the Scuola Siciliana and originally elaborates by bending rhetoric to the rules of physiology and understanding tears as a sight impediment—unlike Giacomo da Lentini, who connects the release of tears to the lifting of a weight from the lover's heart. In the *Rime* tears often appear in combination with sighs. According to the indications of the medical literature, both tears and sighs—at times even consequential to one another[47]—are to be read as the external signs of the pathological conditions by which the lover is bound. In numerous passages of the *Rime*, Guido Cavalcanti insists on the inclusion of these two physiological phenomena, tears and sighs, among the symptoms of love and often binds them in a close sequence. Fully connected with the speaking capacity of the author, sighs naturally turn into tears and then into lines, as in Ballad XXXI (lines 11-12): 'I' sento pianger for li miei sospiri,/quando la mente di lei mi ragiona;' ('I feel my sighs weeping forth when my mind reasons to me about her,' and more references are included in the close reading of the previous pages).

The same sequence of sighs and tears as a physiological process presiding over a rhetorical construction is represented in the *Vita Nova*. In this connection, I quote a few lines from two poems, the two-headed Sonnet *Era venuta nella mente mia* (chapter 23) written for the circumstance of the one-year anniversary of Beatrice's death:

Amor, che nella mente la sentia,
s'era svegliato nel destructo core,
e dicea a' sospiri: «Andate fore!»,
per che ciascun dolente si partia.

---

[47] Sighs and tears are bound as two phases of the same phenomenon in Hildegard of Bingen *Causae et curae*: 'Et ita de humoribus illis, qui in homine sunt, velut amarus fumus per tristitiam egrediens circa cor spargitur, qui tabem, scilicet aquam de sanguine cordis et de sanguine aliarum venarum, cum excussione gemituum superat ac eam sic sursum per venas ducendo ad venulas cerebri quasi fumando mittit et per illlas ad ocuolos ducit, quia et oculi quandam cognationem ad aquam habent. Et ita aqua illa ex oculis fluit et hoc lacrimae sunt. Nam aqua lacrimarum hoc modo de sanguine hominis per suspiria gemituum extrahitur, velut semen hominis ex medulla et de sanguine eius educitur.' Hildegard von Bingen, p. 147. Peri quotes a few more excerpts from medical sources in which tears are explained as a blood by-product: Peri, pp. 59-60.

Piangendo uscivan for dello mio pecto
con una voce che sovente mena
le lagrime dogliose agli occhi tristi.

(Love, who in my mind perceived her, was awakened in the ravaged heart, and said to the sighs 'Go forth'; at which each one sadly departed. Weeping they issued forth from my breast with a voice that often calls up tears of grief to my sad eyes.)

and the Sonnet *Lasso per forza di molti sospiri* (chapter 28), which marks Dante's conversion back to Beatrice after the episode with the *Pietosa*:

Lasso, per forza di molti sospiri,
che nascon de' pensier' che son nel core,
gli occhi sono vinti, e non ànno valore
di riguardar persona che li miri;
e facti son che paion due disiri
di lagrimare e di mostrar dolore,
e spesse volte piangon sì ch'Amore
li 'ncerchia di corona di martiri.

(Alas! through the might of many sighs that issue from the thoughts that dwell in the heart, the eyes are vanquished and have not the strength to look on anyone who gazes upon them. And they have become such that they seem two desires to weep and display suffering, and oftentimes they cry so, that Love encircles them with the crown of martyrs.)

According to the physicians' discussion I recapitulated in IV.2, the shedding of sighs is a physiological necessity, to cool down the chambers of the heart, or to recover after having held one's breath while engaged in obsessive contemplation. Writing, likewise, is by statute a necessity, according to what is verbalized in the *Purgatorio* (XXIV, 52-54) where, with well known lines, Dante announces the existence of a new poetic school and of a new mode of writing, that is, to write from the imperious dictation of Love: 'E io a lui: «I' mi son un, che quando/Amor mi spira, noto, e a quel modo/ch'e' ditta dentro vo significando» ' (I answered: 'I am one who, when Love breathes in me, takes note; what he, within, dictates, I, in that way, without, would speak and shape.') The same nature-driven necessity is attributed to writing in the *Vita Nova*. In the lines of *Donne ch'avete intellecto d'amore* (chapter 10), the manifesto of the new self-celebrating poetry of 'lode,' poetry making is described as an 'isfogar la mente', a 'pouring out of the mind.'[48] The 'ragionar d'Amore' surges forth as the consequence of the

---

[48] 'Donne ch'avete intellecto d'amore,/i' vo' con voi della mia donna dire,/non perch'io creda sua laude finire,/ma ragionar per isfogar la mente./.../' (Ladies who have understanding of

excessive congestion within the pages of the 'book of memory'—'In quella parte del libro della mia memoria...'—from which Dante transcribes his 'libello'.

For both Cavalcanti and Dante, love semeiotics is composed of the characters of an alphabet. This notion belongs to a tradition represented by the poetry of Giacomo da Lentini, since the Notaio introduces in his work the image of the lady painted in his heart: 'In cor par ch'eo vi porti,/pinta come parete,/e non pare difore./' (It seems that I bear you in my heart depicted as you appear but outwardly nothing shows) and in doing so he articulates the dichotomy heart/body, indicating the latter as an external and manifest sign of the former, in the already quoted lines (see chapter II): 'Assai v'aggio laudato,/madonna, in tutte parti,/di bellezze c'avete./Non so se v'è contato/ch'eo lo faccia per arti,/ che voi pur v'ascondete:/sacciatelo per *singa* [emphasis mine]/zo ch'eo no dico a linga,/quando voi mi vedete'.[49] This promotion of the body to an expressive tool[50] initiated by Giacomo da

---

love, I wish to speak with you of my lady, not that I believe I may exhaust her praise, but to converse to pour out my mind) *Donne ch'avete intellecto d'amore*, 1-4. In the poems included in the *Vita Nova*, *sfogare* is related to writing in two more recurrences: *Venite a 'ntender li sospiri miei* (chapter 21): 'però che gli occhi mi sarebbon rei,/molte fiate più ch'io non vorria,/lasso, di pianger sì la donna mia,/che sfogasser lo cor, piangendo lei.' (because my eyes would be my debtors, many times more than I would desire, alas, of weeping for my lady, so as to relieve my heart, weeping for her.); and *Gli occhi dolenti per pietà del core* (chapter 20): 'Gli occhi dolenti per pietà del core/ànno di lagimar sofferta pena,/sì che per vinti son rimasi omai./Ora, sì voglio sfogar lo dolore/che a poco a poco alla morte mi mena,/convenemi parlar traendo guai.' (The eyes grieving for the heart's pity have from weeping suffered pain so that overwhelmed they desist in the end. Now, if I wish to relieve my grief which little by little leads me toward death, I must speak, dragging up woes.)

[49] 'I have praised you highly, my lady, in all places for the beauty you possess. I do not know if you have been told that I do it with artifice, for you always hide yourself. Learn from the outward signs what I shall tell you in words, when you see me.' Giacomo da Lentini, *Meravigliosamente*, 10-13; 46-54.

[50] 'Questa identificazione del linguaggio con la fisicità della persona implica, da una parte, la semeiotizzazione del corpo, dall'altra, la materializzazione della parola. È la via che conduce allo stilnovo e a Dante [...], cioè al potenziamento parallelo delle funzioni psichiche e degli strumenti espressivi. [...]. Vale la pena insistere su questo processo di promozione espressiva del corpo perché ad esso è legata, credo, la linea di sperimentazione principale della lirica medievale, nella quale il desiderio e la sua patologia rinviano immediatamente alla percezione del corpo come principio di sofferenza e quindi, per questo, come campo privilegiato di indagine ermeneutica e rappresentazione letteraria.' Pinto, p. 180. Franco Mancini's monograph includes interesting textual references to the distinction between *figura* and *persona* and indicates possible sources for the theme of the beloved's image painted in the heart. In particular, as a synonym for *figura*, he focuses on the term *insegna* (from Giacomo da Lentini *Or come pote sì gran donna intrare*) which, he claims, is directly derived from a scriptural source: 'Ed è proprio il

Lentini is fully elaborated by Guido and, up to a certain extent, by Dante, when the two authors delegate their communication to the phenomena caused by love's venture. In Guido's lines the *signa ex parte corporis* perform the 'ragionar d'amore' that the lover, given his pathological condition, can no longer perform;[51] in Dante's Sonnet *Lasso per forza di molti sospiri* (chapter 28), those *signa* carry the name of the 'Gentile' and the many words referring to the event of her death:

> Questi penseri, e li sospir' ch'io gitto,
> diventan nel cor sì angosciosi,
> ch'Amor vi tramortisce, sì lien dole;
>   però ch'elli ànno in lor, li dolorosi,
> quel dolce nome di madonna scripto,
> e della morte sua molte parole.

(These thoughts, and the sighs I send forth, become in the heart so anguished that Love there faints, so much does he suffer from them; for they have in themselves, the sorrowful ones, that sweet name of the lady inscribed, and of her death many words.)

Such similarities of topoi however, are explained neither by the theoretical conclusions drawn by the two authors about the nature of Love, nor by their final rhetorical solutions.

As an example, I compare here the different functions performed by the release of sighs. In Cavalcanti, such release stands for the lessening of the poet's rhetorical capacities to recount the love experience, which are reduced to a great extent by the internal battle of the spirits. Deprived of his verbal expression, he is forced to entrust communication to the anonymous and 'objective' voices resounding in the *Rime*, the voices that 'speak woe.' The same subject matter is elaborated differently by Dante, who in Sonnet *Spesse fiate vegnomi alla mente* (chapter 9) maintains control over the message, although the control is commended to his last 'spirto,' who survived as a result of its speaking of Beatrice:

> ch'Amor m'assale subitanamente,
> sì che la vita quasi m'abandona;

---

termine *insegna*, - rilevato anche da cesura - a svelarci (in sì ricco preludio a *Meravigliosamente*) la remotissima origine di quella che sarà la distesa metafora della donna dipinta nel cuore: origine che la clausola "poi porto *insegna* di tal creatura" consente di riconoscere nel versetto del *Cantico dei Cantici* (8, 6): "Pone me ut *signaculum* super cor tuum" che la Bibbia di Gerusalemme traduce: "Mettimi come sigillo sul tuo cuore".' Mancini, pp. 20-21.

[51] See, among many others, IV, 1-4, and VI, 1-4.

> campami uno spirto vivo solamente,
> e que' riman, perché di voi ragiona.
>
> (for Love assails me suddenly, so that life almost abandons me: there survives in me but one live spirit, and that remains because it speaks of you.)

The sighs that are released again in chapter 28, only after the conclusion of the episode with the 'Pietosa' episode, stand out as a sign of the recovery of language: they repeat the name of the woman. They do not relate, as in Cavalcanti, to the poet's death:[52]

> E dico che d'allora innanzi cominciai a pensare di lei sì con tutto lo vergognoso cuore, che li sospiri manifestavano ciò molte volte, però che quasi tutti diceano nel loro uscire quello che nel cuore si ragionava, cioè lo nome di quella gentilissima, e come si partio da noi.
>
> (And I say that from then on I began to think of her so much with all my shameful heart that my sighs manifested this many times; in fact, almost all of them said, in their issuing forth, what was said within my heart; that is, the name of that most gentle one, and that she had departed from us.)

Different conclusions distinguish Guido and Dante on the ground of the rhetorical functions of tears, as well. Four chapters in the *Vita Nova* are crucial for the reading of tears as poetic instruments, those in which Dante recounts his temporary infatuation with the 'Pietosa' (chapters 24-27). Dante first generally defines 'weeping compassion': 'Onde con ciò sia cosa che quando li miseri veggiono di loro compassione altrui più tosto si muovono a lagrimare, quasi come di sé stessi avendo pietate' (with that, because when the unhappy see that others have compassion for them, they are more quickly moved to tears, as if they had pity for themselves) and proceeds to describe a specific episode in which he feels the need to cry: 'Io senti' allora cominciare li miei occhi a volere piangere.' (I then felt my own eyes begin wanting to weep, chapter 24). The 'begin wanting to weep' is what leads to his being smitten with the 'Pietosa' since, according to the love symptomatology he experienced with Beatrice, tears stand as the proof of the authenticity—the 'nobiltà'—of an object of Love. The sight of the 'Pietosa' seems, at first, to be able to trigger and allow the poet to give vent to the internal pressure which is the effect of Love. Dante, in fact, looks for her with the precise intention of starting that chain reaction, of pressure and

---

[52] In Cavalcanti's *Rime* spirits speak the beloved's name in just one poem, the Ballad XXXIV, 25-28: 'Parole mie disfatt' e paurose,/là dove piace a voi di gire andate;/ma sempre sospirando e vergognose/lo nome de la mia donna chiamate.'

release, which is the necessary condition to the shaping of the text. The 'Pietosa', Dante tells us in chapter 25, 'parea che tirasse le lagrime fuori delli miei occhi' ('who seemed to draw tears from my eyes by her sight). Her misleading power is unveiled, however, at the moment when the author, in *Color d'amore e di pietà sembianti* (chapter 25), diagnoses his own expressive block, both physiological and rhetorical: 'E voi crescete sì lor [of his eyes] voluntate,/che della voglia si consumâr tutti,/ma lagrimar dinanzi a voi non sanno.' (And you so increase their longing that by this desire they are wholly consumed; but weep in your presence thay cannot). Regardless of the fact that the absence of tears demonstrates that the 'Pietosa' is not a true object of contemplation, Dante's eyes, by hypostatization, are autonomous of his mind's control. His eyes keep looking for the Pietosa until they finally rouse the author's invective against them, addressed as 'maladecti occhi' (cursed eyes) which stubbornly persist in the search for a false 'gentile.' In fact, his eyes remain dry before her because they have been sidetracked by their thoughtlessness ('vanità').[53] The Sonnet *L'amaro lagrimar che voi faceste* follows (chapter 26) in which the heart scolds the eyes, guilty of infidelity to the memory of the 'Gentilissima.' The sonnet records and announces as well the overcoming of the author's expressive impasse: the poem ends with the verb 'sospirare' which is not only a prelude to weeping, as showed in the examples above quoted, but also the manifesto of the style of the loda and an invitation to compose one. We read in *Tanto gentile e tanto onesta pare* (chapter 17): 'e par che della sua labbia si mova/un spirito soave pien d'amore/che va dicendo all'anima: sospira.' (And it seems that from her lips moves a spirit, soothing and full of love, that goes saying to the soul: sigh).

The same topic of an object of contemplation that is false (because sterile) is discussed in the following Sonnet *Gentil Pensiero che parla di voi* (chapter 27), in which takes place a dialogue between the heart and the soul (which, Dante tells us, stand for desire and reason). Resulting from reason's hostile take-over, a strong 'ymaginatione' arises: Beatrice appears, no longer related to historical circumstance, 'giovane in simile etade in quale prima la vidi' (she seemed young and of the same age as when I first saw her). She unerringly provokes the reappearance of the *signa ex parte corporis*, and thus, also that of writing. First sighs, then, tears: 'Per questo raccendimento de' sospiri si raccese lo sollenato lagrimare, in guisa che li miei occhi pareano due cose che desiderassero pur di piangere.' (Through this rekindling of my

---

[53] Here is Gorni's gloss to the term *vanitate* in a subsequent occurrence (28, 5): '*La vostra vanità è sempre un vizio del vedere. Ancora qui al c. 6 la colpa degli occhi è di aver vaneggiato.*'

sighs was rekindled my alleviated weeping in such a way that my eyes appeared to be two things that desired only to weep.)[54] Sighs and tears stand as the signs of a renovated writing capacity as if they were the inscribed pages that illustrate the author's painful venture, in the above-quoted lines from Sonnet *Lasso per forza di molti sospiri*: 'Questi pensieri, e li sospir' ch'io gitto,/.../ànno in lor, li dolorosi,/quel dolce nome di madonna scripto,/e de la morte sua molte parole.'

If the recovery of the ability to weep in Dante corresponds to the recovery of the capacity for composition, in Cavalcanti it has the opposite meaning. In a survey of the *Rime*'s medical sources conducted in the previous pages, I presented the medical indications according to which Cavalcanti elaborates the phenomenon of weeping as a cause of *oppilatio* (the exact medical term that describes a phenomenon of obstruction of the channels carrying the visual spirits from the eyes to the brain). This is why, in Guido, tears mark the conclusion of the visual process and of the compositional process. The difficult and painful moving of the visual spirit thwarted by tears in Ballad XIX indicates the limit of both vision and writing: the former is not elaborated intellectually, as the latter is confined within the body and has, accordingly, *signa ex parte corporis* as its tools. To this confinement Dante juxtaposes the pilgrim's tears, which, in the *Purgatorio* (XXXI, 16-21) herald the liquid naturalness of poetry making in the presence of the 'Gentilissima'. A bursting forth of words, unrestrained as the flight of an arrow from a drawn bow:

> Come balestro frange, quando scocca
> da troppa tesa, la sua corda e l'arco,
> e con men foga l'asta il segno tocca,
> sì scoppia' io sott'esso grave carco,
> fuori sgorgando lacrime e sospiri,
> e la voce allentò per lo suo varco.
>
> (Just as a crossbow that is drawn too taut snaps both its cord and bow when it is shot, and arrow meets its mark with feeble force, so, caught beneath that heavy weight, I burst; and I let tears and sigh pour forth; my voice had lost its life along its passage out.)

---

[54] *Vita Nova*, Chapter 28.

Appendix

I include here a list of terms from the *Liber Canonis*, followed by the corresponding textual passages. I selected the terms on the grounds established by Guido Cavalcanti's poetry: a reading of love as an experience included in the realm of perceptions. This *Appendix* constitutes a Cavalcantian analytical index of the *Canon* as well as a general footnote apparatus for the *Rime*. In part, this material has been employed for the close reading presented in Chapters III, IV, and V.

The edition is the following: Avicenna, *Liber Canonis de Medicinis Cordialibus Cantica*, Venetiis, apud Iuntas, 1582. The sequence of the sections referring to each term replicates the index of this edition.

ACCIDENTIA

accidens est res quae sequitur hanc dispositionem, quae est non naturalis, sive sit naturali contraria, sive non sit contraria, 28. D. 5.

accidens vocatur respectu suae essentiae aut comparatione eius cui accidit 28. D. 14

accidentia quae accidunt ex doloribus 42. B. 13
Dolor virtutem dissolvit & membra a suis propriis operationibus prohibet, adeo ut membra spiritualia ab aeris prohibeat attractione, aut eius destruat operationem & facit eum intersectum, aut frequentem & omnino non secundum naturalem cursum; & est cum in primis calefacit membra, postea infrigidat, propter illud, quod resolvit & fugat de spiritu & vita.

accidentium quedam sunt essentialia quaedam accidentalia 43. A. 3

accidentium a natura sine voluntate provenientium quaedam sunt quae excitant sensum & quaedam quae non excitant 43. B. 5

Ex cognitionibus vero quae habent ex motibus & quietibus, trahitur res quam modo narrabimus. Significationes vero, que sumuntur ex modo quietis, sunt sicut apoplexia, & epilepsia, & syncopis, & paralysis. & quae ex moto sumuntur sunt sicut horripilatio, & tremor, & singultus, & sternutatio, & oscitatio, & alices, & tussis, & saltus, & spasmus cum incipit spasmari. & earum sunt quaedam quae proveniunt ex operatione naturae principaliter, sicut singultus; & quaedam quae proveniunt ex operatione naturae accidentaliter, sicut spasmus & tremor.

ACTIO

Actio & passio ut succedat oportet ut sint agens & patiens bene disposita 434. C. 6

Et quando faciunt necessario virtutes agentes caelestes & virtutes patientes terrestres, humectationem vehementer aeri, elevantur vapores & fumi ad ipsum, & sparguntur in ipso & putrefaciunt eum cum caliditate debili, & quando fit aer secundum hunc modum, venit ad cor, quare corrumpit complexionem spiritus, qui est in ipso, & putrefit quod circundat ipsum de humiditate, & accidit caliditas egressa a natura & spargitur in corpore causa fluxibilitatis suae & fit febris pestilentialis. & comunicat multitudini hominum, qui iterum habent in seipsis proprietatem praeparationis. Agens enim solum cum pervenit & patienti non est praeparatio, non accidunt actio & passio. & praeparatio corporum ad illud in quo sumus de passione est, ut sint plena humoribus malis; nam munda non forsitan patiuntur ex illo & corpora debilia iterum patienta sunt ex ea, sicut illa, quae multiplicant coitum & corpora dilatatorum pororum humida multae balneationis.

actio cum ignoratur a quo procedit, scitur quod procedit vel a virtute naturali, vel ab animali, vel ab intellectiva, vel a virtute accidentali 560. G. 3

Cum ergo actio nullo attribuitur praedictorum, nec est manifesta ratio a qua procedat esse ipsius, putat quod omnia principia eius ignota sint, cum tamen non ita sit. Etenim intelligens, bene scit, quia procedit, vel a virtute naturali, vel animali, vel intellectiva, vel accidentali. Caetera, quae dicuntur super actione magnetis scilicet quod trahit ferrum cum calididitate sua, vel frigiditate, vel alia existente in ipso magnete [...] omnia inquam falsa sunt.

ANHELITUS
anhelitus motus aequalis naturalis vacui nocumento completur motu velaminis 258. E. 15

Anhelitus completur duobus motibus inter quos sunt duae morae, secundum quod res se habet in pulsu; nisi quia motus anhelitus est voluntarius, qui potest alterari cum voluntate a cursu naturali, & pulsus est naturalis purus. & intentio quidem in anhelitu est, ut impleat pulmonem aere frigido, donec praeparetur pulsibus cordis, & non cesset cor sumere ex eo aerem frigidum, & reddat ipsi vaporem fumosum, quousque accidant illi attractationi duae res: quarum una est conversio ipsius a frigiditate, cum calefactione eius quod ei vicinatur & eius quod ei commmiscetur; & altera est conversio ipsius a claritate sua, propterea quod admiscetur ei vapor fumosus: tunc enim removetur ab eo intentio, qua sit conveniens ad hoc ut extendatur pulsus ab eo; quare necessaria fit eius eductio & permutatio ipsius. [...] & quemadmodum in pulsu est magnus & parvus, & longus & brevis, & velox & tardus, & calidus & frigidus, & frequens & rarus, & fortis & debilis, & intercisus, & continuus, & spasmosus & tremulus, & parvae repletionis venarum, & multae earum, & est res vel dispositio diversitatis: & dispositio laudabilis, & dispositio illaudabilis, & omnibus illis sunt causae, & omnibus illis sunt significationes super rem aliquam, & est eis diversitas secundum complexiones, aetates & genera, & accidentia corporea & animalia, similiter anhelitui sunt istae res numeratae & quae sunt eis similia & unaquequae res earum habet causam, & omnis res ex eis habet significationem. Anhelitus igitur alius est magnus & alius est parvus; & alius est longus, & alius est brevis; & alius est velox, & alius est tardus; & alius est rarus, & alius est frequens [...] & est anhelitus eius plurimae interfectionis & reversionis & fit multae elevationis [...]. Et ex speciebus quidem anhelitus sunt quae habent nomina propria, sicut anhelitus intercisus [...]. & nocumenta quae accidunt in membris anhelitus & ex eis ingreditur nocumentum in anhelitu, aut sunt in membris anhelitus, aut in principiis eorum, aut in eis quae communicant cum vicinitate. & membra quidem anhelitus sunt epiglottis, & pulmo, & canam [...]. Membra autem communicantia cum vicinitate sunt sicut stomachus, & hepar, & matrix, & intestina [...]. Aut aegritudo officialis est paralysi & spasmo. Aut resolutio singularis ex scissione aut putrefactione aut ulceratione aut corrosione.

Aut ex apostemate frigido, aut calido, aut duro. Aut ex dolore. & tu quidem scivisti per illud quod narravi tibi, quod anhelitus est fortis significationis, & currit cursu pulsus, postquam tu observas in eo consuetudinem, sicut necesse est tibi, ut observes rem naturalem consuetam in pulsu etiam.

anhelitus dolentis in membris pectoris qualis est 260.H.1
Et sicut scivisti ex eis quae praeterierunt tibi ex me declaratio eius; ipse enim declinat ad parvitatem & brevitatem, & quandoque duplicatur, & quandoque est difficilis, & quandoque tardatur, quando non est inflammatio: & fit frequens, sicut scivisti. & sunt parvitas eius, & brevitas ipsius, plus quam eius tarditas: quoniam ducens ipsum ad retentionem & parvitatem dilatationis est plus quam ducens ipsum ad facilitatem; & ut noceatur cum magnitudine dilatationis vehementius, quam ut noceatur cum velocitate. Nam inflammatio cordis, & calefactio non excusant ex velocitate, quamvis laedatur cum ea.

ANIMALIS (VIRTUS)
Animalis virtus est una illarum quae deserviunt arti custodiendi sanitatem 56.G.4
Et quod custodiendi sanitatem ars existit illa quae corpus humanum perducit ad hanc aetatem, quae vocatur terminus vitae naturalis secundum observationem convenientium. Huius autem custodiae administrationi duae attributae sunt virtutes, quibus deservit medicus: una earum est naturalis, & vocatur nutritiva [...]. & altera est animalis, & ipsa est virtus pulsativa, quae restaurat quod ex spiritu resolvitur, cuius substantia est aerea & ignea.

Virtutis fortitudo est causa apertionis oppilationis & ruptionis abscessus, & expulsionis superfluitatum 318.G.3

Virtutes in anima sunt novem: scilicet visiva, auditiva, gustativa, tangitiva, olfactiva, motiva, imaginativa, & rationalis, & memoria 588.C.1

CEREBRUM
cerebrum est principium virtutis sentiendi & movendi 9E.16.F.10

cerebrum sive per se sive post cor habeat principium sentiendi existit principium actionum animalium 9. E. 14.

cerebrum suscipit calorem naturalem & spiritus a corde 9. D. 6.
De membri autem suscipientis & non tribuentis inventione non dubitamus: sicut caro est quae sentiendi virtutem vitae suscipit & non est alicuius virtutis principium, quam alii ullo modo tribuat. De aliis vero duabus divisionis partibus, in una earum, medici a magno philosophorum diversificati sunt. Philosophorum nanque magnus dixit quod membrum tribuens & non recipiens est cor: ipsum enim est omnium virtutum prima radix, & omnibus aliis membris suas tribuit virtutes, quibus nutriuntur, & vivunt, & quibus appraehendunt, & quibus moventur. Medici autem, & quidam primorum philosophorum, has virtutes in membris partiti sunt, & non dixerunt quod sit membrum tribuens & non suscipiens. & philosophi quidem sermo cum subtiliter certificatur, est veracior. Sed medicorum sermo, in primis cum attenditur, est magis manifestus. Postea in alia divisionis partes, diversificati sunt medici inter se, & philosophi inter se. Una enim secta dixit quod ossa & caro non sentientia & eorum similia non permanent nisi per virtutes proprias, quae sunt in eis quae non ab aliis principiis eis influxerunt, sed per illas virtutes, cum nutrimentum eis transmittitur, sibi sufficiunt; & neque ipsa alii rei virtutem tribuunt, neque etiam alium membrum eis aliam tribuit virtutem. Alia vero secta dixit, quod virtutis istae non sunt eis propriae; sed ab hepate & corde in generationis principio eis influxerunt, & in eis fixae permanserunt. [...] Cor quidem est principium virtutis vitae & cerebrum quidem est principium virtutis sentiendi & movendi, & hepar quidem est principium nutriendi.

cerebrum est frigidum 4. E. 6.
Vitae etenim principium sunt cor & spiritus: quae quidem ambo vehementer calida existunt ad superfluitatem declinantia & vita quidam existit per caliditatem & augmentum per humiditatem. Et etiam caliditas in humiditate existit & ab ea nutritur. Membra vero principialia sunt tria, sicut declarabimus, & ex eis quidem est unum frigidum, quod est cerebrum, cuius frigiditas non pervenit ad cordis & hepatis caliditatem temperandam. Et ex eis unum est siccum aut siccitati propinquum: & ipsum est cor; sed eius siccitas non pervenit

ad humiditatem cerebri & hepatis temperandam. Neque etiam cerebrum tantum est frigidum, neque cor tamen est siccum, sed cor comparatione aliorum duorum est siccum & cerebrum aliorum duorum comparatione est frigidum.

cerebri basis est os quod omnia alia ossa sustinet 11. D. 10.
Basis autem cerebri est os, quod omnia alia sustinet ossa, & vocatur basilare: quod quidem durum propter duo iuvamenta fuit creatum: unum est quod durities ad portandum iuvat, & aliud quod durum minus suscipit putrefactionem superfluitatum.

cerebrum est sedes virtutis animalis 25. H. 10.
Virtutum & operationum ad invicem, aliae ex aliis cognoscuntur. Omnis enim virtus operationis existit initiu: neque aliqua operatio provenit nisi ex virtute: ideoque utrasque in uno posuimus capitulo. Virtutum autem genera, & operationum ex eis provenientium, apud medicos sunt tria. Quae sunt genus virtutum vitalium, & genus virtutum naturalium: & genus virtutum animalium. Et multis quidem philosophorum, & medicis omnibus, & praecipue Galenus videtur quod unaquaeque virtutum, membrum principale habet, quod eius existitit minera, & a quo eius procedunt operationes.

cerebrum est principium sentiendi 26. A. 6.
Vitalis vero virtus est illa quae spiritus esse rem conservat, qui sensus & motus vehiculum existit, & ipsum reddit aptum ad eorum impressiones recipiendas, cum ad cerebrum pervenit & facit ipsum potentem dandi vitam ubicunque expanditur. Et huius quidem virtutis sedes & operationis ipsius processus est cor. Omnibus autem philosophis maiori, idest Aristoteli videtur quod omnium istarum operationum principium existit cor; sed primarum operationum earum manifestatio in his praedictis existit principiis, quemadmodum apud medicos cerebrum est sentiendi principium & post hoc quisque sensus habet membrum, in quo eius apparet operatio. Praeterea cum considerant, sicut debent & certificant inveniunt rem sicut videtur Aristoteli: & non quemadmodum ipsis videtur; & inveniunt sermones suos extractos ex praemissis probabilibus non necessariis, in quibus non assequuntur, nisi quod ex rebus appareret. Medico autem in quantum medicus, non attinet, ut consideret, quae sit harum duarum

sententiarum veritas, sed illud considerare philosophus, aut physicus debet. Medicus autem cum conceditur ei membra haec praenominata istarum virtutum principia existere, non curat in eo, quod de esse medicationis considerat, an ex aliis habeantur principiis, quae sunt ipsis priora, vel non: verum illius ignorantia est de his, in quibus non conceditur philosopho.

cerebri pars anterior est sedes sensus communis 27. E. F. G.
In virtute autem animali duae copulantur virtutes: quarum ipsa est sicut genus, una est sicut virtus compraehensiva, & altera virtus motiva. Et compraehensiva quidem est, sicut duarum virtutum genus. Una virtus compraehensiva est manifeste, & altera virtus compraehensiva occulte. Et virtus quod manifeste compraehensiva est sensibilis: quae est genus secundum quosdam quinque virtutum, & octo secundum alios. Quod, si dixerimus quod sint quinque, erunt virtus videndi, & virtus audiendi, & virtus gustandi, & virtus tangendi, & virtus odorandi. Et si dixerimus quod sint octo, erit huius causa quod pluribus certificatorum videtur quod tactus sit plures vitutes scilicet quatuor, & ponunt proprie unumquodque quatuor generum tactus virtutem per se; licet in membro sensibili sint comunia: sicut gustus & tactus in lingua, & visus & tactus in oculo. Hoc autem certificare est philosophi. Et virtus quidem compraehensiva occulte scilicet animalis, est sicut genus quinque virtutum, una est virtus quae vocatur sensus communis, & phantasia, & apud medicos quidem sunt una virtus, sed apud certificantes, qui sunt ex philosophis, duae sunt virtutes. Sensus enim communis est illa quae omnia sensu percepta recipit & ab eorum formis patitur, quae in ipsa coniunguntur. Phantasia vero est illa quae eas custodit postquam coniunguntur & retinet eas post sensus absentiam. Et quae harum duarum est recipiens, alia est a custodiente. Hoc autem certificare est philosophi. Sed qualitercunque fuerit eius sedes & operationis eius principium est anterior cerebri ventriculus. Et secuda quidem est virtus quam medici vocant cogitativam. Sed certificatores vocant quandoque imaginativam, quandoque cogitativam. Si enim administraverit eam, seu usa fuerit virtus existimativa animalis, quam postea nominabimus, aut ex se ipsa promoverit ad suam operationem, vocant eam imaginativam. Et si virtus rationalis usa fuerit & reduxerit eam ad illud quod ei prodest, vocatur virtus cogitativa. Quocunque tamen modo

fuerit, inter hanc virtutem & primam existit differentia quod prima est recipiens & custodiens id quod ad eam pervenit de formis sensu perceptis, & ista est illa quae se exercet in eis quae in imaginatione recondita sunt, exercitio componendi & dividendi, & praesentes sibi efficit formas, quemadmodum perveniunt a sensu, & alias formas ab eis diversas, sicut hominem volare & montem smaragdinum. Sed phantasia non appraesentat nisi quantum recipit a sensu, & huius quidem virtutis sedes est ventriculus cerebri medius, & haec quidem virtus est instrumentum virtutis quae procul dubio in animali est occulta compraehensiva. Et est existimativa, & ipsa quidem est virtus qua animal iudicat quod lupus est inimicus, & filius est dilectus, & qui annonam praebere consuevit, est amicus, a quo non est fugiendum.
[...]. Quidam autem hominum sunt qui praesumunt, & hanc virtutem imaginativam vocant. Sed tamen non curamus: quia de nominibus non disputamus, sed intentiones & differentias intelligere debemus.
[...]. Tertia vero illarum, quas nominant medici, est quinta, aut quarta, cum certificaverimus, quae est virtus conservativa & memorialis: & est thesaurus eius, quod pervenit ad existimativam de intentionibus imperceptis sensu extra formas eorum sensu perceptas, sicut phantastica est thesaurus eius quod pervenit ad sensum ex formis sensus perceptis, & eius quidem locus est posterior cerebri ventriculus. Hic vero est locus considerationis philosophicae, utrum virtus conservativa & memorialis virtus, quae reducit illud quod est absens ad memoriam ex eis, quae ab existimativa sunt reposita, sit virtus una, aut virtutes duae. Medico tamen non est inde curandum, quoniam nocumenta, quae eis qualitercunque sint accidunt, sunt homogenea: sunt enim nocumenta, quae in ventriculo cerebri posteriori accidunt, vel de genere complexionis, vel de genere compositionis.

cerebri pars posterior est locus memoriae 27. H.
Hic vero est locus considerationis philosophicae utrum virtus conservativa & memorialis virtus, quae reducit illud quod est absens ad memoriam ex eis, quae ab existimativa sunt reposita, sit virtus una aut virtutes duae. Medico tamen non est inde curandum, quoniam nocumenta, quae eis qualitercumque sint accidunt, sunt homogenea: sunt enim nocumenta quae in venticulo cerebri posteriori accidunt, vel de genere complexionis, vel de genere compositionis.

cerebri pars anterior est sensus visus & auditus 181. D. 15.

Veruntamen cerebri substantia etiam in lenitate & duritie inaequalis existit: nam pars eius anterior est lenior, & ipsius pars posterior est durior. [...] Anterius autem cerebrum non est factum lene nisi quoniam plurimum nervorum sensus, & proprie qui sunt visus, & auditus, oritur ex eo. Sensum enim speculator est & speculatoris inclinatio ad partem anteriorem est dignior.

cerebri complexio non naturalis 184. F. G.
Si [*humiditas* and *siccitas*] aequabuntur, provenit secundum plurimum putredo....

cerebri dispositiones iudicantur etiam ex significatione oculorum 185. C. 8.

cerebri dispositiones significant supra linguae significationem 185. C. 8. E. 2.

cerebrum patitur ex quibusdam membris compatientibus secum in passione 573. H. 1.

cerebri venter medius est locus melior cogitationi & imaginationi 181.H.10.

cerebrum esse sanum vel esse laesum habetur ex operationibus, utrum sint laese vel non 182.H.

COLOR
niger & viridis sunt laudabiliores visui: albus vero & citrinus disgregat oculorum lucem 586.E.6.

colores significat supra complexionem corporis 44.E.15.F.1.

colores albi non sunt nisi in substantia frigida 91.A.16.

COMPLEXIO
complexionis consideratio est duobus modis 4.B.8.

Complexio est qualitas quae ex actione ad invicem, & passione contrariarum qualitatum in elementis inventarum, quorum partes ad tantam parvitatem redactae sunt, ut cuiusque earum plurimum contingat, plurimum alterius provenit. Cum enim ad invicem agunt & patiuntur suis virtutibus, accidit ab earum summa, qualitas in toto earum similis, quae est complexio. & quoniam virtutes primae quae sunt in elementis praedictis sunt quattuor: caliditas, frigiditas, humiditas, & siccitas, tunc manifestum est quod complexiones in corporibus generatis & corruptis sunt per eas.

species omnis habet complexionem propriam ei 4.F.2.
Quaecumque igitur species in terra habitabili commorantium habebit complexionem eis propriam, aeri sui climatis convenientem: & habebit latitudinem. Cuius quidem latitudo duas habet extremitates superfluitatis & diminuitionis, seu intentionis & remissionis. Quartus autem modus est medium quod est inter duas extremitates latitudinis complexionis climatis. & ipsum est complexio complexionibus illius partis speciei temperatior. Modus vero quintus est angustior primo & tertio, & est complexio, quam debet habere individuum designatum, qua vivum & sanum reperitur; quae etiam latitudinem habet ad quam duae terminantur superfluitatis seu additionis & diminuitionis extremitates. Debes autem scire quod omne individuum debet habere complexionem sibi solummodo propriam, in qua alium ei associare vel communicare raro contingit, aut est impossibile.

complexiones sunt novem 3.B.

COR
Libellus Avic. de medicinis cordialibus 557.F.

1. De origine spiritus 557 E
Creavit Deus ex concavitatibus cordis sinistram ut esset armarium spiritus, & minera generationis illius. Creavitque spiritum latorem virtutum animae incolentem cum eis in membra corporis & fecit appendiculum primum virtutum animo spiritum, eiusque manationem secundaria ipso mediante in membris corporis.

2. De diffinitione & natura spiritus & eius utilitate 557 I

Et propterea indicatur de spiritu quod sit substantia luminosa seu lucida: propter quod dicitur de visivo spiritu, quod sit radius aut lux. & exinde anima gaudet ex intuitu lucis & tristatur in tenebris: quoniam illud est conforme naturae vel principio ipsius & hoc est in contrarium.

3. De principalibus passionibus spiritus cordialis & primis causis ipsorum, scilicet potentia & dispositione 558 B

Sapientes, philosophorum & medici eos sequentes concorditer ponunt quod gaudium & tristitia & timor & ira sunt ex passionibus propriis spiritus cordialis. & quod quaelibet passionum intenditur & remittitur non solum propter agens, sed etiam propter intensionem & remissionem dispositionis in substantia patientis. Assignant etiam sapientes subtiliter differentiam inter potentiam & dispositionem, dicentes quod potentia respicit utrunque contrariorum aequaliter; dispositio vero non; quamvis enim gaudere & tristari possit homo, nihilominus aliquis est tamen ad laetitiam praeparatus: aliquis vero ad tristitiam tantum. & simile iudicium est de timore, & ira [...]. Videtur enim quod dispositio sit perfectio potentiae respectu alterius oppositorum. Ex quo patet quod licet spiritui conveniat in quantum inest ei potentia tristari vel gaudere simul seu aequaliter, non tamen ei convenit ex parte ipsius praeparationis, nisi unum ipsorum. Rursus etiam ex hoc patet quod potentia ad haec duo inseparabiliter inhaeret spiritui ex generatione ipsius. Dispositio vero, quae ipsum ad alterum oppositorum inclinat, non inseparabiliter ex generatione inhaeret ei, sed accidere potest ex supervenientibus causis.

4. De gaudio & intrinsecis causis delectationis & tristitiae & eorum diversitate 558 C

Gaudium est delectatio quaedam, omnis autem delectatio est apprehensio adventus perfectionis appropriatae alicui virtuti apprehensivae, sicut in sensibus apprehensio dulcis gustui.

5. De causis exterioribus delectationibus & tristitiae & earum diversitate 558 B

Perfecte dispositio ad aliquem effectum sufficit debilissima causa illius effectus, sicut sulfur ad inflammationem: ipsum enim adeo igne modico inflammatur, quod cum duplo eius lignum inflammari non potest. [...]. De causiis autem gaudii & laetitiae fortibus, & manifestis non est necessarium facere mentionem. Aliae vero sunt sicut intuitus coeli inter laetificantes, cuius signum est, quia contrarium tristitiam causat, scilicet in tenebris permanere. Aut sicut conversari cum consimilibus, cuius signum est quod solitudo attristat. De laetificantibus similiter obtinere desideratum. Et explere intentionem secundum exigentiam intenti sine impedimento. Et praeponere facere quicquam placidum. Et similiter confidentia. Et memoria praeteriti delectabilis & futuri spes. Et meditatio in rebus ambitiosis. Et mutua confabulatio dilectorum. Et evasio a tormento. Et extraneitas rerum & admiratio & elevatio mentis. Et obviatio amicorum & amicabilium vicinorum.

6. Quod unaquaeque passio cordis disponitur ad generationem suiipsius 559 B

Non est autem opinandum quod causae disponentes ad gaudium vel tristitiam sint causae quae coniungunt substantiae spiritus in quantitate & qualitate, immo quandoque accidunt causae aliae animales utpote operationes animales quae disponunt spiritus ad unam istarum rerum, & videtur quod sint ipsae disponentes spiritus ad illud etiam mediante adventu alicuius ex illis causis quae sunt intrantes in qualitate spirituum & quantitate ipsorum, ita quod per eas aequatur complexio spirituum & substantia ipsorum & multiplicatur quantitas ipsorum & distinguitur seu bonificatur natura ipsorum: quare disponunt ad gaudium aut accidit aliqua ex causis contrariis ei, quia disponit ad tristitiam, & illae causae extrinsecae sunt causae primae & istae substantiales, idest accidentes substantiae spiritus, sunt causae secundae, & proximae & istae causae accidentales remotae non existimantur quod non possint computari vel comprehendi in numero, aut difficilis est earum numeratio. Verum summa earum sicut puto comprehenditur in una intentione & est quia omnis actio contrarium habens si saepius iteretur, reddit virtutem eius cuius est potentiorem ad imprimendum effectum. Omnis autem fortificatio virtutis fit quaedam dispositio ad effectum hoc autem sufficienter inductione manifestant. Etenim corpus si pluries calefiat, disponitur ad calefactionem velocem; similiter si pluries infrigidetur, aut rarificetur, aut spissetur, & in interioribus virtutibus accidit illud. Etenim ex frequenti actione & passione fortes habitus generantur in eis; sic enim morales habitus acquiruntur. Huius autem causa forsitan est, quia passio inhaerens continue alicui rei quando accidit est conveniens substantiae eius; quod autem est alicui conveniens, suo contrario disconveniens est, & contrario disconveniens quando reiteratur multoties, tunc diminuitur dipositio vel praeparatio ei opposita & additur in dispositione vel preparatione contraria, quae est ei conveniens. Declaratio vero supradictae intentionis fit per inductionem & syllogismum, seu per rationem assumptam ex per se notis. [...]. Tristandi vero frequentia duo consequuntur, videlicet debilitas naturalis virtutis, & secundum scilicet inspissatio spiritus, propter frigiditatem accidentem apud extinctionem caloris naturalis, causatam a vehementi coadunnatione & coarctatione spiritus. Ad haec vero duo sequuntur contraria eorum, quae paulo ante iam diximus. Est igitur manifestum quod laetandi frequentia disponit spiritum ad laetitiam & tristandi ad tristitiam. Et quod in preparatis ad laetitiam contristantia non imprimunt, nisi fortia sint, & tamen laetificantia debilia imprimunt in eis. Dispositio vero eorum qui sunt praeparati ad tristitiam est e contrario.

7. De differentia debilitatis cordis seu pusillanimitatis & tristitiae & eorum contrarium 559 E

In hoc capitulo consideratur dispositio quae est debilitas cordis & alia dispositio quae dicitur tristitia seu fastidium & strictura pectoris, quae ambae dispositiones similantur, sed tamen inter eas est differentia. Similiter in hoc capitulo consideratur dispositio quae est fortitudo cordis & alia dispositio quae dicitur dilatatio pectoris, & ambae istae dispositiones similantur; inter eas tamen est differentia, quae quidem differentia inter ipsas est ambigua & occulta, propterea quia ambae istae dispositiones ad se invicem consequuntur secundum plurimum. Putatur enim de duabus primis quot sint passivae dispositiones; de aliis vero duabus quid sint active, attamen inter extrema utriusque divisionis est diffrentia manifesta. Primo quidem quia non se consequuntur ad invicem: non enim omnis debilis corde est tristis, nec omnis tristis est corde debilis, & iterum non omnis fortis corde est gaudens, nec omnis gaudens est fortis corde. Secundo vero quoniam ipsorum rationes seu descriptiones sunt diversae. Debilitas enim cordis est dispositio sumpta respectu terribilium rerum secundum quod cor parum tolerat ipsas. Strictura vero pectoris & tristitia sumitur respectu contristantium rerum secundum quod cor parum tolerat; & terribile nocitivum quidem est corporale, tristans vero nocitivum animale est. Tertio similiter differunt quantum ad consequentia, quae sunt animae diversa: nam debilitas cordis movet ad fugam; tristitia vero & pectori strictura quandoque movet ad resistentiam & ad repellendum & causat effectum eius quod est contrarium fugae, scilicet invadendi contra nocivum, praeterea debilitas cordis tepescere facit motivas virtutes; tristitia vero excitat & movet easdem. Et sic in debilitate cordis duae sunt passiones, scilicet una laetitionis, & alia desiderii sive affectus ad motum elongantem. In tristitia vero seu in strictura pectoris unica est passio, scilicet nocumenti vel laesionis; nec naturaliter sequitur eam affectus ad fugam; immo quandoque eligitur ipsa fuga, propter intenitonem aliam absque ipso appetitu inclinante ad recedendum a re nociva, & erit ille appetitus volontarius seu electivus, & forsitan eligetur invasio & repugnantia, & non fuga. Quartum iterum differunt quantum ad consequentia corporea diversa. Debilitatem nanque cordis apud obviationem proprii nocivi sequitur remissio naturals caloris & victoria frigoris. Tristitia vero apud obviationem proprii obiecti, vel nocivi, inflammatio naturalis caliditatis.

Cor non est lacertus ut quidam volebat 276 C
Et iam repertus est cor cuiusdam † {simii} habens duo capita. Et ex virtute vitae cordis est, quoniam quando aufertur ab animali, invenitur pulsari usque ad horam. Iam autem erravit qui existimavit quod cor sit lacertus, quamvis sit similium rerum in eo. Verum motus eius non est voluntarius.

Cordis tremor 278 C 12
Tremor cordis est motus iectigativus accidens cordis. Et causa eius est omne, quod laedit cor ex eis qua sunt in ipso, aut in panniculo eius: aut continuantur ei ex membris vicinis communicantibus ei. Et quandoque fit a materia humorosa, quandoque fit a malitia complexionis purae [...]. Et ille qui est a malitia complexionis purae, ideo est quia omnis complexio dominans facit debilitatem; et omnis debilitas effici in corde, dum perseverat in ipso residuum virtutis, agitationem quandam quasi ipsum expellat a se ipso aliquod nocumentum. Et tremor quidem cordis quando superfluit, permutatur

ad syncopim; et quando magis superfluit, permutatur ad mortem. Et unaquaeque complexionum simplicium facit illud. Apostema vero calidum in principio perseseverans facit apparere tremorem cordis, deinde syncopim, postea mortem. Et frigidum est propinquum dispositioni eius, sed quuandoque interponit spatium aliquantulum. Et similiter resolutio singularis. Et similiter oppilatio existens in cursibus sanguinis, et spiritus in corde, et quae sequuntur ipsum et in venis duris partium pulmonis. Factus autem a causa extranea, est sicut factus a doloribus fortibus, & permutationibus materierum apostematum vicinorum praedictorum [...]. Factus autem a subtilitate sensus cordis est, quoniam habenti illum accidit tremor cordis ex qualibet ventositate generata in spatio, quod est inter ipsum & inter panniculum eius, aut in corpore panniculi eius, aut in vena eius & ex qualibet qualitate frigida aut calida adveniente ei.

Cordi tremor facit ut homines sint de eo solliciti 69 A 12
Ille cui tremor cordis assidue acciderit de se ipso sit sollicitus, ne subita intercipiatur morte. [...]. Et similiter cum perduraverit, ut sensus sint turbidi, & motionum adsit debilitas cum repletione. Cum membra omnia stupida fuerint multum, tunc regantur cum evacuatione phlegmatis, ne ad paralysim et spasmum perveniant. Cum facies vehementer rubuerit & oculus & lachrymae fluxerint & lumen effugerit & capitis dolorem habuerit, minutione regendus erit & solutione ventris et his similibus, ne incidat in phrenesim. Cumque multa absque causa fuerit tristitia, & timor, regendus erit adusti humoris evacuatione, ne ad melancholiam deveniat [...]. Et ad summum omnis res, quae de suo mutatur usu, scilicet desiderium aut egestio aut urina [...] cum augmentantur aut diminuuntur aut suam mutant qualitatem, pronosticantur aegritudinem.

Cordis tremor factus ex oppilatione vel subtilitate sensus quibus cognoscitur 278 G 6
Et fortitudo pulsus & magnitudo ipsius sunt significationes primae significantes ipsum: & certificat ipsum si fuerit corpus cum frequentia huiusmodi tremoris cordis, incolume & virtus conservata & consuetudo in operationibus sana. Et illi quibus plurimum accidit, istae sunt super quorum facies apparent vestigia passionum

animalium, quamvis parum sicut irae aut gaudii, aut tristitiae aut aliarum.

IMAGINATIVA (VIRTUS)

Imaginationum causae sunt colores quibus sentiuntur coram visu 232.D.3

Sunt colores qui sentiuntur coram visu ac ipsi sint misti in aere, & causa in eis est statio rei non perviae inter glacialem & inter ea quae vident; & illa res aut est ex eis, quorum simile non comprehenditur in consuetudinibus omnino, & neque comprehendit ipsum, nisi qui est fortis visus egredientis a consuetudine in comprehendendo; aut est ex eis quae comprehendit visus, quando medius fit, & non est in fine acuitatis: sed est secundum semitam consuetudinis. Et intentio primi est, quoniam cum visus est fortis, comprehendit debile & occultum ex rebus quae volant in aere prope visum, quae sunt ex atomis & aliis, a quibus aer non evacuatur; quare apparet ei vel confuse videntur ab eo; & propter suam propinquitatem quam habent cum aere & ipsorum parvitatem, non verificat eas; & similiter cum sunt in interiore parte vestigia vaporum parvorum, a quibus non evacuatur ex eis complexio & natura omnino. Veruntamen haec duo occultantur a visibus, quae non sunt in ultimo acuitatis & non imaginantur, nisi ei qui est vehementis acuitatis in visu; & ista sunt ex eis quae non comparantur ad nocumentum.

Imaginatio ab acuitate sensum 232.F.6

Signa earum quae sunt ex acuitate sensus sunt ut sint leves non secundum modum unum & figuram unam: & associantur homini tempore sanitatis sui visus absque diminutione subsequente ipsam [...]. Et quando continuatur sanitas oculi & incolumitas eius qui habet imaginationes sex mensibus, est secundum plurimum in securitate. Et imaginationes quae sunt antecedentes aquam non cessant gradatim in conturbatione visus, usquequo descendit cum eis aqua subito, & raro pertransit sex menses. Cum autem vides imaginationes removeri & redire & addi & diminui, scias quod non sunt aquosae. Cumque videris fixarum tempus prolongari & non procedit vel non continuatur in debilitate visus, scias quod ipsae non sunt aquosae.

233.H

Signa portendentia aquam sunt imaginationes pradictae, quae non sunt a causis aliis. Et nos quidem iam exposuimus esse earum in capitulo imaginationum & quod accidit cum eis conturbatio sensibilis, & proprie quando est in uno oculorum, & quod imaginantur ei res luminosae, sicut candelae duplices. Inter aquam vero & oppilationem intrinsecam, distat, quoniam quando unus duorum oculorum comprimitur, dilatatur alter in aqua, sed non dilatatur alter in oppilatione. Et illud quoniam causa in illa diilatatione est expulsio spiritus, qui est in oculo compresso ad alterum cum fortitudine; sed cum invenit oppilationem ante ipsum, seu ipsi oppositam non penetrat, & hoc secundum plurimum, & secundum minus dilatatur alter, nisi aqua sit vehementis grossitudinis, & non fuerit oppilatio, sed in Alintisar non est aliquid de hoc.

Imaginatio & memoria inest spiritui 568.A
Spiritus dividit in naturalem genitum
ex vapore laudabili mundo.
Et dividitur in eum qui iam existit in corde
& est ille per quem permanet vita.
Et dividitur in eum qui in cerebro fertur
& in panniculis eius retinetur.
Insunt autem huic spiritui imaginatio, ratio seu
intellectus & memoria, cum complentur
et perficiuntur ipsius scpecies in ventriculis cerebri.
In quolibet ex spiritibus est virtus propria
alia ab illa quae est in alio.

INTELLECTUS
Intellectus quandoque a sensu & a phantasia distrahitur ab actibus rationis propter corruptionem complexionis spiritus. 559.B.3.
Non est autem opinandum quod causae disponentes ad gaudium vel tristitiam sint causae quae coniungunt substantiae spiritus in quantitate & qualitate, immo quandoque accidunt causae aliae animales utpote operationes animales quae disponunt spiritus ad unam istarum rerum, & videtur quod sint ipsae disponentes spiritus ad illud etiam mediante adventu alicuius ex illis causis quae sunt intrantes in qualitate spirituum & quantitate ipsorum, ita quod per eas aequatur complexio

spirituum & substantia ipsorum & multiplicatur quantitas ipsorum & distinguitur seu bonificatur natura ipsorum; quare disponunt ad gaudium aut accidit aliqua ex causiis contrariis ei, quia disponit ad tristitiam, & illae causae extrinsecae sunt causae primae & istae substantiales, idest accidentes substantiae spiritus, sunt causae secundae & proximae & istae causae accidentales remotae non existimantur quod non possint computari vel comprehendi in numero, aut difficili est earum numeratio. Verum summa earum sicut puto comprehenditur in una intentione & est quia omnis actio contrarium habens, si saepius iteretur, reddit virtutem eius cuius est potentiorem ad imprimendum effectum. Omnis autem fortificatio virtutis fit quaedam dispositio ad effectum hoc autem sufficienter inductione manifestatur. Et enim corpus, si pluries calefiat, disponitur ad calefactionem velocem, similiter si pluries infrigidetur aut rarificetur aut spissetur & in interioribus virtutibus accidit illud. Et enim ex frequenti actione & passione fortes habitus generantur in eis; sic enim morales habitus acquiruntur. Huius autem causa forsitan est, quia passio inhaerens continue aliqui rei quando accidit est, conveniens substantiae eius; quod autem est alicui conveniens, suo contrario disconveniens est, & contrario disconveniens quando reiteratur multoties, tunc diminuitur dipositio vel praeparatio ei opposita & additur indispositione vel praeparatione contraria, quae est ei conveniens. Declaratio vero supradictae intentionis fit per inductionem, & syllogismum seu per rationem assumptam ex per se notis.

IRA

Ira & timor sunt passiones virtutis vitalis 27.D.12

Erit igitur haec virtus secundum philosophorum sententiam virtus animalis, sicut virtutes naturales quas nominavimus apud eos virtutes vocantur animales. Quod si noluerint dicere animam secundum hanc intentionem, sed velint dicere virtutem, quae est principium comprehendendi & movendi, quod ex aliqua provenit compraehensione voluntarie; & naturalem velint dicere pro omni virtute ex qua operatio provenit in suo corpore secundum huius formae diversitatem; non erit virtus animalis, sed erit naturalis & altioris ordinis, quae sit virtus quam medici vocant naturalem. Et si naturalem vocaverit illam quae rem nutrimenti ministrat &

converterit, sive ad hoc ut remaneat individuum, sive ut remaneat species, non erit haec naturalis, sed erit tertium genus. Et quia ira & timor & similia eorum huius virtutis sunt passiones, tunc licet eorum principia sit sensus & existimatio & virtutes appraehendentes; huiuc tamen comparatae sunt virtuti. Huius autem virtutis declarationem certificare & an sit una, an plures quae una in sapientia continetur naturali, quae philosophiae pars existit.

Ira commovet virtutem & spiritus dilatat & pulsum facit magnum & velocem 51.A.5

Ira quidem propterea quod virtutem commovet & spiritum subito dilatat, pulsum facit magnum ad superiora se elevantem velocem & spissum, in quo non oportet diversitatem cadere, quoniam passio existit similis, nisi timor ei admisceatur, qui una vice superet & haec alia superet vice; & similiter si verecundia ei admisceatur, aut contrarietas ab intellectu, qui tacere praecipiat & ne ferveat ad malum inferendum illi cui irascitur. Et ex delitiis quidem, propterea quod ad exteriora paulatim movent, non pervenit pulsus ad illud quod pervenit ex ira in velocitate & spissitudine; immo est cum eius magnitudo sufficit necessitati & est tardus & rarus. & similiter pulsus laetitiae quoniam ipse sit magnus secundum plurimum cum lenitate, & attinet tarditati & raritati. In tristitia vero, propterea quod calor suffocatur & submergitur, & fortitudo debilitatur, oportet ut sit pulsus parvus & debilis, rarus & tardus. Timor vero, qui subito venit, pulsum facit velocem & diversum & inordinatum.

Ira calefacit 59.F.3

Ira namque vehementer calefacit & tristitia multum exiccat, & pigritia virtutes laxat animales, & complexiones ad phlegmatis proprietatem inclinat. In temperamento ergo morum custodia sanitatis animae & corporis simul constitit.

Ira raro interficit 277.F.3

Causarum in corde imprimentium aliae sunt quae sunt ei propriae & aliae sunt ei communes & aliis; sicut causae efficientes complexiones & causae efficientes apostemata & efficientes solutionem singularis & reliquae similes eis, quae sunt ex eis quas numeravi tibi in libris universalibus. Verum cordi appropriantur causae accidentes propter anhelitum & causae accidentes propter passiones animales. Propter anhelitum quidem, quoniam quando constringitur aut calefit valde aut infrigidatur valde, sequitur ex eo ut accipiat cor nocumentum. In passionibus autem animalibus, oportet ut redeatur ad ea quae diximus in universalibus & iam ostendimus impressionem earum in corde mediante spiritu, & quaecumque earum superfluit impressionem praefocationis caloris innati ad interiora. Aut sparsionis eius ad exteriora quandoque consequitur, ut faciat pervenire syncopim, immo consequitur ut interficiat. Et ira quae est ex summa earum, est minor omnibus illis in hoc. Ira enim raro interficit. Vigiliae vero & exercitium & similia illis debilitant cor cum resolutione.

Ira & gaudium & tristitia sunt de passionibus spiritus cordialis 558.B.8

Sapientes philosopshorum & medici eos sequentes concorditer ponunt, quod gaudium & tristitia & timor & ira sunt ex passionibus propriis spiritus cordialis. Et quod quaelibet passionum intenditur & remittitur non solum propter agens, sed etiam propter intensionem & reminissionem dispositionis in substantia patientis. Assignant etiam sapientes subtiliter differentiam inter potentiam & dispositionem, dicentes quod potentia respicit utrunque contrariorum aequaliter, dispositio vero non; quamvis enim gaudere & tristari possit homo, nihilominus aliquis est tamen ad laetitiam praeparatus, aliquis vero ad tristitiam tantum. Et simile iudicium est de timore & ira & caeteris passionibus.

Ira est modus ad expellendum 559.G.3

Sanguis autem grossus & turbidus & additae caliditatis disponit ad tristitiam & ad iram etiam perdurantem. Ad tristitiam quidem quia generatur ex eo spiritus turbidus, ad iram vero quia velociter inflammatur propter caliditatem suam; quod autem efficit perdurantem est spissitudo eius. [...]. Ira vero causata ex sanguine cholerico & subtili velociter exictatur & deletur propter intensam caliditatem spiritus ex eo generati & eius tenuitate. [...]. Ira enim est motus ad expellendum, laetificantia vero delectationi proportionata sunt. In delectatione vero fit inclinans motus ad attrahendum, idicirco in tali homine ex rebus magis creatur ira, & est vehementer spissus spiritus eius & propter etiam eandem causam est parvi timoris.

Ira quando cessat velociter non perdurat forma nocivi in imaginatione 559.H.8
Odium autem vel rancor est perseverantia formae nocivi in imaginatione seu phantasia. Et perseverantia simul imaginationis affectus ad vindictam sumendam ex eo. Hoc autem est ideo, quoniam ira habet aliquam firmitudinem, sed motus ad vindictam non est valde fortis. Et ira quidem est non contra valde fortem, nec contra debilem valde. Sciendum est enim quod ira, quando cessat velociter, non perdurat in imaginatione, seu phantasia, forma nocivi, sed cito deletur, & ideo non causat rancorem. Et similiter quando isti duo scilicet affectus et motus ad vindictam sunt vehementes valde, tunc accidunt duo prohibentia odium, seu rancorem. Et quando isti duo scilicet appetitus & motus ad vindictam sunt, & diversio imaginationis a consideratione intentionum specierum nocivi, & a specie & consideratione eorum quae sequuntur ad ipsum, & ab impressione seu firmatione ipsorum in memoria. De natura enim motivae virtutis est ut ab apprehensivis virtutibus retrahat animam & e converso, & de natura exteriorum est ut divertant ab interioribus & e converso. Secundum vero est quia, quando valde intenditur affectus vel appetitus ad vindictam & non frangitur a timore, perveniat ad hoc ex affectus impressione, ut efficiatur quaesitum quasi apprehensum, & iam obtentum apud imaginationem ipsius. Forma enim ad quam vehemens sit motus & versus eam valde festinatur, imaginat vel repraehesentatur apud imaginationem quasi obtenta & iam existens. Cum vero in imaginatione imprimitur forma quasiti, sive desiderati, sicut forma iam existentis, pervenit in imaginatione, forma eius, sicut forma rei ad quam terminatur motus. Vel destruitur ab imaginatione affectus seu appetitus & deletur ab ea forma. Ita quod in memoria non perdurat & ideo non fit rancor.

LACHRYMAE
De Lachrymis 227.D.
Haec aegritudo est ut sint oculi semper humidi humiditate aquosa. Et quandoque currunt lachrymae. Et earum quidem aliae sunt nativae, aliae accidentales. Et de accidentalibus sunt quae sunt inseparabiles in sanitate & sunt aliae sequentes aegritudinem, quae removentur si removeatur aegritudo, sicut fit in febribus. Causa autem in

accidentalibus est debilitas retentivae [...]. Et principium quidem illius humiditatis est cerebrum & cursus eius ad oculum in una duarum viarum praedictarum multoties.

De aqua 233.F.
Descensus aquae est aegritudo oppilativa, & est humiditas extranea stans in foramine vueae, inter humorem albugineum & siphac corneae, seu siphac corneum, quare prohibet penetrare formas ad visum. Et ipsa quidem quandoque diversificatur in quantitate & diversificatur in qualitate. [...]. Diversitas vero illius in qualitate quandoque est in essentia, quoniam alia est subtilis clara pervia, quae non prohibet lumen & solem, & alia eius est grossa valde. Et quandoque est in colore, quoniam alia eius est ei aerei coloris, & alia eius alba est gypsei coloris, & alia eius alba est margaritalis; & alia eius alba declinat ad blavedinem, seu glaucedinem parva et ad colorem lapidis turchois, & aureitatem; & quaedam est citrina, & quaedam est nigra, & quaedam est cineritia. Et illa quidem quae est magis receptibilis curae ex parte coloris est aerea et alba margaritalis, et quae declinat ad galaucedinem parum et ad colorem lapidis turchois †.

MEDICINA
De subiectis medicinae 3.D.
Quoniam medicina corpus humanum ex parte unde sanatur et a sanitate removetur considerat, et cuiusque rei scientia non acquiritur, neque completur cum causas habuerit, nisi per causas sciatur, ergo debemus in medicina scire sanitatis & aegritudinis causas. Et quia sanitas & aegritudo & earum causae plerunque sunt manifestae, plerumque occultae, quae non sensu, immo per significationes accidentium compraehenduntur; quare oportet etiam in medicina scire accidentia quae in sanitate accidunt & aegritudine. Iam autem declaratum fuit in scientiis veridicis quod rei scientia non acquiritur nisi per scientiam causarum & principiorum ipsius, si causas habuerit & principia; si non habuerit, non completur: seu non acquiritur, nisi ex parte sciendi eius accidentia & concomitantia essentialia. Causarum vero quatuor sunt species: materiales, efficientes, formales & finales. Causae vero materiales sunt res subiectivae, in quibus fundatur vel invenitur sanitas & aegritudo, subiectum quidem proprinquum membrum & spiritus. Subiectum vero remotum, seu longinquum,

humores; & eis longiora sunt elementia. Et haec duo sunt subiecta secundum compositionem, licet sint etiam cum alteratione; & unumquodque quod sic subiicitur in compositione eius & alteratione ipsius, ad aliquam pervenit unitatem. Et haec unitas, ad quam huiusmodi revertitur multitudo, aut est complexio aut forma. Complexio vero est secundum alterationem & forma secundum compositionem. Efficientes autem causae sunt causae permutantes & conservantes humani corporis dispositiones, sicut sunt aeres & quae eis continuantur, & comestiones & aquae & potus & quae eis continuantur [...]. Formales vero causae sunt complexiones & virtutes quae post eas eveniunt & compositiones. Causae autem finales sunt operationes.

MELANCHOLIA
Melancholiae causa vel est in cerebro vel est extra cerebrum
204.C.11.
Dicitur melancholia mutatio existimationum & cogitationum a cursus naturali ad corruptionem & ad timorem & ad malitiam propter complexionem melancholicam facientem pavidum seu tristantem spiritum cerebri interius & facientem ipsum timidum propter tenebras ipsius, sicut tenebrae extrinsecae solicitant & timere faciunt secundum quod complexio frigiditatis & siccitatis contraria est spiritui debilitans ipsum, sicut complextio caliditatis & humiditatis, ut complexio vini est conveniens spiritibus & confortans. Cumque melancholia componitur cum rixa & saltu, contentione, seu pugna permutatur & nominatur mania. [...]. Et melancholiae quidem causa aut est in ipso cerebro aut extra cerebrum. Et illa quae est in ipso cerebro aut est ex malitia complexionis frigidae & siccae sine materia permutante subsantiam cerebri & complexionem spiritus luminosi ad tenebram. Aut est cum materia.

204.E
Et scias quod sanguis cordis quando est tersus, subtilis, clarus, laetificans, resistit corruptioni cerebri, & rettificat ipsum, immo non est mirum si sit secundum plurimum principium illius ex corde. Licet non confirmetur haec aegritudo nisi in cerebro, non enim est novum & longinquum mirum, si cordis complexio primum corrumpatur & sequatur eam cerebrum, aut corrumpatur cerebri complexio &

sequatur eam cor, & corrumpatur complexio spiritus in corde & fiat tristis, seu pavidus, & corrumpat quod ex eo penetrat ad cerebrum & iuvet cerebrum ad se corrumpendum. Et quandoque accidit in fine aegritudinum materialium & proprie acutarum melancholia & est signum mortis & tunc accidit homini illi, ut recordetur mortis & mortuorum plurimum.

Melancholia fit quandoque ex corruptione spiritus vitalis 204.E.6.
Et quandoque est causa generationis eius extra cerebrum. Et principium quidem generationis est in cerebro, sicut cum in stomacho est apostema calidum & adurit vapor eius humiditates cerebri. [...] Eius vero quae fit a frigiditate & siccitate sine materia causa est malitia complexionis melancholicae in corde, cum materia aut sine materia, cui communicat in ipsa cerebrum, quoniam spiritus animalis continuus est spiritui vitali & ex substantia ipsius. Quare complexio eius corrupta melancholica corrumpit complexionem cerebri & convertit ad melancholiam.

Melancholia accidit etiam ex corruptione cordis 204.E.9.

Melancholicus representat sibi res in actu faciens illa sibi apparentes ex forti imaginatione 559.A.16.

Melancholicus videtur in somnis ut interficiatur 172.B.12.

MEMORIA
202 B
Species nocumenti contingentis in operationibus cerebri sunt propter duas causas & cognoscuntur tribus modis. Cum enim sensus hominis est incolumis & imaginatio formarum rerum in somno & vigiliis est sana, deinde formae, seu species, & dispositiones quas videt in vigiliis suis aut in somno suo, & quae sunt ex eis de quibus possibile est ipsum sermonem facere vel narrare, iam sunt remotae ab eo & cum audit eas & videt, non remanent apud eum, tunc laesio illa est in memoria & in posteriore cerebro. Quod si in hoc non est impedimentum, sed loquitur ea quae non sunt dicenda & timet ab eis, a quibus timere non oportet [...], & sperat quod non est sperandum &

inquirit quod inquirendum non est & facit quod faciendum non est & non est potens narrare quod narrandum est de rebus, tunc laesio est in cogitativa & in parte media cerebri. Si vero ipsius memoria & ipsius loquela sunt sicut esse debent & non contingit in his quae agit & loquitur aliquid contrarium rectitudini & imaginatur res sensibiles [...] & videt singularia mendosa [...] aut debiliter imaginatur formas rerum in somno & vigiliis, tunc laesio est in imaginatione & in ventre anteriore cerebri.

202.D.
Quae vero fit ex humore melanchonico est cum tristitia & opinione mala, & cum signis quae dicemus in capitulo suo. Et si fuerit humor melanchonicus, cholericus est cum moribus Alsebaie. Si vero fuerit ex humore melanchonico sanguineo, est illic laetitia & risus cum exuberatione venarum. Facta autem a cholera citrina, est cum inflammatione & caliditate, & rixa, & malitia morum, & agitatione vehementi, & imaginatione ignis & scintillarum, & adustione angulorum oculorum interiorum, & citrinitate coloris, & inflammatione capitis, & extensione cutis frontis, & profundatione oculorum, & saltu ad pugnam. Et in illa quidem quae fit ex rubea sunt accidentia ista vehementiora & magis perversa. Et huiusmodi quidem generis est permistio rationis quae fit in febribus; & plurimum fit in pestilentialibus.

202.G.
Quoniam caliditas est faciens cogitationem quae est unus ex motibus spiritus quo movetur ab anteriore parte cerebri usque ad eius postremam & e contrario. Et caliditas quidem excitat motum & iuvat ipsum. Et congelatio prohibet ipsum.

Memoriae corruptio quid sit 202.H.15.
Et oblivio quidem & corruptio memoriae secundum plurimum non accidunt, nisi ex frigiditate & humiditate.

OPPILATIO
Oppilationes multae sunt in hyeme 40.F.13
Oppilatio accidit aut propter causam extraneam, quae in canali cadit, & hoc aut erit extraneum in suo genere, sicut lapis, aut extraneum in

quantitate sui, sicut faex multa, aut extraneum in sua qualitate & hoc erit aut propter suam grossitiem, aut viscositatem, aut quia est congelatum, sicut sanguis similis sanguisuscae congelatus. [...]. In hieme quoque multae sut oppilationes, propterea quod superfluitates multum retinentur & propterea quod frigus stringit.

Oppilationes in venis inducunt colorem corporis citrinum 46.B.14

Oppilationes ad multas aegritudines perducunt 63.A.6

Oppilationes ex multitudine humorum & ex viscositate humorum quibus curantur 81.G.14

Oppilationes quae sint peiores & deteriores 81.H.15
Et ex oppilationibus quidem peiores sunt oppilationes venarum, & deteriores eis sunt illae quae sunt in arteriis, & adhuc peiores sunt illae quae in membris existunt principalibus.

Oppilationum signa 46.B.14
Cum materiae fuerint coarctatae, seu conculcatae, & significationes eas demonstrant, & sentitur extensio, & non sentiuntur significationes repletionis in toto corpore; oppilationes proculdubio ibi adesse intelleguntur. Veruntamen gravitas in opipilationibus sentitur, cum oppilationes in canalibus existunt, per quas multas currere materias est necesse, sicut in oppilationibus quae in hepate sunt.

Oppilationum prohibitio est via sanitatis conservationis 589.G.7

PALPITATIO
Palpitatio accidit corpori ex parte multiplicationis repletionis 208.B.13

Palpitatio est dispositio sicuti lassitudo 208.B.

PERTURBATIO
De significationibus universalibus operationum cerebri 183.B

Gustus autem & tactus hoc cursu procedunt, nisi quia ipsorum mutatio a cursu naturali secundum plurimum significat corruptionem propriam in instrumentis ipsorum propinquis; & raro est secundum communitatem cerebri, & proprie, sicut quando est communis, sicut stupor toti corpori. Et sensus quidem communicant in specie debilitatis, & fortitudinis, significantes dispositionem in cerebro perseverantem, quae est perturbatio & claritas. Non est enim omnis debilitas cum perturbatione, quoniam quandoque est debilitas cum claritate, sicut homo, si videat aliquid propinquum et parvi radii bene et clare, et videat res parvas, deinde cum elongatur aut multiplicantur ipsarum radii, deficiat. Nam perturbatio & claritas quandoque sunt simul cum debilitate, & claritas quandoque est procul dubio cum fortitudine. Verum perturbatio semper significat materiam & claritas significat siccitatem, & haec quidem perturbatio fortasse subito figitur, & est ex ea oppilatio & significat materiam vaporosam in venis & reti eius.

SENSATUM

1. Sensatum omne contrarium subito secundum quod est contrarium est faciens dolorem 41.G.3.

Verus autem fermo in hoc capitulo est ut complexionis mutatio ponatur genus, ex quo dolor essentialiter provenit, licet cum eo quandoque continuitas separatio contingat. Huius tamen declaratio verificata, in medicina non continetur, sed in parte sapientiae naturali, ideoque ad ipsius summam parumper innuemus. Dicemus igitur, quod est, cum dolor est similium partium in membro dolente & continuitatis solutio nullo modo similium erit partium. Cum enim inveniatur dolor in partibus in quibus non est solutio continuitatis, non ergo erit ibi dolor propter solutionem continuitatis, immo propter complexionis malitiam. [...]. Amplius dolor procul dubio est sentire impressorium contrarium subito secundum quod est contrarium & dolere faciens, est sensatum contrarium subito.

2. Sensatum omne non efficit in instrumento sensibili, nisi formam quae est sibi similis 207.C.12.

3. Sensatio omnis fit cum quadam alteratione 558. D.

SPIRITUS

spiritus & membrum sunt subiectum propinquum sanitatis & aegritudinis 3.D.10
Causarum vero quattuor sunt species: materiales, efficientes, formales & finales. Causae vero materiales sunt res subiectivae, in quibus fundatur vel invenitur sanitas & aegritudo, subiectum quidem proprinquum membrum & spiritus.

spiritus distribuitur per arterias membris corporis 9.B.13.
Et post ligamenta sunt arteriae, quae sunt corpora quae a corde nascuntur, concava, in longitudinem extensa, nervosa, & in sui substantia ligamentalia habentia motiones, dilatando se & constringendo, quae ex quietibus discernuntur. Quae quidem ad hoc fuerunt creatae, ut cor eventetur & fumosus vapor ab eo expellatur & spiritus membris corporis distribuatur. Post sunt venae, quae arteriae similes existunt, sed sunt ab hepate & sunt quietae. Quae quidem fuerunt creatae ad hoc, ut sanguis membris quae sunt in corpore partiatur.

spiritus es subtilis ad superiora mobilis 23.F.13.

spiritus existit vehiculum sensus & motus 26. A.
Vitalis vero virtus est illa quae spiritus esse rem conservat, qui sensus & motus vehiculum existit, & ipsum reddit aptum ad eorum impressiones recipiendas, cum ad cerebrum pervenit & facit ipsum potentem dandi vitam ubicumque expanditur. Et huius quidem virtutis sedes & operationis ipsius processus est cor.

spiritus generatur ex humorum subtilitate secundum aliquam complexionem 27.A.8.
Virtutes autem *alhaivanie* intelligi volunt per illas, virtutem illam, quae cum in membris recepta fuerit praeparabit ea ad recipiendum virtutem sensus & motus & operationis vitae, quibus etiam adduntur timoris & irae motiones per id quod in eis reperitur de dilatatione & constrictione, quae accidunt spiritui; qui huic proportionatus est virtuti. Nos autem explanabimus summam hanc & dicemus quod quemadmodum ex humorum spissitudine secundum aliquam complexionem substantia generatur spissa, quae est membrum aut

pars membri, ita ex humorum vaporibus et eorum subtilitate, secundum aliquam complexionem, substantia generatur subtilis, quae est spiritus. Et sicut apud medicos hepar primae generationis est principio, ita cor generationis secundae, principium exsistit. Et hic spiritus cum secundum complexionem provenit, quam debet habere praeparatur ad hanc viurtutem recipiendam, quae praeparat omnia membra ad recipiendum alias virtutes animales & etiam reliqua. Virtutes enim animales in spiritu quidem & in membris non proveniunt, nisi postquam haec vitalis provenit virtus. Ideoque licet virtutes animales alicuius membri destruantur. Vivum tamen membrum adhuc existit, nisi haec virtus in eo fuerit destructa. Nonne vides quod membrum stupidum aut paraliticum unumquodque secundum habitudinem est non habens sensum neque motum, aut propter complexionem quae prohibet ipsum eos recipere aut propter oppilationem, quae accidit inter cerebrum & ipsum in nervis, qui ad ipsum perveniunt & tamen ipsum est vivum. [...]. In membro ergo paralitico est virtus, quae eius custodit vitam, donec, cum remotum fuerit quod prohibet, profluat ad ipsum virtus sensus & motus. [...]. Et si virtus nutritiva, in quantum est nutritiva, esset ipsa virtus quae praeparat ad sentiendum & movendum, vegetabilia praeparata forent ad sensum & motum recipiendum. Restat ergo ut sit praeparans alia res, quae propriam sequantur complexionem, quae vocatur virtus vitalis. Et ipsa quidem est prima virtus, quae in spiritu provenit, cum spiritus ex subtilitate humorum procedit. Deinde spiritus secundum philosophum Aristotelem per eam recipit principium primum & animam primam, ex qua aliae profluunt virtutes. Harum vero virtutum operationes non proveniunt a spiritu in principio rei, sicut etiam sensus apud medicos non provenit per spiritum animalem, qui est in cerebro, nisi ad cristalloidem penetret, aut ad linguam, aut ad alia. Cum ergo pars spiritus in ventriculum pervenerit, cerebri complexionem recipiet & erit conveniens ut ex eo proveniant virtutum operationes, quae in eo primo repertae sunt, & similiter in hepate & similiter in testiculis. Et apud medicos quid nisi postquam spiritus in cerebro ad aliam convertitur complexionem non praeparat ad recipiendum animam quae est principium motus & sensus, & similiter in hepate, licet prima complexio iam iuverit ad recipiendum virtutem primam vitalem, & similiter in unoquoque membro. Apud eos enim unumquodque operationum genus aliam habet animam. Et neque est anima una, ex qua virtutes profluunt, aut erit anima aggregans hanc summam, quoniam etsi prima complexio iam adiuverit ad virtutem primam *alhaivanie* recipiendam, ubi vel in hora qua advenit spiritus & virtus, quae est eius perfectio, tamen haec virtus apud eos sola non sufficit, ut spiritus per ipsam omnes alias suscipiat virtutes, nisi propria provenerit complexio. Praetera dixerunt quod virtus haec propter hoc quod ipsa est praeparans vitam est etiam motus substantiae spiritualis subtilis principium ad membra & principium constrictionis & dilatationis, propter attractionem aeris & eius expulsionem. Affert enim adiutorium in comparatione vitae, quod est passio, et in comparatione operationum animae, & pulsus praeebet auxilium, quod est actio. Et haec quidem virtus virtutibus naturalibus similatur, ideo quod non a voluntate proveniunt, quae ab ea proveniunt. Et similatur virtutibus animalibus propter operationum earum diversitatem. Ipsa enim dilatat & constringit simul, movet ergo duobus motibus contrariis. Philosophi autem, cum animam dicunt, animam terrenam dicere volunt, perfectionem corporis naturalis instrumentalis. Et volunt dicere principium omnis virtutis, ex qua metipsi motus proveniunt & operationes diversae. Erit igitur haec virtus, secundum philosophorum sententiam, virtus animalis, sicut virtutes naturales, quas nominavimus, apud eos virtutes vocantur animales. Quod si noluerint dicere animam secundum hanc intentionem, sed velint dicere virtutem, que est principium comprehendendi & movendi, quod ex aliqua provenit compraehensione voluntarie. Et naturalem velint dicere pro omni virtute, ex qua operatio provenit in suo corpore secundum huius formae diversitatem; non erit virtus animalis, sed erit naturalis & altioris ordinis quam sit virtus, quam medici vocant naturalem. Et si naturalem vocaverit illam, quae rem nutrimenti ministrat & converterit, sive ad hoc ut remaneat individuum, sive ut remaneat species, non erit haec naturalis, sed erit tertium genus. Et quia ira & timor & similia eorum huius virtutis sunt passiones, tunc licet eorum principia sit sensus & existimatio & virtutes appraehendentes, huic tamen comparatae sunt virtuti. Huius autem virtutis declarationem certificare & an sit una, an plures quam una, in sapientia continetur naturali, quae philosophiae pars existit.

spiritus secundum Aristotelem per virtutem recipit principium primum & animam primam 27.B.15.

spiritus mundificatio sit respiratione & egressione anhelitus 31.A.6.
Aer est elementum nostrorum corporum & spirituum & praeter hoc, quod est elementum nostrorum corporum & spirtuum, est etiam quid successive nostris adveniens spiritibus, & est causa meliorationis eorum, non tantum sicut elementum, sed etiam sicut faciens, scilicet temperans. Iam antem declaravimus in his quae praecesserunt, quid velimus intelligi cum spiritum dicimus. Non enim dicere volumus illud quod philosophi animam vocant. Et hoc quidem temperamentum, quod ex aere nostris advenit spiritibus, ex duabus pendet operationibus, quae sunt mundificatio & eventatio. Eventatio vero est temperamentum complexionis spiritus calidi, cum superfluit propter coarctationem secundum plurimum & alteratur, & per temperamentum intelligimus temperamentum comparativum, quod scivisti. [...]. Cumque aer ad ipsum pervenit, impellit ipsum & miscetur cum eo, & prohibet ipsum ne ad igneitatem convertatur coarctativam vel suffocativam, ex qua ipse ad malitiam pervenit complexionis, per quam removetur a preparatione recipiendi impressiones animales in eo, qui est causa vitae & prohibet ne resolvatur ipsiusmet substantia vaporalis humida. Mundificatio vero fit apud reversionem vel egressionem anhelitus, propter associationem eius quod ei attribuit virtus separativa ex vapore fumoso, cuius comparatio ad spiritum est comparatio humoris superflui ad corpus. Temperamentum ergo eius est propterea quod spiritui advenit aer cum attrahitur, & mundificatio est propter eius exitum cum expellitur.

spiritus motus ad exteriora fit subito, ut ex ira 36.D.12.

spiritus motus ad interiora fit, vel subito vel paulatim 36.D.14.
Et motum quidem eius ad interiora sequitur frigiditas eius, quod est exterius, & caliditas interior. Et est cum multa coangustatione constringitur et infrigidatur interius & exterius & syncopis magna, aut mors sequitur ipsum. Et motus quidem ad exteriora aut fit subito, sicut fit cum est ira, aut fit leviter & paulatim, sicut contingit cum adsunt delitiae et gaudium temperatur. Motus vero ad interiora aut est

subito, sicut cum timor adest, aut est leviter et paulatim, sicut cum adest tristitia.

spiritus retentio fit ex oppilatione 213.H.3

Immo si necessarium fuerit, tunc accidet uni membro & videtur quod paralysis & mollificatio secundum plurimum fit propter retentionem spiritus. Causa vero retentionis est oppilatio, aut separatio pororum & transitum perducentium ad membra cum sectione. Oppilatio autem aut est secundum semitam contrictionis pororum aut secundum semitam prohibitionis ex humore oppilante: aut secundum semitam rei aggregantis ambas res, & est apostema, quare causa mollificationis & paralysis faciens abscissionem spiritus a membris est contrictio pororum. [...]. Repletio vero oppilativa est ex materiis humidis currentibus, quibus membrum humectatur seu madefit, & currunt in vacuitates omnium nervorum aut stant in principiis nervorum aut ramis nervorum, & oppilant viam spiritus currentis in eis. [...]. Et scias quod multoties expellitur materia humida ad extremitates, propter dominium caliditatis in corpore, aut motu subito ex timore, aut pavore, aut ira, aut delitiis, aut angustia.

spiritus visibilis penetrat ad oculum per viam duorum nervorum concavorum 220.B.7.

Virtus visuum & materia spiritus visibilis penetrat ad oculum per viam duorum nervorum concavorum, quos novisti per anatomiam. [...]. Et hic quidem humor positus est in medio, quoniam est dignior locis, qui sunt cum custodia. Sed & post ipsum positus est humor alius adveniens ei ex cerebro, ut nutriat ipsum. Inter ipsum enim & inter sanguinem purum est gradatio. Hic autem humor similis est vitro liquefacto, & color vitri liquefacti est clarus & declinat ad parvam rubedinem.

spiritus subtilitas ut plurimum accidit ex siccitate 231.A.5.

spiritus grossitudo fit propter humiditatem 230 H

Debilitatem visus et eius nocumentum efficit. [...]. Aut est propter rem appropriatam ipsi spiritui visibili & membris quae ipsum sequuntur, sicut nervo concavo & sicut humoribus & tunicis. Et spiritui quidem visibili quandoque accidit ut inspissetur & ut subtilietur & accidit ei ut ingrossetur & accidit ei ut multiplicetur. Et accidit ei ut minoretur. Multiplicatio autem est melior res & magis iuvativa. Et subtilitas quidem plurimum accidit ex siccitate, & quandoque fit ex vehementia separationis accidentis cum sol aspicitur, & simile ei ex resplendentibus. [...]. Et paucitas quidem quandoque est a principio creationis & quandoque est propter vehementiam siccitatis [...] & propinquitatem mortis quando resolvit spiritum.

spiritus est corpus compositum & non simplex 257.D.

spiritus producitur ex parte subtili humorum & ex vaporibus ipsorum 557.E

spiritus est lator virtutum animae in membra animalium tendentium mediante spiritu 557.E.13.

spiritus praeparatur ad receptionem animae ex forma complexionali 557.F.6.

spiritus licet sint plures numero, nihilominus unus ipsorum est generatione primus qui generatur ex corde, secundum philosophorum opinionem 557.G.2.

virtutes animae omnes manant in spiritus ex corde, secundum quosdam philosophos, absque hoc quod spiritus indigeat membro alio 557.H.3

spiritus diffinitio 557.H.8.
[...] & ista quidem dispositio in humano spiritu reperitur, & spiritus quidem in summa est res generata ex commistione elementorum vergens in similitudinem caelestium corporum. Et propterea iudicatur de spiritu, quod sit substantia luminosa, seu lucida: propter quod dicitur de visivo spiritu, quod sit radius atque lux. Et exinde anima gaudet ex intuitu lucis & tristatur in tenebris: quoniam illud est conforme naturae vel principio ipsius & hoc est in contrarium.

spiritus passiones sunt ira, gaudium, tristitia & timor 558.B.7.

spiritus quilibet habet virtutem propriam 568.A.

spiritus dividitur ille qui existit in corde & ille qui in cerebro 568.A.6.

spiritus evacuatio causatur etiam a forti motu 569.C
Causa vero harum aegritudinum est quicquid
in eo frigiditatem generat, & quandoque solvit
ex eo dissolubile, cuius virtus aut est
in potentia, velut contingit in hyusquiamo
assumpto, aut in actu sicut in nive.

Fames est cum pabulum spirituum terminatur
& sicut contingit cum terminatur,
& consumitur oleum in lampade vel crucibulo,
vehemens etiam saturitas & crapula calorem
suffocat & extinguit.

STUPOR
De stupore 218.H
Usus huius dictionis stupor in libris est diversus: plurimum enim ponitur dictio stuporis synonyma dictioni *alrhase*, idest tremoris. Nos vero & plurimi hominum utuntur ea secundum hunc modum, & quidem stupor est morbus officialis faciens evenire in sensu tactuali nocumentum scilicet aut destructionem aut diminutionem cum tremore, si est debilis, aut mollificationem, si est confirmatus, quoniam virtus sensibilis non prohibetur a penetratione, nisi etiam motiva virtus prohibeatur, sicut exposui multoties, quamvis in quibusdam horis inveniatur stupor, absque difficultate motus, propter diversitatem nervorum, motus & sensus. [...]. Aut debilitat & corrumpit eius complexionem propter calorem vehementem [...]. Aut propter grossitiem substantiae nervorum, quare spiritus in ipsa non penetrant bene. [...]. Aut propter grossitiem substantiae nervorum, quare spiritus in ipsa non penetrat bene. Et propter hoc contingit in tactu pedis cum comparatione ad tactum manus, sicut stupor. Aut fit propter oppilationem, ex humoribus grossis scilicet, aut a sanguine, aut phlegmate, aut melancholia [...] aut propter oppilationem ex coarctatione apostematis & exiturae, aut coarctatione vehementi &

ligatura, & coarctatione situs torquente vel involvente nervos, aut propter contusionem eorum vehementem, aut propter dolorem cum quo effunditur ad membrum sanguis, aut humor alius plurimus, quare oppilat transitu, & huius plurimum est a sanguine. Et propter hoc cum permutatur situs eius & removetur & recedit ab eo, quod ad ipsum est effusum, redit sensus. [...]. Causae vero stuporis quandoque sunt in ipso cerebro, & tunc si est universalis, communis in corpori toti, est mortalis in die uno.

TREMOR

Tremor excutit vehementer quod in cerebro comprehenditur de superfluitatibus 209.F.9

Tremor enim excutit vhementer quod in cerebro compraehensum est de superfluitatibus. Sudor autem iuvat tremorem sua expulsione. Et quemadmodum apoplexia convertitur ad paralysim, similiter plurimum β epilessiae convertitur ad paralysim. Quidam autem existimant quod phlegmaticae associantur tremor & agitatio, quoniam phlegma non consequitur in spissitudine sua, ut oppilet meatus integre. Melancholia vero integre oppilat, quare in ipsa accidit parva agitatio. Et alii existimant quod eius cum qua multiplicatur agitatio, forsitan causa est humor parvae quantitatis, aut paucae penetrationis in meatibus & ponitur res e converso. Nullus vero utrorumque sermo in eo est determinatus.

Tremor fit ex omnibus causis quibus virtutes animales contrahuntur 218.D.15

Tremor est morbus instrumentalis eveniens propter defectum virtutis motivae a motu lacertorum cum continuitatem resistentis gravitati impedienti & ingredienti vel aggredienti cum sua motione motionem voluntariam. Quare commiscentur motus voluntarii cum motibus non voluntariis [...]. Et est nocumentum in virtute motiva, sicut stupor est laesio in sensibili. Huius autem causa aut est in virtute, aut in instrumento, aut in utrique simul. In virtute vero, cum debilitatur. Propterea, quod accidit timor, vel propter praesentiam rei timorosae, vel terribilis horribilis sicut aspectus ex loc alto, aut ambulatio super parietem, aut peroratio coram eo, ex quo aliquis verecundatur & qui timetur, aut reliqua, ex quibus contrahuntur virtutes animales, aut angustia, aut tribulatio, aut gaudium pertubans ordines motuum virtutis facit accidere tremorem. Et ira quandoque facit illud, quoniam facit contingere diversitatem in motu spiritus.

Tremor superveniens causonidi tunc solvit permistionem sensus 218.F.11
Cui accidit in febre causonide tremor, tunc sensus permistio resolvit eam ab ipso. Et Galenus quidem non concedit hunc aphorismum. Veruntamen, non est ex eis quae modum non habent. Et scias quod tremor magis perversus est qui a sinistro incipit. Et tremor quidem in sensibus medicamine non removetur.

Tremor est perversus magis qui a sinistro incipit 218.F.12.

VISIO
Visione fieri extramittendo secundum Avicenna 231.C.11.D 1.

De signis 231.C.
In eo quidem quod est communitate corporis signum est illud, quod dedimus, quod significat complexionem totius corporis. Et illud quod fit communitate cerebri est, quoniam illic est aliquod signorum significantium nocumentum in cerebro, cum hoc ut sint reliqui sensus laesi cum illo. Illud enim fiduciam facit communitatis cerebri. Et quandoque appropriatur visui plurimum proprietatum eius, & cum odoratu, fine auditu. Sicut percussio coarctativa, quando cadit in parte anteriore cerebri. Et quandoque est auditus, cum sua dispositione, & remanet oculus apertus, & non potest claudi palpebra super ipsum, verum non videt. Et signum quod ipsi spiritui appropiatur est quoniam si spiritus est subtilis & est paucus, videt rem ex proximo cum perscrutatione, & non videt quod elongatum est cum perscrutatione. Etsi fuerit subtilis plurimus, videt cum perscrutatione rem propinquam & elongatam. Verum eius subtilitas, cum est superflua, non fingitur in re splendida, seu lucida valde. Immo fugat eum lumen forte & separat eum. Et si est grossus & plurimus non deficit ei perscrutatio intuendo longinquum, & non perscrutatur visionem propinqui, & causa in hoc apud loquentes de radio est quod visus non fit, nisi egressione radii, & cum obviat ei quod videtur, & quod motus vadens ad locum longinquum subtiliat grossitiem eius & aequat essentiam ipsius quemadmodum hiuiusmodi motus resolvit

spiritum subtilem, quare forsitan non operatur aliquid. Et apud illos qui dicunt pervium vehere formas visibilium causa est alia ab illa, est quod glacialis motus fit fortis, cum videt illud quod elongatur, & illud est ex eis quae subtiliant spiritum grossum habitantem in ipso, & resolvit spiritum subtilem, & proprie paucum. Verificatio autem certioris in his duobus sermonibus, pertinet ad sapientes, non medicos.

Visiva virtus disponitur mediante complexione humiditatis chrystallinae
557.G
Et existit tamen harum omnium virtutum principium secundum dictum philosophum, in corde, quemadmodum apud eos, qui diversificantur a sententia eius, principium virtutis visivae, auditivae et gustativae, est in cerebro; sed nihilominus secundum eos spiritus disponitur ad recipiendum has virtutes secundum veritatem & perfectionem, in membriis aliis, ita quod visiva mediante complexione crystallinae humiditatis quando complexioni spiritus coniungitur.

De anatomia oculi
220.B.
Virtus visuum & materia spiritus visibilis penetrat ad oculum per viam duorum nervorum concavorum, quos novisti per antomiam. Cumque nervi & panniculi, qui eis associantur, ad orbitam descendunt, dilatatur extremitas cuiusque eorum, & repletur & ampliatur ita quod compraehendit humores qui sunt in pupilla, quorum medius est glacialis, & ipse quidem est humor clarus [...]. Et hic quidem humor positus est in medio, quoniam est dignior locis quam sunt cum custodia. Sed & post ipsum positus est humor alius adveniens ei ex cerebro, ut nutriat ipsum; inter ipsum enim & inter sanguinem purum est gradatio. Hic autem humor similis est vitro liquefacto, & color vitri liquefacti est clarus & declinat ad parvam rubedinem.

De destructione visus 233
Destructio visus quandoque accidit ex causis debilitatis visus, cum superfluunt, quare confideretur illic. Nos vero iterum dicamus & dimittamus, quod est cum communitate cerebri & aliorum, quoniam illud illic intellectum est. Destructio visus aut fit partibus oculi

manifestis in suis substantiis incolumibus, aut fit illud, cum iam acciderit eis nocumentum sensibile, aut non sensibile, & quae itinere eorum procedunt. Noster vero sermo est de primis. Nam si partes oculi apparentes fuerint incolumes in substantiis suis, sed iam acciderit eis nocumentum ex parte alia non manifesta hominibus & vulgo, tunc aut erit foramen secundum dispositionem sanitatis suae, aut non erit; quod si fuerit foramen secundum dispositionem sanitatis suae, aut erit illic oppilatio aquosa, aut erit oppilatio non illic, immo in nervo concavo; aut propter rem cadentem in foramine eius, aut propter cooperimentum accidens ex siccitate, aut mollificatione: aut apostematibus in lacertis suis compressis in se ipsis.

VULNUS
vulnus in corde non sperat sanare 463.E.13.

vulnera quandoque sunt mortalia, secundum loca in quibus existunt 463.E.15.

In corde autem non speratur salus, cum in eo accidit vulnus. Et plurimum ille cui accidit vulnus in ventre suo, cum accidit ei nausea, aut singultus, aut solutio ventris, moritur.

Abstract

Questo studio affronta i testi di un poeta che appartiene ad una impareggiabile categoria di pensatori. L'esile raccolta di poesie di Guido Cavalcanti che va sotto il titolo di *Rime* porta inscritta un'impresa intellettuale di vaste proporzioni. Tradizionalmente considerato all'interno della disputa con Dante Alighieri, Guido in realtà sceglie un fronte di opposizione molto più ampio, che coincide con la roccaforte teologica al centro dell'Europa occidentale di quegli anni. Spiegando l'amore, cioè la conoscenza, nei termini di un'operazione dei sensi, Cavalcanti descrive un cammino che si interrompe prima della visione divina offerta al pellegrino della *Divina Commedia* al termine del suo viaggio. La perfezione terrestre, l'unica a cui gli essere umani possono ambire, rappresentava un imperdonabile affronto di Guido nei confronti del suo 'primo amico', Dante, come del resto nei confronti di un intero *milieu* culturale. Nonostante la sua appartenenza ad una minoranza culturale, nonostante che una importante università europea avesse programmaticamente oscurato le fonti da lui impiegate per costruire i propri versi, Guido Cavalcati procede ad affidare alle sue poesie un messaggio che ridisegna la geografia dell'anima rendendola mortale (una proposizione di gravi conseguenze nella cultura del tredicesimo secolo), così cristallizzando un sapere in procinto di essere bandito nella storia delle idee dell'Europa.

Guido Cavalcanti è qui studiato principalmente dal punto di vista dei suoi esperimenti linguistici. L'indagine all'interno del laboratorio retorico delle *Rime* è introdotta dai primi due capitoli. Nel primo si delinea la doppia tradizione di Cavalcanti, che emerge dai suoi versi, ma anche dal personaggio creato da novellieri e scrittori di cronache appena dopo la sua morte, come un autore leggendario, e sfuggente. Gli autori che in modo più consistente contribuirono a questa tradizione, Dante Alighieri e Boccaccio, furono determinanti nel costruire il profilo di Guido attorno ad una lacuna testuale; eppure, leggendo il *corpus* testuale delle *Rime*, si dimostra che questa è la strategia dello stesso Guido, che si dipinge in uno dei suoi sonetti come una sequenza di impalpabili sospiri. Nel secondo capitolo si introducono le rime dette convenzionalmente 'minori', cioè quelle che accompagnano la canzone maggiore. In *Donna me prega* Cavalcanti formula il principio, che sta a fondamento teorico del suo intero lavoro, secondo cui un individuo è tale solo entro i confini delle proprie percezioni. Questa interpretazione definitiva - prodotta da un'ampia tradizione esegetica che si estende dal commento del medico fiorentino del quattordicesimo secolo Dino Del Garbo fino agli studi più recenti - dichiara una affiliazione filosofica con l'Aristotelismo radicale, una corrente di pensiero le cui teorie vennero dichiarate eretiche al momento stesso della loro formulazione. La conclusione di Cavalcanti, che l'amore è un'esperienza contenuta entro il corpo, è una indicazione che le sue fonti appartengono al mondo della filosofia naturale. Tra queste fonti, il presente studio adotta il *Liber Canonis* di Avicenna, un manuale medico di vasta circolazione e impiego tra il tredicesimo e il quattordicesimo secolo. In questo stesso capitolo viene delineata l'evoluzione, tra arte pratica e scienza teorica, della disciplina medica.

Il terzo capitolo presenta le 'voci del corpo' che costituiscono il fuoco della indagine testuale. Le rime 'minori' rappresentano il protagonista cavalcantiano come figurativamente decapitato, cioè, non in grado di trattenere le idee che egli stesso ha prodotto mediante le proprie percezioni. Questo confinamento nello spazio delle percezioni sensoriali, e nello spazio della materia a cui le percezioni si applicano, produce alcune conseguenze sul piano della lingua: i grammatici contemporanei a Guido avevano concluso che le parole sono il prodotto di concetti astratti. A soluzione di tale difficoltà, in una sezione delle sue *Rime* Guido impiega un linguaggio speciale prodotto dal corpo dell'amante nel corso della sua ventura amorosa, cioè mentre il suo corpo è agito dalla vista della donna e così esposto ad una catena di violente risposte fisiologiche. Le 'voci del corpo' sono composte da queste involontarie risposte, adoperate come unità semantiche. In particolare vengono qui considerati i sospiri e le lacrime, spiegati attraverso le indicazioni di Avicenna, e in contrasto con la tradizione poetica esistente. Gli ultimi due capitoli sono specificamente dedicati all'analisi testuale, inclusa la ricostruzione di una nuova prospettiva del colloquio tra Guido e Dante legata al tema del pianto.

L'*Appendice* consiste di una serie di estratti del *Liber Canonis* selezionati sulla base del vocabolario cavalcantiano. Alcuni di questi estratti costituiscono il materiale principale adottato per l'esegesi delle *Rime*.

Bibliography

Concordanze della lingua poetica delle origini (CLPIO). Ed. D'Arco Silvio Avalle. Milan-Naples: Ricciardi, 1992.

Agamben, Giorgio. *Stanze. Il fantasma nella cultura occidentale.* Turin: Einaudi, 1977.

Agrimi, Jole, and Chiara Crisciani. *Edocere medicos.* Naples: Guerini, 1988.

Albertus Magnus. *De motibus animalium; De spiritu et respiratione.* Ed. Auguste Borgnet. Vol. IX, *Parvorum Naturalium Pars I.* Paris: Bilbiopolam, 1890.

Alessio, Gian Carlo. *Il commento di Gentile da Cingoli a Martino di Dacia* in *L'insegnamento della logica a Bologna nel VIX secolo,* eds. Dino Buzzetti, M. Ferriani and A. Tabarroni. Bologna: Presso l'Istituto della Storia dell'Università, 1992.

Alexandri Aphrodisei e graeco in latinum traducta per Georgium Valla et Aristotelis Problemata Theodoro interprete, et Plutarchi Problemata, Venetiis: per Antonium de Strata Cremonensem, 1488.

Ardizzone, Maria Luisa. *Guido Cavalcanti. The Other Middle Ages.* Toronto, Buffalo, London: Toronto University Press, 2002.

-- ed. *Guido Cavalcanti tra i suoi lettori.* Florence: Cadmo, 2003.

Arnaldi de Villanova. *Opera medica omnia. III. Tractatus de amore heroico, Epistola de dosi Tyriacalium medicinarum.* Ed. Michael R. McVaugh. Barcelona: Edicions de la Universitat de Barcelona, 1985.

Aristoteles latinus. *De Interpretatione.* Eds. Gerard Verbeke, and L. Minio-Paluello. Bruges-Paris: Desclée de Brouwer, 1965.

Aristoteles latinus. *De generatione animalium.* Ed. H. J. Drossaart Lulofs. Bruges-Paris: Desclée de Brouwer, 1966.

Aristoteles latinus. *Physica*. Eds. Fernand Bossier, and J. Brams. Leiden-New York: E. J Brill, 1990.

Averroes. *Commentarium magnum in Aristotelis De Anima libros*. Ed. F. Stuart Crawford. Cambridge, MA: The Mediaeval Academy of America, 1953.

Averroes. *Compendia Librorum Aristotelis qui Parva Naturalia vocantur*. Ed. H. Blumberg. Cambridge: The Mediaeval Academy of America, 1949.

Avicenna latinus. *Liber de Anima seu Sextus de Naturalibus*. Édition critique de la traduction latine médiévale par S. Van Riet. Louvain: Éditions Peeters, and Leiden: E.J.Brill, 1968.

Baránski, G. Zygmunt. *"Chiosar con altro testo". Leggere Dante nel Trecento*. Florence: Cadmo, 2001.

-- *Guido Cavalcanti and his First Readers* in *Guido Cavalcanti tra i suoi lettori*, ed. Ardizzone, pp. 149-175.

Bauemker, Clemens. *Des Alfred von Sareshel (Alfredus Angelicus): Schrift De motu cordis*. Münster: Verlag der Aschendorffschen Verlagsbuchhandlung, 1923.

Benvenuti de Rambaldis de Imola. *Comentum super Dantis Alighierij Comoediam*, Tomus primus. Florentiae: Typis G.Barbèra, 1887.

Bertola, Ettore. *La dottrina dello spirito in Alberto Magno* in *Sophia* 19, 3-4 (1951): 306-312.

Birkenmajer, Aleksander. *Le rôle joué par les médecins et les naturalistes dans la réception d'Aristote au XIIe et XIIIe siècles* in *Etudes d'histoire des sciences et de la philosophie du Moyen Age*. Warszawa: Wydawnictwo Polskiej Akademii Nauk, 1970, pp. 73-87.

Black, Deborah. *Logic and the Linguistic Art* in *Aristotle and His Medieval Interpreters*, eds. Richard Bosley and M. Tweedale. Calgary: Universiy of Calgary Press, 1991, pp. 25-71.

Boccaccio, Giovanni *Decameron*. Ed. Enrico Bianchi. Milan-Naples: Riccardo Ricciardi, 1952.

Bombaglioli, Graziolo. *Commento all' 'Inferno' di Dante*. Ed. Carlo Luca Rossi. Pisa: Scuola Normale Superiore, 1998.

Bono, James J. *Medical Spirits and the Mediaeval Language of Life* in *Traditio* 15 (1984): 91-130.

Boncompagni. *Rhetorica Novissima*, prodit curante Augusto Gaudentio in *Scripta anecdotica antiquissimorum glossatorum*, II. Bononiae: in aedibus Petri Virano olim fratrum Treves, 1892.

Bruni, Francesco. *Semantica della sottigliezza* in *Studi medievali* XXIXX (1978): 1-36.

Bursill-Hall, Geoffrey L. *Speculative Grammar of the Middle Ages*. The Hague and Paris: Mouton, 1971.

Buti, Francesco. *Commento sopra la Divina Commedia di Dante Alighieri*. Pisa: Fratelli Nistri, 1858.

Bruni, Francesco. *Semantica della sottigliezza. Note sulla distribuzione della cultura nel Basso Medioevo* in *Studi medievali* N.S. 19 (1978): 1-36.

Calvino, Italo. *Leggerezza* in *Lezioni Americane*. Milan: Garzanti, 1988.

-- *La penna in prima persona* in *Saggi 1945-1985*. Milan: Mondadori, 1999. t.1 pp. 361-364.

Carrera, Alessandro. *"Per gli occhi venne la battaglia in pria". Fenomenica dello sguardo tra Cavalcanti e Leopardi* in *Guido Cavalcanti tra i suoi lettori*, ed. Ardizzone, pp. 241-262.

Carruthers, Mary. *On Affliction and Reading, Weeping and Argument: Chaucer's Lachrymose Troilus in Context* in *Representations*, 93 (Winter 2006) University of California Press: 1-21

Ceard, Jean, ed. *La folie et le corps*. Paris: Presses de l'École Normale Supérieure, 1985.

Chenu, Marie-Dominique. *Auctor, Actor, Author* in *Bulletin du Cange* 3 (1927): 81-86.

-- *'Spiritus'. Le vocabulaire de l'âme au XII siècle* in *Revue des Sciences philosophiques et theologiques* 41 (1957): 210-230.

-- *Authentica et magistralia* in *La Théologie au Douzième Siècle*. Paris: Librairie Philosophique J. Vrin, 1976, pp. 351-365.

Cicciaporci, Antonio. *Memorie della vita e dell'opere di Guido Cavalcanti. "Rime" di Guido Cavalcanti edite e inedite aggiuntovi un volgarizzamento antico non mai pubblicato del comento di Dino del Garbo sulla canzone "Donna me prega"*. Florence: Nicolò Carli, 1813 pp. v-xxxiii.

Colish, Marcia. *The Mirror of Language*. Lincoln and London: University of Nebraska Press, 1983 (revised edition).

Compagni, Dino. *Cronica*. Ed. Davide Cappi. Rome: Nella sede dell'Istituto, 2000.

Contini, Gianfranco. *Poeti del Duecento*. Milan-Naples, Ricciardi, 1960.

-- *Cavalcanti in Dante* in *Varianti ed altra linguistica*. Turin: Einaudi, 1970, pp. 433-445.

-- *Letteratura italiana del Quattrocento*. Florence: Sansoni, 1976.

Corti, Maria. *Dante a un nuovo crocevia*. Florence: Libreria commissionaria Sansoni, 1981.

-- *Scritti su Cavalcanti e Dante*. Turin: Einaudi, 2003.

D'Alverny, M.Therese, ed. *Avicenne en Occident*. Paris: J.Vrin, 1993.

Dante Alighieri. *La Commedia secondo l'antica vulgata*. Ed. Giorgio Petrocchi. Turin: Einaudi, 1975.

-- *The Divine Comedy*, transl. with an Introduction by Allen Mandelbaum. Berkeley-Los Angeles: University of California Press, 1980-84.

-- *Opere minori*. Vol. II. Eds. Domenico De Robertis and C. Vasoli. Milan: Riccardo Ricciardi, 1995.

-- *Rime*. Ed. and Intro. (1933) Gianfranco Contini. Turin: Einaudi, 1995.

--*Vita nuova*. Eds. and trans. Dino Cervigni and E. Vasta. Notre Dame, IN, and London: Notre Dame University Press, 1995.

-- *Opere minori*. Vol. III, Part 1. Eds. Pier Vincenzo Mengaldo and B. Nardi. Milan: Riccardo Ricciardi, 1996.

----*Vita nova*. Ed. Guglielmo Gorni. Turin: Einaudi, 1996.

De Robertis, Domenico. *Antonio Manetti copista* in *Editi e rari*. Milano: Feltrinelli, 1978, pp. 183-215.

-- *Un altro Cavalcanti?* In *Guido Cavalcanti tra i suoi lettori*, ed. Ardizzone, pp. 13-25.

De Vaux, Roland. *La première entrée d'Averroës chez les Latins* in *Revue des Sciences Philosophiques et Théologiques* 22 (1933): 193-245.

Donno, Daniel J. *Dante's Argenti: episode and function* in *Dante: the Critical Complex* VII (2003): 117-131.

Eco, Umberto, R. Lambertini, C. Marmo, and A. Tabarroni. *On Animal Language in the Medieval Classification of Signs* in *On the Medieval Theory of Signs*, eds. Umberto Eco and C. Marmo. Amsterdam, Philadelphia: John Benjamins Publishing Company, 1989, pp. 3-41.

Favati, Guido. *La glossa latina di Dino del Garbo a 'Donna me prega'* in *Annali della Scuola Normale superiore di Pisa* XXI (1952): 70-103.

-- *Inchiesta sul Dolce Stil Novo*. Florence: Le Monnier, 1975.

Fenzi, Enrico. *La canzone d'amore di Guido Cavalcanti e i suoi antichi commenti*. Genova: Il Melangolo, 1999.

Freccero, John. *Ironia e mimesi: il disdegno di Guido* in *Dante e la Bibbia*, ed. Giovanni Barblan. Florence: Leo Olschki, 1988, pp. 41-54.

Fredborg, Karin Margareta, L. Nielsen, and J. Pinborg. *An unedited part of Roger Bacon's 'Opus Majus': 'De Signis'* in *Traditio* 34 (1978): 75-136.

Gorce, Matthieu-Maxime. *Averroisme* in *Dictionnaire d'Histoire et de geographie ecclesiastique*, ed. Alfred Baudrillart. Paris: Librairie Letouzey et Ané, 1931.

Grabmann, Martin. *L'aristotelismo italiano ai tempi di Dante con particolare riguardo all'Università di Bologna* in *Rivista di filosofia neoscolastica* 38 (1946): 260-77.

Grant, Edward. *The Foundation of Modern Science in the Middle Ages*. Cambridge: Cambridge University Press, 1996.

Hildegard von Bingen. *Causae et curae*. Ed. Paulus Kaiser. Lipsia: Teubner, 1903.

Jacopo della Lana. *Comedia di Dante degli Allagherii col commento di Jacopo della Lana bolognese*. Bologna: Tipografia Regia, 1866.

Jacquart, Danielle. *'Theorica' et 'practica' dans l'einsegnement de la médecine à Salerne au XXIe siècle* in *Vocabulaires des écoles et des méthodes d'einsegnement au moyen âge*, ed. Olga Weijers. Études sur le vocabulaire intellectuel du moyen âge, 5, Turnhout: Brepols, 1992, pp. 102-110.

Klein, Robert. *"Spirito peregrino"* in *Form and Meaning. Essays on the Renaissance and Modern Art*. New York: The Viking Press, 1979, pp. 62-85.

Kristeller, Paul Oskar. *A philosophical Treatise from Bologna dedicated to Guido Cavalcanti: Magister Jacobus de Pistorio and his Quaestio de felicitate* in *Medioevo e*

Rinascimento: Studi in onore di Bruno Nardi, vol. 1. Florence: Sansoni, 1955, pp. 427-463.

-- *Philosophy and Medicine in Medieval and Renaissance Italy* in *Organism, Medicine and Metaphysics*, ed. E.F. Spicker. Dordrecht: D. Reidel, 1978, pp. 29-40.

-- *The school of Salerno. Its development and its contribution to the history of learning* in *Studies in Renaissance Thought and Letters*. Rome: Edizioni di storia e letteratura, 1984, pp. 495-551.

Landino, Cristoforo. *Comento sopra la Comedia*. Ed. Paolo Procaccioli. Rome: Salerno Editrice, 2001.

Lausberg, Heinrich. *Elementi di retorica*. Bologna: Il Mulino, 1969.

-- *Handbook of Literary Rhetoric*. Leiden, Boston, Köln: Brill, 1998.

Lindberg, David C. *Theories of Visions from Al-Kindi to Kepler*. Chicago: The University of Chicago Press, 1976.

Luzi, Mario. *L'inferno e il limbo* in *Nauralezza del poeta*. Milan: Garzanti, 1995 pp. 56-65.

Maierù, Alfonso. *Bolognese Terminology in Medicine and Arts* in *University Training in Medieval Europe*. Leiden, New York, Köln: E. J. Brill, 1994, pp. 71-92.

-- *La logica nell'età di Cavalcanti* in *Guido Cavalcanti tra i suoi lettori*, ed. Ardizzone, pp. 27-49.

Malato, Enrico. *Dante e Guido Cavalcanti*. Rome: Salerno Editrice, 1997.

Mancini, Franco. *La figura nel cuore fra cortesia e mistica. Dai Siciliani allo Stilnovo*. Naples: Edizioni Scientifiche Italiane, 1988.

Maramauro, Guglielmo. *Expositione sopra l' 'Inferno' di Dante Alighieri*. Eds. Saverio Bellomo and P. Pisoni. Padova: Antenore, 1998.

Marmo, Costantino. *Semiotica e linguaggio nella scolastica.* Parigi, Bologna, Erfurt 1270-1330. Rome: Istituto Palazzo Borromini, 1994.

Minnis Alastair, and A. B. Scott, eds. *Medieval Literary Theory and Criticism c.1100-c.1375. The Commentary Tradition.* Oxford: Clarendon Press, 2000.

Mortara Garavelli, Bice. *Manuale di Retorica.* Milan: Bompiani, 2003.

Nardi, Bruno. *L'averroismo bolognese nel secolo XIII e Taddeo Alderotto* in *Rivista di storia della filosofia* 4 (1949): 11-22.

-- *Studi di filosofia medievale.* Rome: Edizioni di storia e letteratura, 1960.

-- *L'amore e i medici medievali* in *Saggi e note di critica dantesca.* Milan-Naples: Ricciardo Ricciardi, 1966, pp. 238-267.

-- *Dante e la cultura medievale*, ed. Paolo Mazzantini. Bari: Laterza, 1990.

L'Ottimo commento della Divina Commedia. tomo I, Pisa: Presso Niccolò Capurro, 1827.

Pagani, Ileana. *La teoria linguistica di Dante.* Naples: Liguori Editore, 1982.

Panvini, Bruno, ed. *Le Rime della Scuola Siciliana.* 2 vols. Florence: Leo Olschki, 1962.

Parodi, Giovanni. *La miscredenza di Guido Cavalcanti e una fonte del Boccaccio* in *Bullettino della Società Dantesca Italiana* 22 (1915): 35-47.

Peri, Massimo. *Malato d'amore. La medicina dei poeti e la poesia dei medici.* Messina: Rubbettino Editore, 1996.

Pesenti, Tiziana. *Arti e medicina: la formazione del curriculum medico* in *Luoghi e metodi di insegnamento nell'Italia del Basso Medioevo (secc. XII-XIV: dalle scuole monastiche ed episcopali alle prime università)*, eds. Luciano Gargan and O. Limone. Galatina: Congedo, 1989, pp. 155-177.

Pietro Alighieri. *Il Commentarium di Pietro Alighieri nelle redazioni Ashburnhamiana e Ottoboniana.* Eds. Roberto della Vedova, and M. Silvotti. Florence: Leo S. Olschki, 1978.

Pinborg, Jan *Speculative Grammar* in *The Cambridge History of Later Medieval Philosophy*, Normann Kretzmann, A. Kenny, J. Pinborg eds. Cambridge: Cambridge University Press, 1982, pp. 254-269.

Pinto, Raffaele. *La parola del cuore* in *La poesia di Giacomo da Lentini. Scienza e filosofia nel XIII secolo in Sicilia e nel Mediterraneo occidentale*, ed. Rossend Arqués. Palermo: Centro di Studi Filologici e Linguistici Siciliani, 2000, pp. 169-191.

Pound, Ezra. *Cavalcanti* in *Literary Essays*. Intro. T.S. Eliot. London: Faber & Faber and New York: New Directions, 1954, pp. 149-200.

Pozzi, Giovanni. *Schola cordis: di metafora in metonimia* in *Lombardia Elvetica. Studi offerti a Virgilio Gilardoni*, eds. Virgilio Gilardoni and P. Caroni. Bellinzona: Edizioni Casagrande, 1986.

Renan, Ernest. *Averroès et l'averroïsme*. Paris: Michel Levy Frères, 1866.

Rosier, Irène. *Interjections et Expressions des Affects dans la Sémantique du XIIIe Siecle* in *Histoire Épistémologie Language* 14/II (1992): 61-84.

Sacchetti, Franco. *Il Trecentonovelle*. Ed. Valerio Mariucci. Rome: Salerno Editrice, 1996.

Schmidt, Paul Gerard. *Perché tanti anonimi nel Medioevo?* In *Filologia Mediolatina* VI-VII (1999-2000): 1-8.

Siraisi, Nancy. *Taddeo Alderotti and his Pupils. Two generations of Italian Medical Learning*. Princeton: Princeton University Press, 1981.

-- *Medieval and Early Renaissance Medicine*. Chicago: The University of Chicago Press, 1990.

Tanturli, Giuliano. *Proposta e risposta. La prolusione petrarchesca del Landino e il codice cavalcantiano di Antonio Manetti* in *Il Rinascimento* XXXII (1992): 213-225.

-- *Filologia cavalcantiana fra Antonio Manetti e Raccolta Aragonese* in *Sotto il segno di Dante: scritti in onore di Francesco Mazzoni*, eds. Domenico De Robertis and L. Coglievina. Florence: Le Lettere, 1998, pp. 311-320.

Taylor, Charles. *Sources of the Self. The Making of Modern Identity*. Cambridge: Harvard University Press, 1989.

Tonelli, Natascia. *De Guidone de Cavalcantibus Physico* in *Per Domenico De Robertis. Studi offerti dagli allievi fiorentini*. Florence: Le Lettere, 2000, pp.459-508.

-- *Fisiologia dell'amore doloroso in Cavalcanti e Dante* in *Guido Cavalcanti laico*, ed. Rossend Arqués. Alessandria: Edizioni dell'Orso, 2004.

Van Steenberghen, Fernand. *La Philosophie au XIII siècle*. Philosophes Médiévaux t. 9. Louvain: Publications universitaires, 1966.

-- *Le problème de l'entrée d'Averroès en Occident* in *L'Averroismo in Italia*. Rome: Accademia Nazionale dei Lincei, 1979, pp 81-89.

Verbeke, Gerard. *L'evolution de la doctrine du pneuma du stoicisme a S. Augustine*. Paris-Louvain: Éditions de l'Institut Supérieur de Philosophie, 1945.

-- *Introduction sur la doctrine psychologique d'Avicenne* in Avicenna latinus, *Liber de Anima seu Sextus de Naturalibus*. Édition critique de la traduction latine médiévale par S. Van Riet. Louvain: Éditions Peeters, and Leiden: E.J.Brill, 1968.

Villani, Giovanni. *Cronica*. Ed. Giovanni Aquilecchia. Turin: Einaudi, 1979.

Villani, Filippo. *De origine civitatis Florentiae et de eiusdem famosis civibus*. Edidit Giuiano Tanturli. Patavi: in aedibus Antenoreis, 1997.

Vitale, Giacomo. *Ricerche intorno all'elemento filosofico nei poeti del "dolce stil novo."* in *Giornale dantesco* XVIII q. v-vi (1919): 162-185.

Wack, Mary Frances. *Lovesickness in the Middle Ages*. Philadelphia: University of Pennsylvania Press, 1990.

Wolfson, Harry Austryn. *The internal senses in Latin, Arabic, and Hebrew Philosophical Texts* in *Harvard Theological Review* 28 (1935): 69-133.

Weitere Titel der Reihe Interkulturelle Begegnungen:

Il Demone e il Barbiere
Grottesco e Monologo in Isaac Bashevis Singer e Edgar Hilsenrath
Der Dämon und der Friseur
Groteske und Monolog bei Isaac Bashevis Singer und Edgar Hilsenrath
(Interkulturelle Begegnungen 1)
Von Veronica Pellicano
2008, 306 Seiten, Hardcover, Euro 54,90/95,50 CHF, ISBN 978-3-89975-114-7

Mit Singer und Hilsenrath werden in diesem Buch erstmals zwei Autoren literaturwissenschaftlich gegenübergestellt, die sich in ihrer Verschiedenheit nicht ähnlicher sein könnten: märchenhaft jiddisch-dämonisch, skandalös bizarr-grotesk.

Ein europäischer Komödienautor
Carlo Goldoni zum 300. Geburtstag
Carlo Goldoni commediografo europeo nel terzo centenario della nascita
(Interkulturelle Begegnungen 2)
Hg. von Richard Schwaderer/Rita Unfer Lukoschik/Friedrich Wolfzettel
2008, 212 Seiten, Hardcover, Euro 39,90/69,50 CHF, ISBN 978-3-89975-141-0

Die Akten des deutsch-italienischen Kolloquiums spiegeln den ganzen Reichtum der inzwischen hervorgetretenen neuen Aspekte, von Editionsproblemen über zeitgeschichtliche Einflüsse bis zu Fragen der Selbstinszenierung des Autors und der medialen Kommunikation Goldonis dramatischen Werkes. So gelingt es hier einmal mehr, die Modernität Goldonis in deutsch-italienischer Perspektive herauszustellen.

Der Salon als kommunikations- und transfergenerierender Kulturraum
Il salotto come spazio culturale generatore di processi comunicativi e di interscambio
(Interkulturelle Begegnungen 3)
Hg. von Rita Unfer Lukoschik
2008, 334 Seiten, Hardcover, Euro 54,90/95,50 CHF, ISBN 978-3-89975-148-2

Der Sammelband bietet in einer Reihe von Fallstudien diachronische Sondierungen zur Herausarbeitung allgemeiner Grundzüge und Tendenzen des italienischen Salonlebens im Spannungsfeld europäischer Kulturen.

Dabei werden kulturelle und politische Implikationen der in diesem hybriden Raum generierten und als Zusammenwirken performativer Handlungen begriffenen Kommunikation ausgeleuchtet. Die darin erzeugten Begegnungen fremder Lebensentwürfe und Kulturkonstrukte werden ebenso behandelt.

Die Antike in der heutigen Welt
Kolloquium über das Klassische an der J. W. Goethe-Universität Frankfurt a. M.
L'antichità classica ed il mondo contemporaneo
Atti della giornata di studi presso l'Università di Francoforte sul Meno
(Interkulturelle Begegnungen 4)
Hg. von Piero A. Di Pretoro/Rita Unfer Lukoschik
2009, 138 Seiten, Hardcover, Euro 24,90/46,00 CHF, ISBN 978-3-89975-164-2

Im Laufe der letzten Jahre ist die Frage nach der Aktualität bzw. Unzeitgemäßheit der klassischen Welt immer dringlicher gestellt worden. Das in diesem Band dokumentierte deutsch-italienische Frankfurter Kolloquium befasst sich mit diesem Thema und fragt nach der Rolle des antiken Kulturerbes in der heutigen Welt.

In ihren Beiträgen behandeln Althistoriker, Altphilologen und Vertreter der klassischen Archäologie, die an deutschen und italienischen Universitäten lehren, wichtige Aspekte der Kulturgeschichte, in denen die Bedeutung und die Relevanz des klassischen Erbes für die Bildung einer gemeinsamen europäischen Identität im Kontext einer globalisierten Gesellschaft hervorragt.

Deutschland in der italienischen Literatur seit dem Ende des Zweiten Weltkriegs
La Germania nella letteratura italiana dopo la seconda guerra mondiale
(Interkulturelle Begegnungen 5)
Von Anna Griesheimer
2009, 225 Seiten, Hardcover, Euro 39,90/69,50 CHF, ISBN 978-3-89975-165-9

Wirtschaftswunder, Massentourismus oder die Migration von Gastarbeitern beispielsweise haben in den Beziehungen der beiden Länder auf politischer, wirtschaftlicher und gesellschaftlicher Ebene zu grundlegenden Veränderungen geführt. Wie sich diese in der italienischen Literatur widerspiegeln und auf welche Art und Weise italienische Autoren während dieser Jahrzehnte Deutschland darstellen, ist Gegenstand der Studie.

Aus dem in ausführlichen Recherchen zusammengetragenen Material hat die Verfasserin für eine detaillierte Interpretation 18 Schlüsseltexte exemplarisch ausgewählt, darunter Werke von Carlo Levi, Curzio Malaparte und Gianni Celati.

Ihr Wissenschaftsverlag. Kompetent und unabhängig.

Verlagsbuchhandlung GmbH & Co. KG
Erhardtstr. 8 • 80469 München
Tel. (089) 20 23 86 -03 • Fax -04
info@m-verlag.net • www.m-verlag.net

www.ingramcontent.com/pod-product-compliance
Lightning Source LLC
LaVergne TN
LVHW012244070526
838201LV00090B/116